Revolution and the Form of
the British Novel, 1790–1825

intercepted correspondence is the order of the day . . .
Maria Edgeworth, *Leonora* (1805)

LE COTERIE DEBOUCHE. Reproduced by kind permission of the British Museum, London.

Revolution and the Form of the British Novel
1790–1825

Intercepted Letters, Interrupted Seductions

NICOLA J. WATSON

CLARENDON PRESS · OXFORD

1994

Oxford University Press, Walton Street, Oxford OX2 6DP
Oxford New York Toronto
Delhi Bombay Calcutta Madras Karachi
Kuala Lumpur Singapore Hong Kong Tokyo
Nairobi Dar es Salaam Cape Town
Melbourne Auckland Madrid
and associated companies in
Berlin Ibadan

Oxford is a trade mark of Oxford University Press

Published in the United States
by Oxford University Press Inc., New York

British Library Cataloguing in Publication Data
Data available

Library of Congress Cataloging in Publication Data
Watson, Nicola J., 1958–
Revolution and the form of the English novel, 1790–1825:
intercepted letters, interrupted seductions/Nicola J. Watson.
Includes bibliographical references (p.) and index.
1. English fiction—19th century—History and criticism—Theory,
etc. 2. France—History—Revolution, 1789–1799—Literature and the
revolution. 3. English fiction—18th century—History and
criticism—Theory, etc. 4. Epistolary fiction, English—History and
criticism—Theory, etc. 5. English fiction—French influences.
6. Point of view (Literature) 7. Seduction in literature.
8. Letters in literature. 9. Narration (Rhetoric) 10. Literary
form. I. Title.
PR868.P57W38   1994   823'.709358—dc20   93–30203
ISBN 0–19–811297–1

1 3 5 7 9 10 8 6 4 2

Typeset by Cambrian Typesetters
Frimley, Surrey
Printed in Great Britain
on acid-free paper by
Bookcraft Ltd
Midsomer Norton, Bath

TO MICHAEL

letter-writer *extraordinaire*

Acknowledgements

IN THE course of completing this book, I have worked for three successive universities (Oxford, Harvard, and Northwestern), and have shuttled backwards and forwards between England and America on a regular basis. I am therefore especially grateful to those who, in spite of my multiple changes of address, have been kind enough to read parts of this study and offer their advice for revisions and improvements in person or through the mail, in particular Marilyn Butler (King's College, Cambridge), who devoted a great deal of time, energy, and good temper to this project in its earlier stages, but also Stephen Gill (Lincoln College, Oxford), Rita Goldberg (Massachusetts Institute of Technology), Larry Lipking (Northwestern University), Ruth Perry (Massachusetts Institute of Technology), Jane Spencer (Edinburgh University), Susan Staves (Brandeis University), Janet Todd (University of East Anglia), and Jonathan Wordsworth (St Catherine's College, Oxford). Thanks are due, too, to Mary Favret (Indiana University) for many entertaining and stimulating conversations. I have also been extremely fortunate in my editor at Oxford University Press, Andrew Lockett, who has been notably efficient, supportive, and charming, and in my OUP readers, who have been uniformly rigorous and helpful in their commentary.

I am particularly delighted also to have the opportunity to make what payment I can here of the great debt I owe to my parents, Peter and Elizabeth Watson, who have provided not only consistent encouragement beyond all reasonable expectation but also, even more valuably, a study and a garden to work in during my all too short summers in England, not to mention a seemingly inexhaustible flow of very happy and very welcome suppers when I found myself in the last throes of preparing the manuscript. Finally, I should like to express my great and enduring gratitude to Michael Dobson for his indefatigable and much-prized intellectual, editorial, and personal support, and to dedicate this book to him at long last and with much affection.

N. J. W.

Lymington, Hampshire   August 1992

Contents

Introduction:
Revolutionary Letters

In a country where morals are on the decline, sentimental novels always become dissolute. For it is their province to represent the prevalent opinions; nay, to run forward and meet the coming vice, and to sketch it with an exaggerating and prophetic pencil. Thus, long before France arrived at her extreme vicious refinement, her novels had adopted that last master-stroke of immorality, which wins by the chastest aphorisms, while it corrupts, by the most alluring pictures of villainy.[1]

Eaton Stannard Barrett's description of the interconnection between the 'dissolute' discourse of the sentimental novel and the adoption of 'vicious refinement'—a term which here implies revolution in the State as well as indiscipline in the family—displays in miniature the intimate relation between sentimental fiction and radical politics that took on an unprecedented intensity in the imagination of the British reading public during the years of the French Revolution, the Napoleonic wars, and their aftermath of social unrest. Barrett goes on to imagine the fatal rescripting of domesticity by the sentimental plot—exemplified here, as elsewhere, by Rousseau's epistolary novel *La Nouvelle Héloïse*:

Rousseau . . . has undone many an imitating miss or wife, who began by enduring the attempts of the libertine, that she might speak sentimentally, and act virtuously; and who ended by falling a victim to them, because her heart had become entangled, her head bewildered, and her principles depraved . . .[2]

---

[1] Eaton Stannard Barrett, *The Heroine; or, The Adventures of Cherubina* (3 vols., London, 1813), iii. 234. Barrett's spoof, set in the 1790s, depicts the adventures of a young woman who takes a variety of contemporary sentimental novels as templates for her own behaviour, which includes rabble-rousing in Ireland: see Ch. 3 below.

[2] Barrett, *The Heroine*, iii. 235–6. For similar criticisms, see Jane West, *Letters Addressed to a Young Man* (3 vols., London, 1801), i. 186–8. This is merely an individualized and politicized version of a charge common against the sentimental novel in general during the 1790s, put most bluntly and uncompromisingly by the author of *The Evils of Adultery and Prostitution; with an Inquiry into the Causes of their Present Alarming Increase, and Some Means Recommended for Checking their*

As the comments of the polemical writer Laetitia-Matilda Hawkins, made in 1793 after the execution of the French king and at the height of the Terror in France, would suggest, sentimental discourse could further be accused, by extension, of complicity in a parallel scenario of seduction, namely full-blown revolution; she remarks that 'she who . . . will easily be persuaded to consider her husband as an unauthorized tyrant' is likely to be one 'who has early imbibed an aversion towards the kingly character', an aversion which Hawkins argues is related both to 'the dominion allowed to the passions under the specious name of sentiment' and to its corollary, the 'clamour for universal liberty'.[3] By 1799, when England was in the throes of war with France and under threat from both rebellion in Ireland and 'seditious' societies at home, Jane West was even more emphatic in her dramatization of the specifically political consequences of filial and marital disobedience, eroticized and supposedly promulgated by the novel of sensibility:

Should it . . . be told to future ages, that the capricious dissolubility (if not the absolute nullity) of the nuptial tie and the annihilation of parental authority are among the blasphemies uttered by the *moral* instructors of these times . . . they will not ascribe the annihilation of thrones and altars to the successful aims of France, but to those principles which, by dissolving domestic confidence and undermining private worth, paved the way for universal confusion.[4]

Taken together, these comments characterize the fiction of sentimental seduction as at once fomenting revolution and perfectly figuring its logic—seducing its readers into infidelity on all levels. This politicization of sentimental discourse, on the part of radicals, liberals, and conservatives alike, generated a range of new narrative models in response, models which it is the project of this study to map in terms of their political valence. Some writers active during the 1790s following the euphoria engendered by the fall of the Bastille in 1789, including the radical thinkers William Godwin,

---

Progress (London, 1792): 'The increase in novels will help account for the increase of prostitution and for the numerous adulteries and elopements we hear of in the different parts of the kingdom' (54).

[3] Laetitia-Matilda Hawkins, *Letters on the Female Mind* (2 vols., London, 1793), i. 105–6.

[4] *A Tale of the Times* (3 vols., London, 1799), ii. 274–5.

Mary Hays, Charlotte Smith, and Mary Wollstonecraft, attempted to exploit the individualistic aspects of the sentimental novel to underwrite their 'Jacobinical' anatomies of social ills. Others, Maria Edgeworth, Jane Austen, Lady Sydney Morgan, and Sir Walter Scott amongst them, responded to the pronounced conservative backlash that accompanied domestic hardship and unrest, war with France, and the rise of Napoleon by attempting to erase forms associated with the plot of sensibility (notably the epistolary and the first-person memoir) in favour of narrative strategies which highlighted the disciplining of individual desire by social consensus to promote what Barrett describes, praising such new moral novels, as 'national virtue'.[5] Yet others—Charles Maturin, William Hazlitt and James Hogg among them—responded to Waterloo and Peterloo by producing counter-fictions critical of conservative versions of social and national consensus. Solipsistic, fragmentary, and determinedly illegible, these counter-fictions self-consciously pushed sentimental paradigms to their furthest extreme in order to fashion revolutionary subjectivities. In what follows, I shall be tracing the ways in which the residue of the sentimental novel was assimilated within these divergent strands of the novel between 1790 and 1825, regarding these formal innovations as fictional accommodations of the same cultural anxiety—that crystallized by the French Revolution. In particular I shall be examining the fate of the letter within the novel as a pointer to the changing concerns of literary-political discourse over the period, thereby offering a coherent account of one neglected and especially pertinent sub-genre at a crucial moment in its evolution. More generally, I hope thereby to provide a fresh perspective—informed above all by contemporary politics—on the experiments in narrative that characterize the closing years of the eighteenth century and the early decades of the nineteenth, in order to illuminate the hitherto largely unexplained transformation of the eighteenth-century novel into the forms more characteristic of the nineteenth century.[6]

[5] Barrett, *The Heroine*, iii. 236.

[6] The most convincing recent survey of the period's fiction is undoubtedly that of Gary Kelly—*English Fiction of the Romantic Period, 1789–1830* (London, 1989)—which, however, reads in terms primarily of class politics rather than in terms of what Jonathan Arac and Harriet Ritvo have termed 'macropolitics' or 'politics at the level of the State'; *Macropolitics of Nineteenth Century Literature: Nationalism, Exoticism, Imperialism* (Philadelphia, 1991), 1.

I

The perhaps rather startling contention that revolutionary politics
were understood crucially in terms of sentimental fiction—and in
particular the plot of a single novel, *La Nouvelle Héloïse*—calls for
some amplification; before going any further, therefore, I want to
detail some of the ways in which the logic of Rousseau's plot came
to inform much of the discourse stimulated by the Revolution in
England, to the point where even the most passing allusion to its
heroine, Julie, might operate as a convenient shorthand for multiple
anxieties surrounding female sexuality, national identity, and class
mobility. The plot of unfolding revolution was, as I have already
suggested, commonly understood by contemporaries as a plot of
seduction (frequently across class lines);[7] so it was that the 'novel of
sensibility' came to serve as such an important narrative matrix in
the period. While this is a notoriously slippery genre to pin down, it
can be said that for contemporaries the paradigmatic sentimental
plot of seduction, occasioning extravagant displays of feeling
recorded at length in impassioned correspondence, was descended
in its mainstream on the one hand from Samuel Richardson's
Clarissa[8] and on the other from its most influential and notorious
rewrite, *La Nouvelle Héloïse* (1761), which went through a
profusion of editions between 1761 and 1810.[9] In England,

[7] This was, of course, not the *only* way in which contemporaries made sense of
the revolution, as others have pointed out—notably Marilyn Butler in *Jane Austen
and the War of Ideas* (Oxford, 1975), Ronald Paulson in *Representations of
Revolution, 1789–1820* (New Haven, Conn., 1983), and, more recently, Alan Liu in
Wordsworth: The Sense of History (Stanford, Calif., 1989). It is certainly the most
pertinent, however, for an understanding of the development of narrative form and
novelistic plot in this period.

[8] Cf. Ronald Paulson's passing comments that *Clarissa* might usefully be
described as a 'protorevolutionary novel', and (invoking one of the most famous
Jacobin novels of the period) that 'the important precursors of Caleb Williams are
not the overt radical novels but some granddaughters of Clarissa'; *Representations
of Revolution*, 228, 230.

[9] First published in England, in anonymous translation by William Kenrick, as
*Eloisa: or, a series of original letters collected and published by J. J. Rousseau.
Translated from the French* (4 vols., London, 1761). Rousseau's novel, it should be
noted, only became generally notorious during the late 1780s and 1790s. In the
more liberal 1770s and early 1780s, *La Nouvelle Héloïse* had been widely admired
(giving rise to something of a tourist industry) and imitated (to take a random
sample) in *Julia, a Poetical Romance, by the Editor of the Essay on the Character,
Manners and Genius of Women* [William Russell, LL D] (London, 1773); in Henry

sentimentalism already had a long history of association with a broadly radical dissenting tradition: it was therefore perhaps inevitable, given the widespread perception of Rousseau as 'father' of the French Revolution,[10] that the popularity of his controversial novel should have been regarded after 1789 as a cause of that revolution, and that the plot of his novel should have come to be understood as one of the Revolution's paradigms.

The centrality of Rousseau's fiction to the interpretation of contemporary politics in the 1790s is strikingly demonstrated by the moment when the august statesman Edmund Burke, in an early counter-revolutionary polemic, *A Letter to a Member of the National Assembly* (1791), unexpectedly descends to invoking it as a model for what are to him the most cataclysmic political events in modern history:

That no means may exist of confederating against their tyranny, by the false sympathies of this *Nouvelle Héloïse* [the Revolutionaries] endeavour to subvert those principles of domestic trust and fidelity which form the

Mackenzie's *Julia de Roubigné* (2 vols., London, 1777); the anonymous *Julia Stanley* (fraudulently attributed to Mackenzie) (2 vols., Dublin, 1780); the spurious *Letters of an Italian Nun and an English Gentleman. Translated from the French of Jean Jacques Rousseau* (attributed to William Combe) [1781] (2nd edn., 2 vols., London, 1784); William Godwin's *Italian Letters; or, The History of the Count de St. Julian* [1784], ed. Burton R. Pollin (Lincoln, Nebr., 1965); the anonymous *Laura: or Original Letters, A Sequel to the Eloisa of J. J. Rousseau* (2 vols., London, 1790) and *The Palinode; or, The Triumph of Virtue over Love; a Sentimental Novel* (London, 1790). Until the late 1780s, Rousseau's novel had been received largely without moral condemnation, except by commentators to whom the novel was an intrinsically immoral genre. For a full account of the reception of *La Nouvelle Héloïse* in England see James Warner, 'Eighteenth-Century English Reactions to *La Nouvelle Héloïse*', *PMLA* (Sept. 1937), 803–19. Later novels influenced by the paradigm, however, especially those written after the fall of the Bastille, position themselves as explicitly politico-sentimental novels. Such novels include, notably, the American Sarah Wood's *Julia, and the Illuminated Baron. A Novel: Founded on Recent Facts Which Have Transpired in the Course of the Revolution of Moral Principles in France* (Portsmouth, NH, 1800), drafted, according to its preface, in the earlier 1790s.

[10] This perception is expressed e.g. by T. J. Mathias in 1797 in a footnote glossing his lines on 'Equality's vain priest, Rousseau' (of whom he says that '*his work* THE CITIZEN began, | And gave to France the social savage, Man'): 'ROUSSEAU ... was stimulated to pursue his researches into the origin and expedience of *such* government, and of *such* oppression ... till he reasoned himself into the desperate doctrine of political equality, and gave to the world his fatal present, "*The Social Contract*". Of *this* work the French, since the Revolution, have never once lost sight. With them it is first and last, and midst, and without end in all their thoughts and public actions'; *The Pursuits of Literature* (London, 1797), pt. iv, 2–4.

discipline of social life. They propagate principles by which every servant may think it, if not his duty, at least his privilege, to betray his master. By these principles every considerable father of a family loses the sanctuary of his house. . . . They destroy all the tranquillity and security of domestic life . . .[11]

As Burke's rhetoric makes evident, Rousseau's masterpiece of 'philosophic gallantry', consisting as it did of 'metaphysical speculations blended with the coarsest sensuality',[12] offered a convenient narrative of what happened when desire broke loose under the sanction of political philosophy, generating domestic mayhem. Striking not just at the class system but at the roots of the patriarchal family (most especially at the security of patrilineal inheritance),[13] Rousseau's plot of ideological seduction struck, by extension, at the State, which was, for Burke and many others, founded upon it, as even the liberal Thomas Dutton makes clear:

Nor is the nuptial ordinance less salutary in a political than moral point of view; less calculated to promote political than moral good. . . . Government, in its very principle, deduces its primary origin from family rule. . . . *states and nations are but families upon a larger scale.*[14]

Even more radical contemporaries, rudely awakened from their smug euphoria over the fall of the Bastille and the Declaration of

---

[11] *The Works of the Right Honourable Edmund Burke* (6 vols., London, 1882–4), iv. 33. Burke goes on to declare that Rousseau is for the Revolution a figure 'next in sanctity to that of a father'. On Burke's view of Rousseau see also Paulson, *Representations of Revolution,* 62–4.

[12] *Letter to a Member of the National Assembly,* 33.

[13] Cf. Burke's argument in *Reflections on the Revolution in France* (1790) in favour of a political system premised on the patriarchal family and maintained by legitimate inheritance: 'in this choice of inheritance we have given to our frame of polity the image of a relation in blood; binding up the constitution of our country with our dearest domestic ties; adopting our fundamental laws into the bosom of our family affections . . . it has been the uniform policy of our constitution to claim and assert our liberties, as an *entailed inheritance* derived to us from our forefathers, and to be transmitted to our posterity. . . . the idea of inheritance furnishes a sure principle of conservation, and a sure principle of transmission. . . . Whatever advantages are obtained by a state proceeding on these maxims, are locked fast as in a sort of family settlement; grasped as in a kind of mortmain for ever. By constitutional policy, working after the pattern of nature, we receive, we hold, we transmit our government and our privileges, in the same manner in which we enjoy and transmit our property and our lives'; *Reflections on the Revolution in France* [1794], ed. Conor Cruise O'Brien (Harmondsworth, 1982), 119–20.

[14] *Brief Sketch of the Character of George III,* cited in *The Anti-Jacobin Review and Magazine; or, Monthly Political and Literary Censor,* 11 (1802), 186.

the Rights of Man in 1789 by the grisly excesses of the Terror
(inaugurated by the September massacres of 1792 and culminating
in the execution of both Louis XVI and Marie Antoinette in 1793),
increasingly read *La Nouvelle Héloïse* as at once the prime example
of Rousseau's own dismaying, even hysterical, excesses[15] and a
cautionary narrative of the undesirable consequences of excessive
'sensibility'.[16]

A key contested term, as the following chapters will make clear,
'sensibility' came to serve during the 1790s as cultural shorthand
for, on the one hand, a Burkean ideal of feeling, defined in
opposition to the disintegrative force of 'Reason'—defined as the
proper antidote, in fact, to the ideological zeal which the French
supposedly elevated over all family ties (including those between
subject and monarch). On the other hand, however, it could also
serve as the term for that which disqualified both women and the
French (as analogical 'others') from full bourgeois subjecthood,[17]
and thus from responsible citizenship, due to their excess of feeling

---

[15] 'The extreme and febrile sensibility which was the characteristic peculiarity of
Rousseau . . . imported a singular delicacy, freshness, and animation, to every page
of his writings. His feelings, in whatever channel they flowed, rushed on with a
restless impetuosity; but, in the end, they made a wreck of his understanding. His
judgement was lost in the unremitting turbulence of his sensations; and, in some
intervals of insanity, he exhibited the melancholy prospect of genius crumbling into
ruins'; *Monthly Mirror*, 8 (1799), 72. Cf. also Julie Ellison on Coleridge's
disparaging remarks on Rousseau in *The Friend*: 'Rousseau emerges as the victim of
an age that could not discipline or contain his hysterical tendencies' and, as such a
hysteric, may be described as 'the most feminine, as well as the most prurient of
radicals' in a move which dramatizes 'the slippage between revolutionary politics
and the feminine'; 'Rousseau in the Text of Coleridge: The Ghost-Dance of History',
Studies in Romanticism, 28(3) (1989), 420–1, 424. For a modern reading which
also identifies Rousseau with a heroine of sensibility, his own, see Peggy Kamuf,
Fictions of Feminine Desire: Disclosures of Héloïse [1982] (Lincoln, Nebr., 1987),
118–22.

[16] This is not to say that for some contemporary readers *La Nouvelle Héloïse*
could not still seem to offer more benignly 'progressive' possibilities—in particular,
the Clarens sequence might operate as a critique of metropolitan 'court' values
through its representation of an alternative, bourgeois pastoral. What I am primarily
concerned with here, however, are the very different ways in which the *plot* of the
novel functioned in contemporary political discourse, especially when relocated and
reinflected.

[17] In this context, see Nancy Armstrong, *Desire and Domestic Fiction: A Political
History of the Novel* (Oxford, 1987), which relates the figures of the prostitute, the
monstrous woman, and the 'female who lack[s] femininity', to a category of
undomesticated desire especially associated with the working classes (181, 183).
This seems particularly pertinent to the insistent, horrified figuration of the French
tricoteuses and *poissardes* found in contemporary accounts of the Terror.

and correspondent lack of rationality.[18] This excessive sensibility was often identified as revolutionary energy; insistently gendered female, it was held responsible for the horrors committed by the mob during the Terror in contemporary texts by writers ranging across the political spectrum from Mary Wollstonecraft (otherwise implacably opposed to Burke) to the self-styled 'anti-Jacobin' Isaac D'Israeli. Wollstonecraft, for example, remarks on the connection between excessive sensibility and revolutionary violence:

The refinement of the senses, by producing a susceptibility of temper, which from it's [sic] capriciousness leaves no time for reflection, interdicts the exercise of the judgement. The lively effusions of mind, characteristically peculiar to the french [sic], are as violent as the impressions are transitory . . . people who are carried away by the enthusiasm of the moment are most frequently betrayed by their imagination, and commit some errour . . .[19]

Echoing Wollstonecraft almost word for word, D'Israeli suggestively amplifies her notion of 'errour' in terms that recall novelistic discourse on the dereliction of female virtue caused by unwisely cultivated feeling, an amplification which finally characterizes contact with the French as uncannily similar to contamination by the sentimental heroine herself:

In France they feel to inexpressible delicacy, or to inconceivable horror. . . . Women in all things, they are women in vengeance. Impatient of restraint, in war . . . in peace, an orderly constitution could neither excite their love nor their reverence. . . . Europe they may afflict with continued revolutions. . . . for they address themselves to the imagination; they seduce the eye and inflame the heart; they mingle prominent virtues, which conceal their radical viciousness. . . . to fraternize with them were to embrace and perish.[20]

---

[18] For discussions of the varied political valences of sensibility in the 1790s see Stephen Cox, 'Sensibility as Argument' in Syndy McMillen Conger (ed.), *Sensibility in Transformation: Creative Resistance to Sentiment from the Augustans to the Romantics* (London, 1990), 63–82; and Janet Todd, *Sensibility: An Introduction* (London, 1986).

[19] Mary Wollstonecraft, *An Historical and Moral View of the Origin and Progress of the French Revolution* . . . [1974], ed. Janet M. Todd (Delmar, NY, 1975), 468. See also Wollstonecraft's curious account of the march of women upon Versailles, which, despite being designed to refute Burke's hostile account, lapses into very similar descriptions of the women as wearing 'the appearance of furies' and as probably drawn from the ranks of the local prostitutes (427, 452).

[20] *Vaurien: or, Sketches of the Times* (2 vols., London, 1797), ii. 288–90. Cf. Charles Lucas, *The Infernal Quixote: A Tale of the Day* (4 vols., London, 1801), ii. 289.

This casting of revolutionary sensibility within an eroticized rhetoric of seduction and fatal error habitually demonizes anarchic desire, and most typically female desire, and it is not surprising that contemporary English novels deploying plots of adultery habitually equate marital infidelity and French liberty, just as frequently as contemporary right-wing polemics equate the popularity of *La Nouvelle Héloïse* with the collapse of the *ancien régime*.[21] Mary Robinson's progressive novel *The False Friend* (1797), for example, has the unpleasant and reactionary Lord Arcot make just this connection: 'If a wife breaks the fetters of matrimonial restraint, though we all know that women were born to be slaves, why, forsooth, she is only called a lover of liberty.'[22] As Cora Kaplan has suggested, 'female subjectivity, or its synecdotal reference, female sexuality, became the displaced and condensed site for the general anxiety about individual behaviour which republican and liberal political philosophy stirred up':[23] certainly the logic of blurring together sexual and political metaphors that she identifies informs a high proportion of counter-revolutionary polemics published during the 1790s and thereafter. Hence in 1798, at the height of the backlash against all those supposed even remotely to have sympathized with the Revolution (fuelled by the eruption of the French-backed Irish rebellion), the *Anti-Jacobin* is at pains to point out, in its review of William Godwin's radical philosophical treatise *Political Justice* (1793), that a proper policing of female desire both

---

[21] For a discussion of the connection between women's bodies and revolution in revolutionary France, see Dorinda Outram, *The Body and the French Revolution: Sex, Class and Political Culture* (New Haven, Conn., 1989), Ch. 8. For a wide-ranging survey of how revolutionary politics were refracted through a variety of female figures in 19th-c. French and English texts see Doris Y. Kadish, *Politicizing Gender: Narrative Strategies in the Aftermath of the French Revolution* (New Brunswick, NJ, 1991). An important analysis of the ways in which masculinity is figured as under revolutionary threat in the writings of, amongst others, Edmund Burke, Samuel Taylor Coleridge, Matthew Lewis, and John Moore is provided by David Punter, '1789: The Sex of Revolution', *Criticism*, 24 (1982), 201–17.

[22] Mary Robinson, *The False Friend: A Domestic Story* (4 vols., London, 1799), iv. 98–9.

[23] 'Pandora's Box: Subjectivity, Class and Sexuality in Socialist Feminist Criticism', in Gayle Greene and Coppelia Kahn (eds.), *Making A Difference: Feminist Literary Criticism* (London, 1985), 165. See also her passing remarks on the sexualized figuration of the mob in Wollstonecraft's *A Vindication of the Rights of Woman* in 'Wild Nights: Pleasure/Sexuality/Feminism', reprinted in Nancy Armstrong and Leonard Tennenhouse (eds.), *The Ideology of Conduct: Essays on Literature and the History of Sexuality* (New York, 1987), 171–2.

before and after marriage is necessary to preserve the health of the state, offering apocalyptic warnings about the political and social consequences of the liberal attitudes towards sexuality advocated by Godwin:

In the first place, by leaving women to the exercise of what he soon after calls their natural and social rights, it would take away powerful restraints on the promiscuous intercourse of the sexes; an intercourse which has a very direct and speedy tendency to the annihilation of virtuous principle, and consequently to the advancement of *jacobinical morals*. It would loosen and finally dissolve the tie of marriage, destroy one of the chief foundations of political society, and thus promote *jacobinical politics*.[24]

A similar logic informs a satirical afterpiece staged in London in 1799, which savagely parodied Helen Maria Williams's perform-ance as 'Liberty' in a Normandy production of the revolutionary drama *La Fédération, ou La Famille patriotique* by representing her in the role of 'Lechery':[25] likewise, one anti-French broadside illustrates the consequences of the Revolution by personifying 'liberty, equality, and fraternity' as a trinity of pregnant hussies,[26] and the *Anti-Jacobin* hails Mary Wollstonecraft as a '*Penthesilea* of liberty and libertinism'.[27] Given the 'obvious and indissoluble connection, which Providence [has] been pleased to establish

---

[24] *Anti-Jacobin*, 1 (1798), 100. This charge is echoed by John Bowles in his *Reflections at the Conclusion of the War* (London, 1801); discussing the 'alarming progress in adultery' he speculates on the possible causes, giving pride of place to 'that tender and compassionate sympathy with guilt, which has been caught from the German school, and which impels us to consider vice as an object of compassion and indulgence, rather than of horror and detestation'; see *Anti-Jacobin*, 10 (1801), 404. In referring to 'the German school', Bowles is thinking of such texts as Goethe's *The Sorrows of Young Werther*, and Kotzebue's immensely successful plays, *Lovers' Vows* (translated and adapted by Elizabeth Inchbald; see Ch. 2 below) and *The Stranger*, of which Thomas Harral comments, 'Rousseau, Godwin, or Mary Wollstonecraft could not have inculcated a more baneful sentiment!' *Scenes of Life* (London, 1805), Preface.

[25] This performance took place at the château of a friend, M. du Fossé, on 28 Aug. 1790: 'In the last scene, I, being the representative of Liberty, appeared . . . guarding the consecrated banners of the nation, which were placed on an altar on which was inscribed in transparent letters: "À la Liberté, 14 Juillet, 1789" '; Helen Maria Williams, *Letters from France*, ed. Janet M. Todd (8 vols. bound in 2; Delmar, NY, 1975), i. 34. (For further information on M. du F—, see Ch. 1.) On the London satire, *The Vision of Liberty*, in which Williams appears in a procession of the Seven Deadly Sins, see *Anti-Jacobin*, 1 (1799), 146–7.

[26] Reproduced in Klaus Theweleit, *Male Fantasies*, i. trans. Stephen Conway (Minneapolis, 1987), 8.   [27] 3 (1799), 29.

between female chastity and the welfare and safety of civil society',[28] this identification of political liberty and female desire, rendered the more volatile by injudiciously cultivated sensibility, made it possible in the late 1790s to imagine France's projected military invasion of Britain as a mere continuation of that invasion of Britain via the minds and bodies of its women which libertarian literature had supposedly already begun to achieve. As William Barrow's outraged remarks make clear, even national, military history could thus be perceived in terms of the plot of seduction:

It was one of the boasts or the menaces of France in the earliest periods of her revolution that she would in every country of Europe prepare the minds of one sex [men] for a similar revolution by perverting the sentiments and corrupting the morals of the other [women]. That this fatal project has been attempted against our nation, I shall readily be excused the unnecessary task of proving to my fellow-subjects.[29]

II

Given that events in France were frequently understood in these ways, it is not surprising that novelists active in the 1790s and after were, as I shall be showing over the course of this study, heavily preoccupied with recasting Rousseau's plot, as they and their public attempted to come to terms with both the Revolution and the philosophies which its proponents and inheritors sought to enact. Fortunately for the vitality of the results, La Nouvelle Héloïse proved a particularly fertile text to re-emplot in aesthetically and politically multiple ways. Despite almost universal condemnation after 1789 for its immoral tendencies (supposedly exacerbated by the seductive power of its language), the novel usefully suffers from a radical ambiguity, strung as it is between a powerful validation of

[28] John Bowles, A View of the Moral State of Society, at the Close of the Eighteenth Century, Much Enlarged, and Continued to the Commencement of the Year 1804, with a Preface Addressed Particularly to the Higher Orders (London, 1804), 37.

[29] Quoted from William Barrow's Essay on Education (1802) in Anti-Jacobin, 12 (1802), 128–9. See also e.g. one contemporary broadside which imagines the main threat from France as a 'daring and perilous expedient of a female Invasion on the part of the French'. 'Old England to her Daughters' (London, 1803), in Napoleon's Threatened Invasion of England: Original Broadsides, 37. Houghton Library Collection.

individual, transgressive desire and a strenuously extended effort to close that desire down in the name of the father.[30] The heroine, Julie, commits the first and fatal indiscretion of entering upon an interdicted correspondence,[31] thus not only disobeying her father but also effectively putting her body into a circulation that threatens patrilineal inheritance.[32] (One thinks here of that simultaneously hateful and erotic moment in Rousseau's own source-text when Lovelace equates Clarissa's forbidden letters with her sexual body, commenting that 'Had [the two letters] been in [my hand] the seal would have yielded to the touch of my warm finger (perhaps without the help of the post-office bullet); and the folds, *as other plications have done*, opened of themselves, to oblige my curiosity').[33] Julie not only willingly gives in to her socially ineligible seducer, St Preux, becoming pregnant, but, after a miscarriage, is ultimately (and from the point of view of contemporary readings scandalously) reinstated in society through marriage with her father's alternative choice of suitor, his friend Wolmar. Love-letters give way to letters to Claire, Julie's female confidante, who then shows them to St Preux. As Janet Altman Gurkin has remarked of this development:

the untenable lovers' intimacy of the first half of the novel gives way to communal intimacy; private confession becomes semi-public and communal with the omnipresent Wolmar presiding, just as the intimate

[30] For a reading that stresses the importance to the novel of 'the sign of the paternal metaphor' see Nancy Miller, 'The Misfortunes of Virtue II; *La Nouvelle Héloïse*', in *The Heroine's Text: Readings in the French and English Novel, 1722–1782* (New York, 1980), 96–115.

[31] Julie retrospectively identifies her reading of St Preux's first letter as the fatal first step: 'Au lieu de jeter au feu votre première lettre ou de la porter à ma mère, j'osai l'ouvrir: ce fût là mon crime, et tout le reste fût forcé'; *Julie, ou, La Nouvelle Héloïse* [1761] (Paris, 1960), 32. Cf. in this respect her prototype, Clarissa, who locates the source of all her disasters in her crime of letter-writing in spite of paternal interdiction: 'My crime was the corresponding with [Lovelace] at first, when prohibited so to do by those who had a right to my obedience'; Samuel Richardson, *Clarissa; or, The History of a Young Lady* [1747–8] (8 vols., Stratford-upon-Avon, 1930), vi. 138.

[32] See Mary Poovey, *The Proper Lady and the Woman Writer: Ideology as Style* (Chicago; 1984), 6–15, for an excellent discussion at length of this issue. For a register of just how threatening Julie's seduction was to contemporaries' sense of social order, it is only necessary to turn to Clara Reeve's recorded wish to alter the novel to make 'the two lovers stop short of the act that made it criminal in either party to marry another'; *The Progress of Romance* (2 vols., Colchester, 1785), ii. 17–18.

[33] Richardson, *Clarissa*, vol. iii, p. cxiii.

correspondence between Saint-Preux and Julie has vanished in favor of letters that could be read by other members of 'la petite communauté.'[34]

In short, individual and illegitimate discourse is thus disciplined in favour of the social and the legitimate.[35] Rousseau's celebration of his Julie as an 'exemplar to her sex' by virtue of the control over her passions thus displayed (and, indeed, repeatedly exhibited through a series of trials set up by Wolmar after St Preux's eventual return) is, however, radically undercut by the extraordinary denouement, in which the now married Julie, writing from her death-bed—'trop heureuse d'achéter au prix de ma vie le droit de t'aimer toujours sans crime, et de te le dire encore une fois!' (731)—affirms her unextinguished and undying passion for St Preux. Reasserting at the last moment the revolutionary, disruptive potential of female sexuality and its associated epistolarity, Julie's last love-letter in effect entirely overturns the carefully reconstructed fiction of the power of patriarchal social order, revealing all its contracts, premised on the fiat of the father, to be empty.[36] (That English readers in the post-revolutionary years found this letter especially disturbing is vividly displayed by Amelia Opie's obsessive and meticulous inversion of it in her 1804 novel *Adeline Mowbray*—

---

[34] *Epistolarity: Approaches to a Form* (Columbus, Oh., 1982), 49. Other critics have also identified this movement from private to published in *Clarissa*—see e.g. Christina Marsden Gillis, *The Paradox of Privacy: Epistolary Form in Clarissa* (Gainesville, Fla., 1984), 74.

[35] I am indebted here to Peggy Kamuf's elegant reading of the ways in which 'a parent's name—the father's . . . functions to suppress the woman's dissident passion and to bury the evidence of a difference within a singular identity', and also to her understanding of the textual strategies of closure at work in the text, 'gestures of closure at the borders of the fictional work, where, in the liminal space of prefaces and forewords, postscripts and appendices, editorial commentary sets to work sealing cracks in the text'; *Fictions of Feminine Desire*, p. xvii.

[36] Elizabeth MacArthur expresses a similar view on the subversiveness of this development, remarking that epistolarity as the modality of time and desire inevitably undermines the novel's apparent project of instituting a timeless idyll at Clarens. MacArthur notes that in the Clarens section of the novel letters become passive, public, and incorporate several reported voices rather than one single voice of passion, before pointing out that the final 'disruption of the stable social order (and the closural narratological order) results from the resurfacing of Julie's suppressed desire, and it forces both social order and narrative to eliminate her'. MacArthur concludes, as I do, that 'narratibility and epistolary extravagance are linked to female desire'; *Extravagant Narratives* (Princeton, NJ, 1990), 212, 218 n. For yet another reading of the submerged power of female desire in *La Nouvelle Héloïse* see Kamuf, *Fictions of Feminine Desire*, 97–122.

based at once on *La Nouvelle Héloïse* and on the life of her friend Mary Wollstonecraft—whereby the dying heroine instead avows her entire submission to the social order, retrospectively unwriting all her earlier declarations of forbidden love). As Tony Tanner remarks, 'if the "full" word of the father is listened to carefully and is discovered to be in fact an "empty" word . . . what becomes of all the dependence structures and binding contracts—not only between parents and children, husbands and wives, but between words and meanings, signs and things [and, it would be pertinent to add, between State and individual]?'[37] Rousseau's text succeeds, tenuously and temporarily, in containing that power only by strategically witholding Julie's final letter until after her exemplary death. The very fabric of the novel plays out a contest between female sexuality/textuality and the editor's attempts, visibly ineffective, to police it by attempting to provide more authoritative miniature plot and theme summaries and alternative interpretations designed to reduce a proliferation of ambiguity and self-contradiction,[38] not to mention readerly indiscretion in breaking open the mailbag at all. In this context, Rousseau's ominous warning to his young female reader (the contemporary English translation reads: 'A modest girl will never read books of love. If she should complain of having been injured by the perusal of these volumes, she is unjust: she has lost no virtue; for she has none to lose'),[39] a warning which she must already have disregarded, serves to point Peggy Kamuf's observation that 'at stake in this definition of the limits of the book are the structures which keep women—and readers—in their place'.[40] To desire to read is already to be seduced, for to read letters of this nature is to enter into a circuit of desire which, of its nature, exceeds all but the most punitive of closures—the lingering death which is itself one of the most recurrent features of sentimental fiction.

[37] *Adultery in the Novel: Contract and Transgression* (Baltimore, Md., 1979), 142.
[38] For an extended reading of *La Nouvelle Héloïse* along these lines see MacArthur, *Extravagant Narratives*, 230–57; for similar comments regarding *Clarissa* see Terry Castle, *Clarissa's Ciphers: Meaning and Disruption in Richardson's Clarissa* (Ithaca, NY, 1982), 167.
[39] *Eloisa, or a series of original letters*, trans. William Kenrick [1761] (1803 edn.), ed. Jonathan Wordsworth (2 vols., Oxford, 1989), vol. i, p. xxxii.
[40] *Fictions of Feminine Desire*, p. xviii.

The woman's letter, exemplified in Julie's last missive, therefore concentrates in the most heady and potent form the complex of desire and transgression upon which the narrative of revolution, in the 1790s and thereafter, is founded. Insidiously instituting an exchange system which functions in accordance with a logic inimical to the patriarchal logic of property, the letter, as Linda S. Kauffman has pointed out, constantly reiterates an equation of writing with sexual freedom, transgression, and seduction, whether written in the hand of the prototypical Héloïse or of any of her eighteenth-century descendants.[41] To filch Elizabeth J. MacArthur's term, the letter is quintessentially 'extravagant', open-ended, and desirous, the motor of 'endlessly erring narratives', ultimately resistant to the sort of closure or stasis which Wolmar, and his progenitor Rousseau, try to enforce. Moreover, the epistolary, as MacArthur further remarks, thanks to its interest in multiple perspectives, puts into question 'the possibility of objective truth or stable authority'.[42] This uncontainable formal extravagance—doubled by its mirror-reflection, a scenario of insurgent and illicit female desire—provided fertile material for novelists of all persuasions working in the wake of the Revolution, and in the light of successive and competing interpretations of events in France and England alike. Premised upon conflicting models of reading, and containing within itself its own counter-revolutionary mechanisms of rereading, indeed unreading,[43] La Nouvelle Héloïse proved improbably amenable to their revisionary efforts. As the Revolution was read and reread, written and rewritten in the light of subsequent episodes—the inception of the radical London Corresponding Society, the declaration of war with France in 1795, the

[41] Discourses of Desire: Gender, Genre and Epistolary Fictions (Ithaca, NY, 1986), passim.

[42] Extravagant Narratives, 16, 22. One might usefully recall here Neil Hertz's contention that 'semiotic restlessness' connects with the 'dissolution of hierarchical difference' and is particularly associated with the feminine in texts concerned with revolution; The End of the Line: Essays on Psychoanalysis and the Sublime (New York, 1985), 176.

[43] I am thinking here in particular of the letter from Julie to St Preux which, describing her marriage as an internal revolution, sets about systematically rereading all previous letters, methodically dismantling her previous discourse and so putting into question the readability both of the first part and of what follows. For a detailed (if gender-blind) reading of this letter, see Paul De Man, Allegories of Reading (New Haven, Conn., 1979), 210–20.

rise and fall of Napoleon, the outbreak of anonymous seditious letters associated with 'Captain Swing' in 1804,[44] the Luddite disturbances of 1811–12, the social unrest leading up to the Peterloo massacre of 1819, the scandalous sexual misdemeanours of the Prince Regent which culminated with the Queen Caroline affair of 1820, the widespread reform agitation of the 1820s—so too in contemporary fiction would Rousseau's bundle of illicit letters be insistently intercepted, scrutinized, and redirected in censored form.[45]

III

My principal focus in the chapters which follow will accordingly be on the different narrative structures evolved to reappropriate or to contain the potentially revolutionary force of the *Héloïse* plot. I shall be diagnosing this process in large part by tracing the mutations and transmutations of the letter, which, standing metonymically in the place of the figure of the desiring woman (and thus as a condensed 'symptom' of Rousseau's plot), was widely read as an oppositional discourse—a potential disruptor of the existing social or symbolic order.[46] Like the female desire for which they stand, letters in the novels of the post-revolutionary years are always liable to go astray, to engage in duplicity and deception, or

[44] See E. P. Thompson, 'The Crime of Anonymity', in Douglas Hay *et al.* (eds.), *Albion's Fatal Tree: Crime and Society in Eighteenth Century England* (London, 1975), 287 ff.

[45] I should perhaps emphasize that this process of disciplining the letter as a metonym simultaneously for errant female sexuality and for revolution does not originate in the 1790s, although it re-emerges with peculiar force at that time: the same process can be traced e.g. in the structure of Aphra Behn's *Love-letters between an English Nobleman and His Sister* (1685–7), which progresses from a purely epistolary narrative to one disciplined by an omniscient narrator. It is hardly irrelevant that Behn's novel is concerned with the politics of subjectivity on the eve of a revolution that the British would later initially construe as the model for the French Revolution.

[46] In this respect, the letters which appear in the highly politicized novels of the 1790s and early 1800s with which I shall be concerned draw to different degrees on a long 18th-c. tradition of identifying all kinds of letters with generally 'oppositional' writing—whether of the classical republicans, of the common-wealthmen, of the salons, or of the Encyclopaedists' English counterparts (with their strong predilection for the philosophical 'familiar epistle').

to circulate out of control, relativizing competing discourses and thus putting social consensus in jeopardy. In pursuing their itinerary through the changing fiction of this crucial period of transition, I shall be considering not only the ruptures or disjunctions which they may mark for the liberals of the 1790s, but also their carefully signalled attenuation, transformation into generalized figures of errant textuality, and ultimate erasure in favour of more socially responsible, constitutive, and regulatory discourses as the nineteenth century takes shape—discourses which range from gossip at one extreme through the language of the law to national history at the other. In fact, one of the central purposes of this study will be to demonstrate that the rapid disintegration of the epistolary novel in the late 1780s and 1790s, far from being the 'natural' consequence of the increasing sophistication of the novel (as critics have too often casually assumed),[47] was, as the contemporary novelist Sophia Lee argued apropos of her epistolary novel *The Life of a Lover* (1804), intimately bound up with the problematic political resonances of its narrative mode in the revolutionary and post-revolutionary period.[48]

As will rapidly become clear, in mounting this archaeological endeavour to uncover a substratum of revolutionary narrative I have chosen texts without particular regard to their canonicity, and, especially, without privileging certain texts or authors as somehow more originatory than others. In part this is because this study is not designed to offer further 'background' or 'context' to an understanding of, for example, Austen or Scott or Byron (although it will certainly perform that function for readers who view the period from such a perspective), nor to offer a comprehensive survey of the novel between 1789 and 1825 (although it will certainly provide a solid sketch-map, not to mention detailed coverage of much important and hitherto neglected terrain), but rather to examine one specific process of cultural work, a process in which texts of many different kinds and levels of status participated. Because I am interested in how individual texts articulate,

---

[47] See e.g. Frank Gees Black, *The Epistolary Novel in the Late Eighteenth Century* (Eugene, Ore., 1940), 110; Godfrey Frank Singer, *The Epistolary Novel: Its Origin, Development, Decline, and Residuary Influences* [1933] (New York, 1963), 152.

[48] For Lee's extended discussion of this point, see Singer, *The Epistolary Novel*, 157.

negotiate, and modify plot-figures drawn from a common cultural repertoire, and in displaying them as a generic topography of local, contending, discursive practices, I have chosen texts for examination which seem to display these plot-figures with particular clarity, and which stand as extreme examples of any given strategy. Methodologically speaking, this study therefore builds on the seminal analyses of narratives of revolution offered by Marilyn Butler and Ronald Paulson respectively,[49] and with them presupposes narrative representation to be a cultural work that extends along a continuum from the crystallization of the actual into the political 'event', to the reportage of such events, and eventually to specifically 'literary' narrative. In particular I assume that history, as it emerges into both political actions and literary texts, is inevitably emplotted according to pre-existent narratives embedded within the reader of such 'texts'; it is this enabling assumption that underpins my contention that texts as apparently disparate as *Maria; or, The Wrongs of Woman, Persuasion, The Antiquary, Liber Amoris*, and *Confessions of a Justified Sinner* all crucially engage with the same inherited sentimental genealogy of plot, in their efforts to reshape the meaning of the Revolution for contemporary readers.[50]

[49] See esp. Marilyn Butler's insistence that the Revolution does not simply manifest within texts as trope or mode (the main thrust of Paulson's argument) or even as textual rupture (see in this vein, David Punter *et al.*, 'Strategies for Representing Revolution', in Francis Barker *et al.* (eds.), *1789: Reading, Writing, Revolution: Proceedings of the Essex Conference* (London, 1982), 81–100), but, crucially, as narrative that accommodates, contains, and induces revolution: 'Telling it Like a Story: The French Revolution as Narrative', *Studies in Romanticism*, 28 (1989), 345–56, esp. 347–8, 354. In choosing to focus minutely upon the ways in which pre-existing plots and forms were, to borrow Paulson's useful coinage, 'Jacobinized' (or, indeed, 'anti-Jacobinized') by a series of political events, I am pursuing a line of enquiry that Paulson has already set out in his discussion of the Gothic as 'a specific plot that was either at hand for writers to use in the light of the French Revolution, or was in some sense projected by the Revolution and borrowed by writers who may or may not have wished to express anything specifically about the troubles in France'; Paulson, *Representations of Revolution*, 221. In espousing this view of the relation between the literary and the historical, I have generally elided the concerns of other influential historians of the novel in the period, notably Gary Kelly and Nancy Armstrong, whose broadly Marxist paradigms concentrate almost exclusively upon class conflict and (in Armstrong's case) the production of class subjectivity as a ground to the fictions they consider.

[50] Here I am generally indebted to Alan Liu's work on the ways in which revolution was precipitated in a variety of narrative genres, which is itself indebted

Chapter 1 accordingly begins with a survey of the interwoven fates of the letter and the sexually transgressive heroine in radical polemic and fiction from 1790 to 1800, examining the strategies by which radical novelists, including Helen Maria Williams, Eliza Fenwick, Mary Hays, Mary Wollstonecraft, and Charlotte Smith, attempted to appropriate and modify the plot of sensibility provided by *La Nouvelle Héloïse* to ratify the heroine's self-legitimating revolutionary desire as expressed in letters. Chapter 2, by contrast, examines the fate of the letter in those broadly conservative fictions of the 1790s and beyond which conceived of themselves as 'antidotes' to the 'poison' of 'sentimental books | Collations sweet, by philosophic cooks'[51] and thus as contributing to the cause of social and moral regeneration. Here I read a series of fictions by Jane West, Elizabeth Hamilton, Maria Edgeworth and, most notably, Jane Austen, considering their manœuvres to contain the subversiveness of illicit correspondence and thus the heroine's related insurrection; such strategics, visible in their most sophisticated and elaborate form in *Emma* (1816), discipline the errancy of the letter by intercepting, readdressing, and redelivering it to multiple and repeatable rereading. In particular, I trace here the ways in which the sentimental letter begins to vanish, metamorphosing into, and slowly being replaced by, problematic textual

to Fredric Jameson's work in *The Political Unconscious: Narrative as a Socially Symbolic Act* (Ithaca, NY, 1981). I assume, like Liu, that history becomes knowable 'only insofar as it is acted upon by the collective process of arbitrary structuration . . . by which cultures interpret reality' and, further, that 'history is quintessentially narrative, not only because the lay forms of historical action and reportage . . . are "emplotted", but because the governing institutions of history . . . are themselves fully plotted in every sense of the word and can be subverted or revolutionized only by counter-plot. The only way to "know" history is through a category of narrative underlying social institutions and literary forms alike'; *Wordsworth: The Sense of History*, 41, 50.

[51] 'Andrew Clover', *Popular Opinions, or, A Picture of Real Life, Exhibited in a Dialogue between a Scotish Farmer and a Weaver. . . . To Which is added, an Epistle from the Farmer to Elizabeth Hamilton, Author of the Cottagers of Glenburnie, in Scotish Verse* (Glasgow, 1812), 23. 'Clover' identifies as 'philosophic cooks' William Godwin, Thomas Paine, Mary Wollstonecraft, Ossian, Rousseau, Kotzebue, and Helen Maria Williams, amongst many others. The poison/antidote figure was common—cf. Jane West's remark that 'while the enemies of our church and state continue to pour their poison into unwary ears through [the novel], it behoves the friends of our establishments to convey an antidote by the same course'; *The Infidel Father* (3 vols., London, 1802), i, Preface. See also Reeve, *The Progress of Romance*, i. 77; 'Clover', *Popular Opinions*, 82.

artefacts whose itineraries none the less duplicate those of the letter for which they substitute.

My third chapter pursues a related and amplified thematics of 'right reading' in the early novels of Scott and a number of fellow writers, Lady Sydney Morgan and Maria Edgeworth amongst them, novels which subordinate the individual sensibility associated with the letter and the residue of the Rousseauistic plot to social, indeed national and historical, consensus; the chapter is particularly concerned with tracing the recuperative transliteration of epistolary correspondence into the competing fictions of historiography, a transliteration which allows for the selective authentication of one socially healing version of a national past. My last chapter shifts ground to consider the after-life of the letter as it modulates, under the aegis of Rousseau's *Confessions*, into the quintessentially Romantic narratives of the early nineteenth century. Such texts as Charles Maturin's *Melmoth the Wanderer* (1820), William Hazlitt's *Liber Amoris* (1823) and James Hogg's *Confessions of a Justified Sinner* (1824), displaying in their convoluted and destabilized structures the residue of a revolutionary subjectivity premised upon self-authorizing discourse, sharply question the achieved if delicate certainties of the more conservative forms of the novel which form the topic of my two central chapters, by rendering the letter and its analogues, and thus the intricacies of revolutionary desire, effectively unreadable and thus immune from certain sorts of narrative discipline. I conclude with an analysis of Lady Caroline Lamb's affair with Lord Byron, pursuing it through their consciously sentimental correspondence to the publication of Lamb's novel *Glenarvon*, and culminating with a reading of Byron's 'novel in verse', *Don Juan*, to show how this literary correspondence recapitulates the generic negotiations and mutations detailed in the bulk of this book. I argue finally that *Don Juan*'s overall structure purloins a series of novelistic paradigms ranging from the sentimental to the Gothic to recapitulate the itinerary of revolutionary subjectivity embodied in the fate of the letter and its surrogates, and, in so doing, rereads the structures of Regency society.

In the course of my analysis I hope to demonstrate that, if the novel of the 1790s is obsessed with revolution and its failures, the novel of the early decades of the new century is preoccupied above all with projects of recuperation, conversion, and purgation of that great cataclysm, projects that require the radical modification of generic convention. In other words, I shall be arguing that generic innovation can be linked directly to contemporary changes in political, cultural, and ideological structures.[52] In addition I hope to suggest, if only by implication, why and how it is that the letter survives into the nineteenth-century novel almost exclusively as the marker of disruptive female desire, characteristically fixed as a figure of criminal excess and threatening semiotic restlessness within a social and narrative order that consistently attempts to discipline it. My account of the curious demise of the epistolary novel thus aims in part to provide something of a prehistory to the frightening vagaries of the letter and female sexuality in Charles Dickens's *Bleak House* (1852–3), to the letter's flight underground in Charlotte Brontë's *Villette* (1853),[53] to its illegibility and secrecy in a series of detective fictions taking their genesis from Edgar Allan Poe's 'The Purloined Letter',[54] and, above all, to its strikingly privileged position in modern critical discourse.

Today the letter seems able to represent an almost promiscuous range of radical potentialities—the possibility of 'bodily' writing for both the French theorists of *l'écriture féminine* and American feminists, the replacement of the privileged voice by the seductive slippage of writing for Jacques Derrida and his followers, the ultimate 'writerly' text that invites interminably unstable interpretation for novelists such as John Barth, the proof of the itinerary of subjectivity for Jacques Lacan. This flurry of interest, not to mention the success of stage, film, and television adaptations of a series of eighteenth-century epistolary novels (notably *Les Liaisons dangereuses* and *Clarissa*), relies upon an erotics, still in place, of potentially revolutionary writing femininity—an erotics displayed elaborately in my frontispiece illustration of the notoriously successful *demi-mondaine* Harriette Wilson concocting her

---

[52] Although in this study I confine myself to the British context, it is also true that similar strategies *vis-à-vis La Nouvelle Héloïse* are employed elsewhere as, e.g., in Stendhal's *Le Rouge et le Noir* (1831).

[53] For an influential reading of the letter as sign of disruptive sexuality in Brontë's novel, one that would be in broad alignment with my position here, see Mary Jacobus, 'The Buried Letter: Feminism and Romanticism in *Villette*', in *Women Writing and Writing About Women* (New York, 1979), 42–60.

[54] See e.g. the use of the letter as a figure for illicit female desire and, in parallel, illicit politics, in Sir Arthur Conan Doyle, *The Return of Sherlock Holmes* (London, 1905), esp. 'The Adventure of the Second Stain'.

extremely lucrative memoirs from her stock of old love-letters, surrounded by her at once titillated and dismayed admirers.[55] It is, above all, this political erotics of genre at a crisis point in its development that this book sets out to delineate.

[55] For more information regarding the outrageous and refreshingly unrepentant Harriette, see the *Dictionary of National Biography*, and her own *Memoirs of Herself and Others* (London, 1825).

Julie among the Jacobins:
Radicalism and the Sentimental Novel,
1790–1800

Over the course of the 1790s, women novelists known for their revolutionary sympathies—Helen Maria Williams, Charlotte Smith, Eliza Fenwick, Mary Hays, and Mary Wollstonecraft amongst them—made repeated attempts to adapt the controversial plot of *La Nouvelle Héloïse* to radical, often explicitly feminist, political ends. Their experiments, the subject of this chapter, were aimed ultimately at dissociating the feminist author from the disempowered and eroticized heroine of sensibility exemplified by Rousseau's Julie; their failure, as I shall be showing, is demonstrated, finally, by the success with which conservatives were none the less able, at the close of the decade, simply to rewrite Wollstonecraft and her contemporaries themselves as quintessential erring sentimental heroines.

To grasp the political implications of these narrative experiments it is necessary to take into account the legacy of sentimentalism, which, despite its regular and explicit repudiation by so-called 'Jacobin' writers, nonetheless crucially underpinned both radical thinking and the novelistic forms employed to plot it in fictional terms.[1] Sentimentalism, through its connection with associationist and sensationist psychology (developed initially by John Locke in his *Essay Concerning Human Understanding*, 1689, and subsequently refined and put into juxtaposition with the concept of 'natural' virtue by David Hume's *Treatise of Human Nature*, 1739), offered a set of constellated but frequently conflicting versions of the relation of the individual to external (and therefore

---

[1] There is a vast body of literature on the crucially interlocking concepts in the late 18th-c. of sensibility, sentimentalism, and sympathy. For the brief discussion that follows I have relied principally upon R. F. Brissenden, *Virtue in Distress* (London, 1974) (esp. Ch. 2) and Janet Todd, *Sensibility: An Introduction* (London, 1986).

social) reality. As elaborated in the novel of sensibility, most notably the epistolary variant used by Rousseau himself, it supplied what was undoubtedly a potentially radical politics of subjectivity, promulgating a notion of exquisite individual sensibility which, although called into play by the outside world, was essentially self-authorizing rather than produced through subjection to any social structure (most especially the State) whatsoever. This thinking had provided the rationale for Rousseau's influential concept of the 'natural man' (developed in his political treatise *Du contrat social*, 1762, and in his educational treatise *Émile*, published in the same year), who, if preserved uncorrupted from the vitiating institutions of society as presently constructed, would prove to be possessed of innate virtue, and thus to be admirably equipped to fulfil the functions of the democratic citizen. That concept came not only to be central to the philosophical mythologies of the Revolution in France, but also to exert considerable influence upon the thinking of English dissenting radicals, from Catherine Macaulay Graham and Thomas Holcroft to William Godwin and Mary Wollstonecraft.

However, at the same time as constructing this potentially revolutionary subject, the capacious ideology of sensibility also imagined a peculiarly disempowered individual, trapped within his own bodily sensations and unable to imagine or effect any social change whatsoever. Although the anarchy implicit in this model of social isolation was typically warded off by recourse to the notion of 'sympathy' (most elaborately set out by Adam Smith in *The Theory of Moral Sentiments*, 1759—human beings were thought to relate to one another through some sort of natural correspondence or sympathetic communion which was supposed to induce 'benevolence' and so to guarantee the functioning of social structure), the anxiety remained that embracing the cult of sensibility might encourage the effective dissolution of both society and the individual as readily as promoting the beneficent reconstruction of either. Thus sentimental narratives such as Henry Mackenzie's *Julia de Roubigné* (1777) (an influential rewrite of Rousseau's fiction), typically dramatized subjectivity as fragmentary, passionate to the point of irrationality, and peculiarly unfitted to do more than sympathize with, and occasionally relieve, local distress.[2]

[2] See Marilyn Butler's comment that '[t]he most obvious characteristic of sentimental narrative writing is that it shifts the emphasis from the action—what a character does—to his response to the action. . . . The scene is what matters, and the

Mackenzie's novel, in keeping with this fragile and contingent concept of identity, is presented as a translation of letters, some of which are suppressed wholly or partially and the order of which is to a certain extent determined, disconcertingly, by the translator's laziness or incapacity. The letter here characteristically functions at once as a crucial space of the 'play' of self-expressiveness, and, potentially, as the marker of isolated consciousness, unauthorized (in all the meanings of the word) and perhaps unauthorizable, visibly liable to failure of transmission.

The epistolary subject so imagined was quintessentially, if not exclusively, the sentimental heroine. Her language is almost always that of the letter, a framed and eroticized display of the language of the body, of sensibility, an anti-narrative discourse that palpitates with bodily sensations which minutely register social contradictions; the action to which she is subjected and through which she is produced as a sentimental subject is paradigmatically, as in *Julia de Roubigné*[3] and its original *La Nouvelle Héloïse*, the plot of the conflict between paternal fiat and sexual passion, a conflict that

---

focus of each scene is the character's state of mind in response to external stimuli. The total movement of the book, what traditionally would have been the plot, becomes obscure, complex, perversely malign, in imitation of the real-life manner in which the environment impinges upon the individual'; *Jane Austen and the War of Ideas* (Oxford, 1975), 14. See also Robert Markley's remark (apropos of Henry Mackenzie and Laurence Sterne) that sentimentality 'demonstrates . . . the powerlessness and impracticality of the very benevolence it attempts to valorize', producing 'self-absorbed and self-congratulatory mystifications of inequality'—a position remarkably similar to that of Wollstonecraft; 'Sentimentality as Performance: Shaftesbury, Sterne and the Theatrics of Virtue' in Felicity Nussbaum and Laura Brown (eds.), *The New Eighteenth Century: Theory, Politics, English Literature* (New York, 1987), 230.

[3] It may be appropriate here to quote J. M. S. Tompkins's efficient summary of the plot of *Julia de Roubigné* for the benefit of readers unfamiliar with the novel: 'Montauban, middle-aged, Spanish by education, sober and morose by habit, falls in love with Julia de Roubigné, only child of a ruined nobleman. Her father's misfortunes, her mother's death, the obligations under which the whole family stand to Montauban, force her step by step into an alliance to which she can bring only respect and gratitude; yet she withholds her hand until she learns that Savillon, to whom her affections are given, has taken a wife in Martinique. Then she marries Montauban and follows him, with vague, unhappy forebodings, over the dark threshold of her new home . . . Savillon [returns] to France to assure Julia of his constancy, and . . . Montauban, convinced by small ambiguous circumstances of Julia's guilt, in a passion of outraged love and pride poisons first her and then himself'; *The Popular Novel in England 1770–1800* (Lincoln, Nebr., 1961), 341–2.

would eventually, as I have already suggested, come to serve as the dominant plot of radical fictions of the Revolution.

Of all the fictions of the 1790s which attempt to wrench sentimental narrative to a radical political programme, it is thus those by women, themselves inevitably implicated in the potential and the plight of sentimentalism's paradigmatic writing heroine, which are of particular interest: in striving to legitimate a model of female subjecthood analogous to Rousseau's version of the male republican subject, they demonstrate with peculiar clarity the difficulty—experienced to a lesser extent by male colleagues such as William Godwin and Thomas Holcroft—of finding a narrative form capable of authenticating such a concept. Unwilling to jettison Rousseau's plot of seduction (unlike Godwin, whose success in *Caleb Williams* appears to depend on translating that plot into homosocial terms), women writers wrestled with the problem of how to authorize a revolutionary female subjectivity premised upon the authenticity of individual feeling—feeling that, in the terms of contemporary gender ideology and, inevitably, within the plot that articulated that ideology, was always liable to be dismissed or demonized as sexuality errant to the point of madness. To borrow from the summary of the judge's closing remarks from Mary Wollstonecraft's posthumously published and incomplete novel, *Maria; or, The Wrongs of Woman* (1798), 'if women were allowed to plead their feelings ... it was opening a floodgate for immorality. What virtuous woman thought of her feelings?'[4] The struggle was made the more intense by increasing anxieties over the progress of the French Revolution, which was seen as the practical realization and consequence of new ideas about the subject's relation to the State, recognized, quite rightly, as deriving from Rousseau's sentimentalism.

In the course of this chapter I shall be reading this effort by contemporary women to develop a radical novel of sensibility in the fate of the letter itself, which in these fictions comes to operate not only as the locus of authentic female feeling, but also, by extension, as a condensed figure for the plot of the daughter's sexual rebellion against the father and the *ancien régime* for which he stands. For the 1790s and beyond, the letter and the plot of *La Nouvelle*

---

[4] *Maria; or, The Wrongs of Woman* [1798], ed. Moira Ferguson (New York, 1975), 148–9.

Héloïse stand in metonymic substitution for one another, some-times appearing in conjunction, sometimes separately, but always referring to the ghost or cultural trace of the other. In the heady and self-congratulatory days of 1790, the letter could still be imagined by Helen Maria Williams as a Rousseauistic discourse of desire powerful enough to cancel out the patriarchal *lettre de cachet* employed by the *ancien régime*; over the course of the nineties, however, as radicals qualified their initial fervour in the wake of the Terror, the letter gradually dwindled into political inefficacy, finally appearing in Mary Wollstonecraft's unfinished novel *Maria; or, The Wrongs of Woman* (1798) as simply a marker of the ways in which female subjectivity was mediated through the debilitating ideology of sensibility, in this case represented once again in appropriated epistolary fragments of the text of *La Nouvelle Héloïse*. I shall thus be showing how the letter, even in the most determinedly radical of texts, becomes increasingly subject to translation into an alternative and absolutely incompatible—even inimical—discourse, that of society, performed variously in these texts as the language of gossip or, more institutionally, of the law-court.

I

Both conservatives and radicals (and all shades of partisan in between) accused those of other political persuasions of excessive sensibility and of exploiting an essentially sentimental rhetoric, and all equally indignantly denied the charge. If Wollstonecraft, in *A Vindication of the Rights of Men* (1790), could base her critique of Burke's politics upon accusations of muddy sentimental thinking, constructing him as all crocodile tears and about as much sympathy, Gillray, the noted conservative caricaturist, was, for his part, just as comfortable producing a cartoon of Sensibility as a woman crying over a dead bird, with the volumes of Rousseau in one hand and a foot carelessly resting on the French king's severed head.[5] Both conservative and radical factions professed on occasion to regard sensibility as dangerously self-indulgent, conservatives

---

[5] For a full discussion of these charges and counter-charges see Todd, *Sensibility: An Introduction*, 130.

because it was thought to lead to abandoning necessary social restrictions upon the passions and to promote moral relativism, liberals and radicals because they considered that, under the guise of individual philanthropy stimulated by pathos, it simply mystified and upheld 'things as they were', in effect pre-empting any political analysis or revolutionary action based upon the more appropriate grounds of Reason. As a result, attacks on the debilitating effects of the 'cant' of sensibility are often hard to assign to any particular political standpoint; this reviewer of *Edward and Harriet; or the Happy Recovery: A Sentimental Novel* (1788) is making an entirely conventional point in remarking that:

Young women may be termed romantic, when they are under the direction of artificial feelings, when they boast of being tremblingly alive all o'er, and faint and sigh as the novelist informs them they should. Hunting after shadows, the moderate enjoyments of life are despised, and its duties neglected; and the imagination, suffered to stray beyond the utmost verge of probability ... soon shuts out reason, and the dormant faculties languish for want of cultivation; as rational books are neglected, because they do not throw the mind into an *exquisite* tumult. ... false sentiment leads to sensuality, and vague fabricated feelings supply the place of principles.[6]

This humdrum reviewer, however, happens to be Mary Wollstonecraft, who would over the next ten years refine this commonplace into an analysis not so much of the fatal effects of reading sentimental fiction as of the disastrously insinuating power over women of the ideology of sensibility itself, and who would call for the cultivation, above all, of women's reason, a concept that had, after such incidents as the installation by the revolutionaries of a notorious prostitute as the Goddess of Reason in the *ci-devant* cathedral of Notre-Dame, become charged with radical meaning.

None the less, that there was more than a grain of truth in the conservatives' accusations may be demonstrated by a glance at the enormously influential volumes which, along with those of Dr John Moore,[7] provided the British reading public with a comprehensive

---

    [6] *Analytical Review*, 1 (June 1788), 207–8.
    [7] *A Journal during a Residence in France from the beginning of August to the middle of December 1792* (London, 1793–4); *A View of the Causes and Progress of the French Revolution* (London, 1795).

eyewitness account of political events in France throughout the years immediately following the fall of the Bastille, and contributed to their author's lifelong reputation as 'preeminent among the violent female devotees of the Revolution',[8] Helen Maria Williams's *Letters from France* (1790–6)[9]. Produced in part during Williams's heyday as a sought-after radical *salonnière* at the heart of Paris (her English guests alone included the prominent revolutionary sympathizers Mary Wollstonecraft, John Opie, Thomas Poole, Thomas Christie, and the Whig statesman Fox, amongst many others; her friends and correspondents included Charlotte Smith, Anna Barbauld, Anna Seward, and William Godwin),[10] these volumes elaborately exploit the revolutionary power of sentimental discourse as embodied in the letter, casting a sympathetic account of the Revolution in the format of private

---

[8] *Gentleman's Magazine*, 98 (1828), 373.

[9] The bibliographical problems surrounding these volumes are considerable; M. Ray Adams lists her output as follows: *Letters written from France in the Summer of 1790* (1790); *Letters from France* (1792–6) in 4 volumes the 1st of which is a reprint of the initial volume, the 2nd entitled *Letters from France containing many New Anecdotes relative to the French Revolution and the present State of French Manners*, and the third and fourth entitled *Letters from France containing a great variety of interesting and original Information concerning the most Important Events that have lately occurred in that Country and particularly respecting the Campaign of 1792*. It is these 4 initial volumes with which I am concerned here: they are not to be confused with her 2nd series of *Letters from France* (1795–6), also in 4 volumes entitled respectively, *Letters containing a Sketch of the Politics of France from the Thirty-First of May, 1793, till the 10th of Thermidor, Twenty-Eighth of July, 1794* (vols. i and ii), *Letters Containing a Sketch of the Scenes which passed in various Departments of France during the Tyranny of Robespierre and of the Events which took place in Paris on the Tenth of Thermidor* (vol. iii); the 4th volume, untitled, was added to the 2nd edn. of the first 3 volumes in 1796. Nor should the 1st series be confused with yet another volume entitled *Letters on the Events which have passed in France since the Restoration in 1815*, published in 1819. For further bibliographical details, see M. Ray Adams, 'Helen Maria Williams and the French Revolution', in Earl Leslie Griggs (ed.), *Wordsworth and Coleridge* [1939] (New York, 1962), 87–8. I am using here Todd's edition of Williams's *Letters from France*, cited above.

[10] Later friends included Anne Plumptre, Amelia Opie, the Wordsworths, and Lady Sydney Morgan, all known for their 'Jacobinical' opinions at one time or another. Other acquaintance included Madame de Genlis (a noted educationist and author of the influential treatise *Adèle et Théodore*, which Wollstonecraft undoubtedly read in the 1780s before preparing her own educational tract) and Kosciusko (the Polish leader, of whom more later). See M. Ray Adams, 'Helen Maria Williams and the French Revolution', 89–91, 97, 101, 104, 105.

correspondence. Williams uses the letter to translate the cerebral discourse of politics into a feminized discourse of the 'heart';[11] coaxing her fictional correspondent (and by extension the reader) into emotional, and therefore political, complicity, Williams repeatedly insists that politics are a matter of sensibility, and that her revolutionary politics arise naturally and spontaneously as the appropriate (even conventional) reaction of the woman of sensibility to sentimental narrative:

I am glad you think that a friend's having been persecuted, imprisoned, maimed, and almost murdered under the ancient government of France, is a good excuse for loving the revolution. What, indeed, but friendship, could have led my attention from the annals of imagination to the records of politics; from the poetry to the prose of human life? In vain might Aristocrates have explained to me the rights of Kings, and Democrates have descanted on the rights of the people. How many fine-spun threads of reasoning would my wandering thoughts have broken; and how difficult should I have found it to arrange arguments and inferences in the cells of my brain! But however dull the faculties of my head, I can assure you, that when a proposition is addressed to my heart, I have some quickness of perception. (i. 195)

This paradigm for reading the Revolution through sentimental epistolary conventions is expanded and elaborated in two stories inset into Williams's narrative of French current affairs, stories that are evidently designed not only to justify the French Revolution, but also to dramatize it, even to stand in for it. These vignettes

---

[11] For another examination of Williams's hybridization of sentimentalism and political rhetoric, albeit one largely concerned with the relation between sentiment and the sublime, see Julie Ellison, 'Redoubled Feeling: Politics, Sentiment, and the Sublime in Williams and Wollstonecraft', in *Studies in Eighteenth-Century Culture*, 20 (1990), 201–2. While I do not agree with Ellison that 'sentiment sabotages political positions in Williams's *Letters*' (largely because Ellison does not, I think, take the politics of sentimentalism seriously enough, preferring to elevate an anachronistic concept of some more appropriate radical mode), I would concur with her judgement that, nonetheless, sentiment 'operates as a mode of feeling that is the very basis for political engagement and for political writing' (204). See also in this vein Janet Todd's observation that Williams, 'rapturously converted the French ceremonies and revolutionary festivities into enactments of the tableaux of the sentimental fiction she also wrote; French revolutionary policy became crystallized into poignant family relationships and scenes of domestic tenderness' (*Sensibility: An Introduction*, 130). I shall be expanding below on this identification of the fictional conventions informing Williams's account, although I myself am not convinced that the French revolutionary celebrations to which Todd refers were not themselves consciously staged in sentimental terms.

replicate the Revolution in terms of the letter and plot of sensibility, bearing a curious generic resemblance (despite their foundation in fact)[12] to the plot of La Nouvelle Héloïse. They present such a striking example of the importation of the epistolary discourse of the sentimental novel into what is avowedly a politico-historical document that it seems appropriate to look in some detail at them as miniaturized instances of the way in which the sentimental plot served as a political narrative in its own right, before turning to examine at more length the fate of that plot and the associated letter in subsequent radical fictions.[13]

The first story Williams retails deals with the sufferings of a certain M. du F[ossé] under the regime of a father 'who was of a disposition that prefered [sic] the exercise of domestic tyranny to the blessings of social happiness, and chose rather to be dreaded than beloved' (i. 123). Described pointedly as devoid of sensibility, 'cold even to the common feelings of nature', this father is consequently 'formed by nature for the support of the ancient government of France' and maintains 'his aristocratic rights with unrelenting severity' (i. 124) in a domestic microcosm of the *ancien régime* as a whole. By contrast, his son is plentifully endowed with 'the most feeling heart' (i. 125), a heart that leads him to fraternize across class lines with the bourgeois companion to his mother, Monique C— (in a reverse image of the affair between Julie and St Preux), and to freight his unaristocratic ambition of future 'conjugal felicity' (i. 129) upon their mutual attachment. Du Fossé's father reads this liaison as a revolutionary plot; infuriated by their secret marriage, the Baron has his son arrested and imprisoned by

---

[12] M. Ray Adams gives the most circumstantial account of the events lying behind Williams's deployment of this story: see 'Helen Maria Williams and the French Revolution', 98 and *passim*.

[13] For a discussion of these episodes which reaches rather different conclusions, see Mary Favret, 'The Idea of Correspondence in British Romantic Literature', Ph.D. thesis (Stanford Univ., 1988), 56–142. For an analysis of the *Letters . . . from France* that is also interested in Williams's deployment of sentimental epistolary novelistic paradigms and in the implications of this usage by both Wollstonecraft and Williams for their construction of revolutionary female subjectivity, but which ignores these episodes entirely and broadly argues that the sentimental is actively opposed to the revolutionary sublime, see Vivien Jones, 'Women Writing Revolution: Narratives of History and Sexuality in Wollstonecraft and Williams', in Stephen Copley and John Whale (eds.), *Beyond Romanticism: New Approaches to Texts and Contexts* (London and New York, 1992), 178–99. On the relation of the sentimental to the sublime in Williams's texts, see also Julie Ellison, 'Redoubled Feeling'.

means of a *lettre de cachet.* It is appropriate, therefore, that M. du
F—'s return to France (having escaped and married his lover in
England) is eventually enabled by the Revolution itself, which
breaks open the Bastille—an object of peculiar hatred because those
imprisoned there were consigned solely by the arbitrary power of
the *lettre de cachet*:

> Mons. and Madame du F— arrived in France, at the great epoch of French
> liberty, on the 15th of July, 1789, the very day after that on which the
> Bastile was taken. It was then that Mons. du F— felt himself in security on
> his native shore. (i. 189)

The power of the *lettre de cachet*, the letter of the law and of the
father, is implicitly subordinated in this narrative to the power of
the sentimental letter; further to underline M. du F—'s affinity with
the sentimental heroine, Williams quotes his letters from prison to
his wife at length, in the process encouraging her fictional
correspondent, and thus the reader, to identify with his position:

> You, my dear friend, who have felt the tender attachments of love and
> friendship, and the painful anxieties which absence occasions . . . who
> understand the value at which tidings from those we love is computed in
> the arithmetic of the heart; who have heard with almost uncontrollable
> emotion the post-man's rap at the door; have trembling seen the well-
> known hand which excited sensations that almost deprived you of power
> to break the seal which seemed the talisman of happiness; you can judge of
> the feelings of Mons. du F— when he received . . . an answer from his wife.
> (i. 163)

In addition, Williams herself acknowledges the thoroughly novelistic paradigm that endows her politics with the 'air of a romance'
(i. 193), stressing the similarities of her second interpolated
narrative to sentimental fiction (while nevertheless insisting, in the
traditional opening language of any editor of any epistolary novel,
that its efficacy resides in its historicity):

> Perhaps a novel-writer, by the aid of a little additional misery, and by
> giving the circumstances which actually happened a heightened colour—by
> taking his pallet, and dashing with the full glow of red what nature had
> only tinged with pale violet, might almost spin a volume from these
> materials. Yet, after all, nothing is so affecting as simplicity, and nothing so
> forcible as truth. (ii. 156)

This second narrative, so introduced, similarly deals with the
Revolution as displaced into the fortunes of a young couple (the

aristocrat Auguste and the impoverished gentlewoman Madelaine) divided by another *ancien régime* father, who arranges to have their correspondence intercepted, and attempts to consign Madelaine to a convent. The text explicitly identifies Madelaine with Pope's Eloisa, as if covering up the Rousseauistic analogue in favour of Pope's more repressive version of the story.[14] But Madelaine's view of the Revolution when it comes is entirely in line with her sentimental heritage:

Madelaine was a firm friend to the revolution, which she was told had made every Frenchman free. 'And if every Frenchman is free,' thought Madelaine, 'surely every Frenchman may marry the woman he loves.' It appeared to Madelaine, that, putting all political considerations, points upon which she had not much meditated, out of the question, obtaining liberty of choice in marriage was alone well worth the troubles of a revolution . . . (ii. 174–5)

And indeed the Revolution performs the part of a *deus ex machina* by intervening to prevent any nuns from taking the veil, thus preserving Madelaine for the embraces of her now independent lover. The Revolution effectively legitimates and reinstates the lovers' correspondence,[15] in complicity with the conventions of sentimental fiction. The status of these political vignettes as sentimental fiction is neatly confirmed by their subsequent published afterlife, shamelessly extracted and pirated in America on at least

[14] See e.g. ii. 120, where Williams directly quotes from 'Eloisa to Abelard': 'All is not Heav'n's while Abelard has part, | Still rebel nature holds out half my heart!' Although on this occasion the ominous laundering of Rousseau's fiction with Pope's far more oppressive version remains unrealized (Pope's poem conventionally imagines an essentially one-sided and permanently intercepted correspondence, after all), this is not the case in Elizabeth Inchbald's contemporaneous novel *A Simple Story* ([1791], ed. J. M. S. Tompkins (London, 1967)). In the first half of this interesting counter-example (originally drafted in the late 1770s), the wayward heroine Miss Milner is introduced as a typically uncritical reader of *La Nouvelle Héloïse*; the second half, written after the fall of the Bastille, closes down the 'Frenchness' of the first, condemning Miss Milner to her exemplary fate with a series of sardonic quotations from Pope's poem (22). On an analogous invocation of Pope, by Sir Walter Scott, see Ch. 3: for a discussion of the political implications of the replacement of Rousseau's version of the Abelard and Héloïse myth with Pope's in the poetry of Wordsworth and Byron, see Nicola J. Watson, 'Novel Eloisas: Revolutionary and Counter-Revolutionary Narratives in Helen Maria Williams, Wordsworth and Byron', *Wordsworth Circle*, 23 (1992), 18–23.

[15] For an opposed view of this episode, see Favret, 'The Idea of Correspondence', 100, where she argues that 'the revolution erases the need for letters, its movements expose the fiction of the love-letter as . . . obsolete.'

two occasions later in the decade, once as an addendum to a translation ,from the French of a novel by Louis Sebastian Mercier—*Seraphina; a novel . . . To which is added, Auguste and Madelaine. A Real History.* By Miss Helen Maria Williams (of which two separate editions were published in 1797, in Maine and Virginia respectively)—and once appended to another Gallic fiction, the suspiciously Rousseauistic *Ambrose and Eleanor, or the adventures of two children deserted on an uninhabited island. (Translated from the French). To which is added, Auguste and Madelaine. A Real History. By Miss Helen Maria Williams* (of which two editions were also published, this time in Baltimore and Philadelphia respectively, during 1799).

Given Williams's interest in using the sentimental plot within her revolutionary polemic (indeed, *as* revolutionary polemic) it is hardly surprising that her first novel, *Julia* (1790), is also preoccupied with reworking material borrowed from *La Nouvelle Héloïse*.[16] Although this novel initially appears to be hermetically sealed within the sentimental tradition inflected by Rousseau, Mackenzie and Goethe,[17] avowedly interested in tracing 'the danger arising from the uncontrouled indulgence of strong affec-tions' (vol. i. p. iii), it nevertheless betrays its political charge in the curious detour into polemical lyric embedded at its sentimental climax, a poem entitled 'The Bastille, A Vision'. Indeed, it might be said that *Julia* is in this respect the direct inverse counterpart to *Letters from France,* insetting the politics within the sentimental framework rather than the other way round, but similarly premised on their interdependence.

Deploying the device of simple plot inversion, *Julia* replays the crucially important death-bed scene in Rousseau's novel with a different distribution of personnel. In the original, Julie's death in St

---

[16] Williams wrote and published *Julia* in 1790, a matter of weeks before moving to France, establishing her salon, and beginning her series of *Letters from France*: see Janet Todd (ed.), *A Dictionary of British and American Women Writers* (London, 1985) (*DBAWW* hereafter), 323–6.

[17] This remains true despite the novel's routine incidental satire on the public's addiction to sentimental novels, in this case *The Pangs of Sensibility*. See Helen Maria Williams, *Julia: A Novel, Interspersed with some Poetical Pieces* (2 vols., London, 1790), ii. 48–9. The discussion of *The Sorrows of Young Werther* (ii. 202) is of particular interest here because it appears partially to valorize Goethe's highly Rousseauistic text (on which *Julia* certainly structures itself), which conservatives would find increasingly objectionable over the course of the decade.

Preux's arms, witnessed by a voyeuristic Wolmar (who by being a witness moralizes and legitimizes this scene of displaced sexual desire), accommodates in the only way possible both Wolmar's power and St Preux's passion—at the expense of Julie's life. With the fate of the heroine at odds with patriarchal structures functioning as a fiction of revolution, that death-bed encodes in little a form of counter-revolution; hence Williams institutes a strange and protracted game of musical death-beds in a bid to preserve her radical protagonist. Charlotte marries one Frederick Seymour, who has unfortunately fallen in love during their engagement with her close friend, Julia; after a great deal of suffering, elaborately detailed, and after each lover has teetered on the brink of death and subsequently staged a miraculous recovery, the character who eventually draws the short straw is (un-expectedly) Frederick, who expires begging to be buried with Julia and echoing for good measure the dying gasp of Rousseau's heroine, '[i]t will be no crime, Julia!' It seems, briefly, that Julia will follow him in the approved fashion—endorsed in this case by no less a personage than the respected author who was to feature two years later as one of Wollstonecraft's targets in *A Vindication of the Rights of Woman* (1792), the conduct-book writer Dr Gregory,[18] whose narrative prescription for an excess of sensibility Williams meticulously quotes and then paraphrases:

Though a woman with rectitude of principle, will resolutely combat those feelings which her reason condemns; yet, if they have been suffered to acquire force, the struggle often proves too severe for the delicacy of the female frame; and though reason, virtue, and piety, may sustain the conflict with the heart, life is frequently the atonement of its weakness. (ii. 240)

Side-stepping this repressive script at the last moment, Julia avoids the graceful decline into the grave, reinstating her friendship with Charlotte over Frederick's corpse, and organizing to share with her the upbringing of Frederick's son in a neat re-working of that intriguing coda to *La Nouvelle Héloïse* in which Claire, refusing to marry St Preux, is persuaded to live for Julie's daughter. The sentimental heroine manages, in short, the difficult trick of

---

[18] See Mary Wollstonecraft, *A Vindication of the Rights of Woman* [1792], ed. Charles Hayden (New York, 1967), 153 ff.

surviving her unauthorized passion and her exquisite sensibility; and the radical charge of this moment is both glossed and heralded by 'The Bastille; A Vision', the communal reading of which precedes Frederick's death. The poem is described as 'written by a friend lately arrived from France, and who, for some supposed offence against the state, had been immured several years in the Bastille, but was at length liberated by the interference of a person in power' (a provenance which sounds remarkably like that of the du Fossé story in *Letters from France*), and consists in part of an up-to-date preview of recent events in its celebration of the visionary moment when 'the guilty fabric falls!' (ii. 217, 221). This linkage of the inauguration of the French Revolution with the survival of the sentimental heroine seems hardly fortuitous.

In reserving and valorizing the revolutionary power of sensibility in this way, Williams's fictions of revolution are not unique during the years between the fall of the Bastille and the Terror; the plot of *Julia* is conflated with the miniatures sketched in the *Letters from France* and expanded to full effect by the popular novelist Charlotte Smith in one of her most controversial and accomplished novels, her foray into political romance, *Desmond*, published in 1792. *Desmond* is remarkable on the one hand for its canny handling of the erring heroine, who is explicitly associated with the 'Frenchness' of the Revolution, and on the other for its documentary effects (as Margaret Doody comments, 'the character's letters are dated, and the author is evidently careful to ensure that people mention [actual historical] events at the time when they would first have heard of them'[19]—in fact, the action of the novel takes place in 1790); effects that seem designed to replicate the impact of Williams's *Letters from France*.

Desmond pointedly juxtaposes politics and the sentimental plot, binding its analysis of the tyranny of the *ancien régime* and its supposedly on-the-spot reportage in Paris to a demonstration of domestic tyranny which is clearly identified as an analogous system: in this respect *Desmond* makes explicit what is largely implicit in *Julia*, frozen and preserved in its lyric interlude.[20] None

[19] 'English Women Novelists and the French Revolution', in *La Femme en Angleterre et dans les colonies américaines aux XVIIe et XVIIIe siècles* (Lille, 1975), 182.

[20] Diana Bowstead has also paid tribute to its delicate interweaving of political argument and fictional event: see 'Charlotte Smith's *Desmond*: The Epistolary Novel As Ideological Argument', in Mary Anne Schofield and Cecilia Macheski

the less, this novel displays a certain amount of caution, reflecting in its reticences something of the volatile and uncertain political mood of 1792 after the ominous arrest of the king. Smith's discreet adaptation of Rousseau's text retains the central love entanglement—Desmond (who at one point explicitly identifies himself as St Preux) is only partially successful in concealing from the lovely (and married) Geraldine Verney (who doubles Julie) his hopeless passion for her;[21] however, here the similarity to *La Nouvelle Héloïse* begins to break down, for she does not admit to a tenderness for him, either to herself or to the reader, until well into the third volume, and then only a few pages prior to the climactic scene when, on his death-bed (the familiar death-bed, but here unconventionally occupied by a surrogate for Wolmar), Geraldine's profoundly unsatisfactory husband hands her over lock, stock, and barrel (children included) into Desmond's keeping. Geraldine's predicament, delineated in the bulk of the novel—married to a rake, and threatened with prostitution to his friends—previews Wollstonecraft's later use of this motif in *Maria; or, The Wrongs of Woman* (1798); but Smith not only refuses to construct Geraldine as rebellious, but also rejects the opportunity to politicize her predicament in any way other than through the most subtle verbal parallels. Thus, although she allows Geraldine to compare herself to the Parisian mob when preparing to go into France on the orders of her husband, she depicts her emphasizing their fellowship in suffering rather than exploring the possibility of analogous rebellion, a refusal that would seem to register the increasing anxiety in England over the progress of the deliberations of the National Assembly towards the execution of the king:

If I get among the wildest collection of those people, whose ferocity arises not from their present liberty, but their recent bondage, is it possible to suppose they will injure *me*, who am myself a miserable slave, returning with trembling and reluctant steps, to put on the most dreadful of all fetters?—Fetters that would even destroy the freedom of my mind. (iii. 71)

Considering that both the loathsome Verney and his French counterpart Boisbelle join the counter-revolutionary forces in the

<hr />

(eds.), *Fetter'd or Free? British Women Novelists, 1670–1815* (Athens, Oh., 1986), 237.

[21] *Desmond* (3 vols., London, 1792), ii. 240.

attempt first to rescue and then to reinstate the king, Geraldine's self-identification with the mob released from the Bastille is hardly coincidental. The text resonates with its implications: as Desmond himself writes of the royal family's attempted escape prior to his arrest,

I would ask the tender-hearted personages who affect to be deeply hurt at the misfortunes of royalty, whether if this treachery, this violation of oaths so solemnly given [referring to the king's recent compact with the National Assembly], had been successful, and the former government restored by force of arms, the then triumphant monarch and his aristocracy, would, with equal heroism, have beheld the defeat and captivity of the leaders of the people. . . .—Then would the *King's Castles* (Mr. Burke's name for the Bastile) have been rebuilt, and *lettres de cachet* have re-peopled the dungeons!   (iii. 81)

Desmond replaces Edmund Burke's notoriously sentimental figuration of Marie Antoinette as the beleaguered heroine of sensibility with an alternative sentimental plot, 'this treachery, this violation of oaths solemnly given', a formulation that bears a strong resemblance to Geraldine's rationale for possible insurrection against her husband on the grounds of his manifest violations of the marriage-contract. Geraldine, however, resolutely remains a model of suffering duty, the 'good' Julie of the second part of *La Nouvelle Héloïse* rather than the 'bad' Julie of the first, whose sexuality threatens to subvert paternal lines of authority. Smith provides, in her stead, another locus for sexual rebellion in Geraldine's French mirror-image, Josephine de Boisbelle (whose disreputable sister is named, tellingly, Julie); the saving difference resides in the slippage of the imperfect translation between 'Verney' and 'Boisbelle'. These women are obsessively counterpointed, the crucial difference being that although Desmond fathers an illegitimate child on Josephine, he eventually marries Geraldine, a satisfactorily virtuous ending made possible by this convenient doubling. The upshot is that the figure who occupies the place of the sexually transgressive heroine of sensibility is actually Desmond, ultimately redeemed by marriage to Geraldine much as Julie is for a time reclaimed by marriage to Wolmar (men, as Wollstonecraft acidly observes in her Preface to *Maria; or, The Wrongs of Woman*, are allowed to learn from their mistakes). It is therefore possible to pair off all the protagonists satisfactorily at the end of the novel, with an ease and vim reminiscent of comic opera—but Smith remains fully aware of the fragility of these slender rope-bridges. Much of the interest in volume III hinges on whether Geraldine has indeed had a clandestine affair with Desmond and given birth to his illegitimate child, as gossip reports. This scandalous echo of the original affair of Julie and St Preux is finally exorcised by a suspiciously glib substitution of the French for the English, another version of 'translation'; the couple taken for Geraldine and Desmond were in fact Josephine and her brother Montfleuri come abroad to conceal her pregnancy until she should give birth to Desmond's illegitimate child. That the local tattlers were foxed hardly seems surprising; the splitting of the 'good' and the 'bad' woman, always liable to instability, here shows signs of collapsing back into undifferentiation, exactly as in Rousseau's prototype. When Josephine hands over the child to Geraldine the surrogacy achieves such completeness as to call attention to itself with positive stridency.

Although in this novel the 'truth' of true feeling wins out over the libellous stories fabricated by the local gossips, that is to say, although the private letter circulated among the sentimental protagonists is authenticated over what is shown to be mistaken social consensus, that victory became increasingly fragile and finally untenable as the 1790s wore on. In its explicit yoking of the power of the sentimental letter and the enthusiasms of revolutionary politics, *Desmond* records perhaps the last moment at which that authentication seemed possible.

II

In post-Terror England, it becomes harder and harder to authorize the voice of individual feeling as a form of legitimate rational protest; and this problem proves peculiarly acute when tackled within the apparently hospitable structures of the sentimental plot. 'Feeling', briefly energized by its juxtaposition with revolutionary thinking, was none the less prone, when embodied in a sentimental heroine, to add up to seduction and victimization, or, worse, madness. As Janet Todd has remarked, novels of this period are marked with a sense that 'the discourse of certain kinds of subjectivity is dangerous for women—and, if women try to appropriate it . . . they will arrive at a self-destroying impasse',[22] or, to borrow one heroine's words, 'the strong feelings, and strong energies, which properly directed, in a field sufficiently wide, might—ah! what might they not have aided? forced back, and pent up, ravage and destroy the mind which gave them birth!'[23] A heroine's 'energies of mind' (with the notable exception of those of Thomas Holcroft's remarkable and implausible Anna St Ives, in his novel of that name published in the optimistic days of 1792), are all too liable to translate into disastrously extravagant sexuality. Moreover, if the advocacy of emotionalism as the ground of a new model of female subjectivity proved a generally treacherous strategy, so too did the conventional vehicle for the expression of such affect, the letter, seem increasingly problematic as a markedly provisional, relative, and unauthorized mode of utterance. The feminist polemic which contemporary radical heroines write is in perpetual danger of being rendered powerless by their very positions as heroines of sensibility, because their political protests can be readily assimilated to the status of their other utterances— ineffectual, if graceful, effusions of sentiment—a textual blushing, or palpitation. This undermining slippage is made the more inevitable by that very polemic's own insistence on the value and authority of individual feeling. How, then, was a revolutionary polemic premised upon the heartstrings to be metamorphosed from solitary effusion to social programme? It was this problem above all that motivated the experiments carried out in Eliza Fenwick's *Secresy* (1795), Mary Hays's *The Memoirs of Emma Courtney* (1796) and *The Victim of Prejudice* (1799), and finally Mary Wollstonecraft's *Maria; or, The Wrongs of Woman* (1798). These novels set about dismembering and rearticulating *La Nouvelle Héloïse* to ratify the voice of individual affect in the face of social restrictions, a voice that had been conspicuously cut off and contained in Julie's last posthumous avowal of passion. Such attempts are successful according to the formal choices these novels make in their bid to prise open the equation of letters with sensibility, of sensibility with female sexual desire, and of female sexual desire with a plot of certain ruin and death.

---

[22] *The Sign of Angellica: Women, Writing and Fiction, 1660–1800* (London, 1989), 234.
[23] Mary Hays, *The Memoirs of Emma Courtney* [1796] (New York, 1802), i. 118.

The first and only novel produced by Eliza Fenwick, a member of the same radical circles as Mary Hays, Thomas Holcroft, William Godwin, Mary Robinson, Francis Place and Mary Wollstonecraft (whose deathbed she attended),[24] *Secresy*, published in the volatile year of 1795, is remarkable for a peculiar aesthetic and political deadlock, which displays the crippling effect of the epistolary mode upon the urgent feminist project of distinguishing between sensibility as debilitating conservative ideology and as the powerhouse of a new feminist vision. Fenwick stages a conflict between the figure of Julie (representing passionate female sexuality imperfectly repressed) and the apparently opposed figure of Rousseau's other heroine, Sophie, the perfectly obedient, pastorally educated bride of his 'natural' man, Émile. *Secresy* characterizes the story of Sophie as the father's 'script', a script interested in the maintenance of men's power over women's bodies and minds; in contrast, the story of Julie functions as the heroine's script—a script of avowed female desire and revolt against the father. In Fenwick's novel, each plot subverts the other; for while the father-surrogate, Valmont (tellingly named after Laclos's libertine-hero of *Les Liaisons dangereuses*), acts out the story of Sophie upon his niece Sibella's body, educating her upon the principles set out by Rousseau for the production and regulation of the 'natural' woman, Sibella herself, with a voice of her own conferred upon her by the novel's epistolary format, is, perhaps inevitably, acting out the story of Julie. As she moves from a position as a colonized object to vocal subjecthood, Sibella demonstrates that 'natural' (uneducated, insulated, unsocialised) womanhood is in fact independent and active—the exact opposite of her uncle Valmont's ideal woman, whom she indignantly stigmatizes as 'a timid docile slave, whose thoughts, will, passion, wishes, should have no standard of their own, but rise, change, or die as the will of a master should require!'[25] Describing Valmont's educational precepts as fictionalizing tactics—'Blind to conviction, grown old in error, he would degrade me to the subordinate station he describes' (i. 14)—she aspires instead to write her own fiction to counteract his. Attempting to circumvent her uncle's apparently inexplicable

[24] See Todd, *DBAWW*, 123–4.
[25] *Secresy, or The Ruin on the Rock* [1795], ed. Gina Luria (2 vols., New York, 1974), i. 14.

interdiction on marriage with her childhood sweetheart, Clement Montgomery, a connection which hitherto Valmont had appeared to encourage, she initiates her own quasi-marital contract outside wedlock—a private contract which she hopes will be powerful enough to return the newly profligate Clement to his original 'natural' state of grace. This proves to be a fatal mistake; for, so far from converting him, she is colonized by him, becoming pregnant (just as, of course, does her prototype Julie) and eventually going into the prescribed decline.

Secresy stages this struggle between scripts specifically in discursive terms; the tension of the narrative hinges upon the conflict between the letter, identified closely with the heroine, and the plot, associated with Valmont. Adopting this pattern, Fenwick is replicating the conventional equations (operative at least since Samuel Richardson's publication of *Clarissa*) of the heroine with letter, fiction, and reaction, and of her seducer with story, action, and instigation. Although Sibella's guerrilla letters operate from a zone outside Valmont's (largely inferred) Rousseauistic authoritarian discourse, re-voicing it from a female perspective, asserting desire and dissent, the movement of the novel ultimately establishes that the power of the letter is seriously circumscribed; 'a letter', as Caroline Ashburn, Sibella's correspondent and champion remarks, 'cannot waft down . . . drawbridges' (i. 2), much less release Sibella from the imprisonment she suffers during the course of the action. Power continues to reside in the operation of (Valmont's) plot, which, though directly threatened by Sibella's letters and their corollary, her deluded assertion of sexual independence, none the less wins out. It transpires that Clement Montgomery is Valmont's natural son; fittingly, Valmont's plan is to educate Sibella into a pattern of 'natural' submissive womanhood, and then marry her to Clement, so transferring her legitimate name and fortune into his line. Laid bare in the final pages, in Valmont's one and only letter, the cancerous secret of the title, read at first as the daughter's passional, subversive betrayal of the father, is revealed instead as the illegitimacy of patriarchy itself.

The letter's all-too-visible disempowerment, directly analogous to that of the sentimental heroine, as a helpless and eroticized display of emotion rather than a generator of plot, is compounded by its undecidability. In the clash of discourses that the epistolary plays out no one voice is enabled to elect itself unambiguously as the centre of authority; moreover, in this novel, epistolary fictions remain essentially private, removed from the test of social consensus and the possibility of mutual modification into the merely solipsistic. Although the epistolary cannot socialize the writing heroine, and therefore cannot moralize her without her consent (Sibella conspicuously refuses to recant—a gesture practically obligatory on analogous deathbeds[26]—or to underwrite the conventional morality of her death), the balance of power in terms of the 'reality' of an epistolary novel—'reality' being embodied in the progress of the plot in the interstices between the letters—is clearly in favour of the paternal system; the heroine inhabits the metareality of the epistolary, the letter that retards but never quite discards the male plot. As Patricia Spacks observes of the English Jacobin novel in general, ' "bad" characters—those opposed to the interests the text appears to support—generate events and stories by *plotting*', in particular, by rewriting the history and identity of the protagonist; as Spacks further remarks, 'females, in these fictions, cannot plot', being able only, very occasionally, to block plot.[27]

This diminished faith in the letter itself is explicitly developed over the course of Fenwick's narrative. Though Sibella's opening letters display all the rush of released revolution in their new-found voice, they eventually falter into silence, and thereafter her correspondent Caroline's letters, too, begin to lose their subversive power as she struggles to justify her action in aiding Sibella's aborted escape to Valmont and to assign him the blame for the catastrophe. While a qualified moral victory appears finally to rest

[26] Cf. e.g. the exemplary end made of Julia in Maria Edgeworth's version of *Sense and Sensibility*, *Letters of Julia and Caroline* (1795), or the awful warning presented by the flibbertigibbet anti-heroine of Jane West's *Advantages of Education* (1793). Later novels make their heroines recant at humiliating length, notably Jane West's *A Tale of the Times* (1799) and Amelia Opie's *Adeline Mowbray* (1801). See Ch.2.

[27] Patricia Meyer Spacks, *Desire and Truth: Functions of Plot in Eighteenth-Century English Novels* (Chicago, 1990), 178–80, 182. For a discussion of the functions of plot and of plotters in the English Jacobin novel see Ch. 7. As will become clear, however, I am by no means in agreement with Spacks that a movement away from plot (powered, in her view, by a masculinist drive to rational power) towards some narrative model more hospitable to a merge of reason and feeling is generally characteristic of the fiction of the period. Spacks's genealogy depends ultimately upon a denial of the opposed political agendas underlying fictional form in this decade (however much it appears to take them into account), a denial facilitated by a highly selective choice of Jacobin texts.

with Caroline, actual (in this case, financial) power remains firmly in the hands of Valmont and the predatory Clement, who ultimately forsakes Sibella to marry Caroline's rich mother, thereby disinheriting Caroline for good measure. (That the figure conventionally representing 'sense'—Caroline, who has a good deal in common generically with both Austen's Elinor in *Sense and Sensibility* and Maria Edgeworth's Caroline in her *Letters of Julia and Caroline*—should be left unmarried, and with only a qualified moral victory, eloquently testifies to the unsettling and discontented nature of Fenwick's resolution). The inadequacy of female feeling, however moral and however rational, to effect beneficial social relationships, is starkly revealed in a world where the swellings of the heart as incarnated by heartfelt letters fail signally to supplant the dark plottings of the father. Despite her searing indictment of the plots of femininity promoted by Rousseau, Fenwick is unable to imagine an alternative source of female power to 'true feeling', the truth of which seems to be in direct proportion to its helplessness; *Secresy* thus acquiesces, if reluctantly and ambiguously, in rerunning the standard tragedy of sensibility, and comes, inevitably and abruptly, to a dead end.

Perhaps it is not surprising, therefore, that subsequent revisionists of the sentimental plot find it expedient to jettison the pure epistolary in favour of narratives that contain it within the structures of first-person narration. Their attempts to stabilize the epistolary form by arresting the oscillation of *La Nouvelle Héloïse* between the law of the father and the desire of the daughter to the benefit of the heroine breed a number of highly fragmented first-person narratives, which, although they often make extensive use of letters, increasingly display a wish to negate the misreading, misconstruction, and miscarriage endemic to the epistolary. First-person narrative, as a framing mechanism, is more orderly and consequential, and, above all, permits and is premised upon the survival of the heroine.

Mary Hays's *Memoirs of Emma Courtney* (1796), for instance, borrows again from Rousseau to write an impassioned first-person narrative inlaid with Hays's own thinly-disguised real love-letters. Hays, already a radical Dissenter at the start of the 1790s, had become a disciple of Wollstonecraft after reading *A Vindication of the Rights of Woman* in 1792 and appeared as a feminist polemicist in her own right in 1793, when she published *Letters and Essays,*

Moral and Miscellaneous, and again in 1798, when *An Appeal to the Men of Great Britain in Behalf of Women* appeared: the letters which feature in *Emma Courtney* as love-letters from Emma to Augustus Harley were originally written to William Godwin's associate William Frend. Indeed, Godwin himself appears in the novel as Emma's mentor Mr Francis, failing to dissuade the heroine from indulging her epistolary passion.[28] By insetting Emma's letters within the frame of her memoirs, Hays goes beyond the dysphoric tale of fatal passion to institute instead what Nancy Miller has termed a 'euphoric' narrative structure; as Miller points out, the 'I' of memoirs is euphoric in the sense that it presupposes the survival of the heroine and declares her active and continuing productivity.[29] Furthermore, Hays salvages the power of the letter by eventually equating Emma's authorship of her memoirs with the legitimation of her earlier flood of letters: the memoirs reveal that Emma's unsolicited and outrageous epistles to her inexplicably silent heart-throb Harley were justified after all by his belatedly avowed return of her shameless passion, thus re-empowering those disgraceful missives retrospectively. So far from enacting a sentimental tragedy of the awful consequences of errant female sexuality, the novel attempts to develop a discourse, in part borrowed from Godwin and d'Helvétius, that would valorize and utilize an active female desire founded upon acute sensibility. Claiming to be a warning against the over-indulgence of feeling, it actually celebrates and validates the heroine's own infatuated, coercive effusions, with which the reader is virtually forced to identify as a result of the mixed epistolary and memoir format; despite footnotes that attempt a modicum of damage control and Hays's prefatory insistence that 'the errors of my heroine were the offspring of sensibility and ... the result of her hazardous experiment is calculated to operate as a *warning* rather than as an example', despite even the impeccable politics of the plot of the bulk of the novel (which largely endorses Hays's early verdict on *La Nouvelle Héloïse* in *Letters and Essays, Moral and Miscellaneous*, which was

[28] See Todd, *DBAWW*, 156–7. Hays herself, a popular *bête noire* of conservatives, later features in anti-Jacobin *romans à clef*, e.g. as Lady Gertrude Sinclair in Charles Lloyd's *Edmund Oliver* (1798) and as Bridgetina in Elizabeth Hamilton's *Memoirs of Modern Philosophers* (1800–1): see Ch. 2.

[29] See the central argument of *The Heroine's Text: Readings in the French and English Novel 1722–1782* (New York, 1980).

that its lack of 'purity' made it suspect),[30] it is nevertheless entirely clear that Hays reverses the plot of misguided sensibility at the very end and shows her heroine to have been right all along—by implication, as her critics remarked at the time, justifying every excess.[31]

Drawing the parallel with *La Nouvelle Héloïse* very early on, Hays makes it clear that Emma Courtney's reading of Rousseau has been in every sense partial, limited, in fact, to the first one or two volumes before the novel was removed by her father. In this instance paternal censorship has had the opposite effect to that intended; as a result of her father's action, Emma never benefits from the corrective re-insertion of Julie into patriarchy or, indeed, from the punitive cutting-short of her revived desire. Rousseau's novel thus functions at once as the agent of textual seduction, the prelude to physical seduction, and as an index to a version of female subjectivity constructed by this type of fiction. Despite Hays's claims that her 'extravagant' and 'eccentric' protagonist is a new type of heroine, replacing '*ideal perfection*, in which nature and passion are melted away' with 'a human being, loving virtue while enslaved by passion',[32] Emma will in fact describe the trajectory reserved for all passionate women, exemplified by 'the tender Eloisa' (ii. 87). Hence it is ominously overdetermined that Emma should describe her initial reaction to *La Nouvelle Héloïse* in heated and quasi-sexual terms, and should characterize this crucially truncated reading as the narrative template for her own life:

Ah! with what transport, with what enthusiasm, did I peruse this dangerous, enchanting work!—How shall I paint the sensations that were excited in my mind!—the pleasure I experienced approached the limits of pain—it was tumult—and all the ardour of my character was excited. . . . the impression made on my mind was never to be effaced—it was even productive of a long chain of consequences, that will continue to operate till the day of my death. (i. 28–9)

---

[30] 'On Reading Romances', *Letters and Essays* (London, 1793), 94.

[31] Cf. Hays's unconvincing self-exculpatory remark about the reception of this novel, made in the preface to her subsequent *The Victim of Prejudice*: 'I was accused of recommending those excesses, of which I laboured to paint the disastrous effects.' *The Victim of Prejudice* (2 vols., London, 1799), 'Advertisement'.

[32] *The Memoirs of Emma Courtney* [1796] (3 vols., New York, 1802), i. 3.

In keeping with Rousseau's master-plot, she promptly falls in love with one Augustus Harley (whom she describes variously as her St Preux and her Emilius), who tutors her in a secluded pastoral setting, a scenario heavily reminiscent of the affair of Julie and St Preux. The main body of the text is occupied by her initiation of advances (in this she is similar to Sibella) after falling in love with Harley's portrait, and her lovesick epistolary courtship of him, despite silence, evasion and ambiguity on his part. The flux of letters that constitutes *La Nouvelle Héloïse* modulates here into Emma's virtual monologue, which appropriates the text of Harley's (few and reluctant) letters and perversely misreads them, favours her image of Harley over his speaking person, and prioritizes her script for their relationship over his. For the bulk of the novel Emma assiduously manages to evade male syntax in the attempt to realize her desire, circumventing with considerable agility her mentor's attempts to cut her sentimental scenario down to size; Francis's reproof,

> Was there ever a life, to its present period, less chequered with substantial *bona fide* misfortunes? . . . Your conduct will scarcely admit of any other denomination than moon-struck madness, hunting after torture. . . . Evils of this sort are the brood of folly begotten upon fastidious indolence. They shrink into non-entity, when touched by the word of truth. . . .   (ii. 70)

is countered by a thoroughly sentimental insistence on the validity of subjective suffering:

> What does it signify whether, abstractly considered, a misfortune be worthy of the names real and substantial, if the consequences produced are the same? That which embitters all my life, that which stops the general current of health and peace is, whatever its nature, a real calamity to me. There is no end to this reasoning—what individual can limit the desires of another?   (ii. 74)

Despite her campaign, however, her script is ultimately over-written by Harley's secret, already complete, narrative. Like Sibella, Emma has entirely misread the situation—her fantasied ideal pastoral love has been pre-empted by Harley's prior secret marriage, concealed in order to prevent a conditional inheritance from falling forfeit. As in *La Nouvelle Héloïse*, completed plot is identified as patriarchal in that it is male-instigated and concerned primarily with inheritance, striving constantly to silence the woman by placing her within its own narrative syntax. In this perspective

Emma's interminable letters can displace the thrust of that syntax by their repetitive assertion of female subjectivity only for as long as the fiction of mystery can be maintained. Once Emma's fictions are finally proven fantastic, however, she submits to marriage with her other suitable suitor, Montague, a distinctly inferior version of Rousseau's tolerant Wolmar.

There is, however, an unexpected sting in this cautionary tale, which at the last moment throws its caution to the winds. Five years later, the sub-sub-text emerges; Harley reappears, wounded to death, to be nursed by Emma and to confess with his last breath (like Williams's Frederick) his long-standing and enduring love for her in words that echo Julie's letter from beyond the grave:

'Surely,' said he, 'I have sufficiently fulfilled the dictates of a rigid honour!—In these last moments—when human institutions fade before my sight—I may, without a crime, tell you—*that I have loved you . . .*'   (ii. 130)

This revelation not only unexpectedly vindicates Emma's plot of sensibility, but seems suddenly to enable her as narrator. Julie's desire may undercut the artificial Wolmar pastorale in retrospect, but it is throttled at utterance; Emma survives to exact what looks rather like vengeance.

In stark contrast to the main part of the novel, in which frustrated emotion takes the place of action, in the coda which ensues (narrated entirely in the first person) action proliferates uncontrollably and melodramatically. Between pages 130 and 158 of volume III, Emma takes in Harley's orphaned son, hires a nurse for him whom her husband seduces and impregnates, is beaten by her husband (jealous of her grief for Harley), discovers that the nurse has given birth and that Montague has murdered the child, witnesses his suicide, and eighteen years later is mourning the death of her daughter, Emma Montague, who was to have married her adopted son, called (not coincidentally) Augustus Harley. This improbably rapid *débâcle* seems to be directed at re-establishing the much-desired dyad of Emma and Harley, albeit at one remove.

Indeed, the express reason for the memoirs is Emma's need to repossess her adopted son's affections, which have been directed fruitlessly and self-destructively towards another woman (Emma's pretext for forwarding her memoirs has been to warn him against the dangers of a misguided passion). Her efforts to transmute the unstable relation of the lovers into the mother–son relationship can be seen as a restructuring of the original disastrous love-affair. In the act of writing her memoirs her powerless letters are embedded within, and thereby transformed into, a powerful monologic discourse. This discourse addressed to her son springs from the fertilization of her epistolary passion by Harley's written will, his last and most authoritative 'letter', which bequeaths his son to Emma's guardianship—legitimizing him in this way as the offspring of their illegitimate passion, and in the same moment sanctioning her transgressive narrative. Emma's ability to empower herself through her 'son' parallels and comments upon Julie's death, which follows upon her rescue of her son from drowning; whereas Julie, by dying instead of her son, sacrifices her desire finally to patriarchy, Emma forces her son to acknowledge, accommodate, and embody her desire.[33]

If *The Memoirs of Emma Courtney* performs a fragile victory in eventually endorsing the power of the heroine's letters, Hays's second novel, *The Victim of Prejudice* (1799), is profoundly pessimistic in its insistence on the impotence of the text preoccupied with recording the intimate vibrations of individual feeling and experience when faced with patriarchal social scripts. Couched primarily in the form of memoirs punctuated with a few letters, the narrative repeats an idyllic Émile/Sophie scenario, only to shatter it with a series of alternative stories concentrating on male betrayal and exploitation, of which the most important is the tragic narrative of the seduction, fall into prostitution, and eventual execution on a charge of murder of the heroine Mary's own mother (provided in the mother's own, for once, *pace* Nancy Miller, dysphorically posthumous, inset memoir); a trajectory that Mary herself will be violently forced to follow (despite her unassailable virtue) as a result of society's refusal of amnesty to the supposedly contaminated daughter of such a parentage. Raped by an aristocrat rather than seduced (in a sequence heavily reminiscent of *Clarissa*),

---

[33] This ending is not unlike one of the two projected endings to Wollstonecraft's *Maria; or, The Wrongs of Woman*, in which the lost child is restored and the heroine takes refuge in motherhood with her faithful servant at her side. This fantasy of a 'community of women' (to borrow Nina Auerbach's phrase) reinstated by the maternal embrace operates as yet another extraordinary reworking of the coda to *La Nouvelle Héloïse*, in which Claire, Julie's greatest friend, is persuaded to live through the ruse of dressing Julie's daughter as Julie.

Mary is compelled to repeat her mother's story, through the doomed attempt to earn her living, an imprisonment for debt, and finally her attempted suicide (though she is rescued from this last in the nick of time to go into a more respectable, though equally fatal, decline). The voice of feeling in this novel, however eloquent its critique of aristocratic libertinism, has no weight at all against the social script with which the heroine is forced to comply; as her rapist warns her on her threatening to take him to court, 'Who will credit the tale you mean to tell? What testimony or witnesses can you produce that will not make against you? . . . How would your delicacy shrink from the idea of becoming, in open court, the sport of ribaldry, the theme of obscene jesters?',[34] and she finally, despairingly, concurs:

What credit has the simple asseverations of the sufferer, sole witness in his own cause, to look for against the poison of detraction, the influence of wealth and power, the bigotry of prejudice, the virulence of envy, the spleen and corruption engendered in the human mind by barbarous institutions and pernicious habits? (ii. 200)

Isolated in her prison cell, the writing of the memoir is Mary's only recourse in a world that will not accord her any degree of discursive credibility; but with no addressee and no system of delivery, the memoir becomes increasingly unstable until finally it topples into madness, in a telling repetition of Godwin's original projected ending to *Caleb Williams*. These sentimental letters, unlike those imagined by Helen Maria Williams earlier in the decade, have no power to break out of tyrannic incarceration, but only to recapitulate it:

And thou, the victim of despotism, oppression, or error, tenant of a dungeon, and successor to its present devoted inhabitant, should these sheets fall into thy possession, when the hand that wrote them moulders in the dust and the spirit that dictated ceases to throb with indignant agony, read; and if civil refinements have not taught thy heart to reflect the sentiment which cannot penetrate it, spare from the contemplation of thy own misery one hour . . . (i. 1)

Although Hays recuperates her heroine's reason in an unexpected supplemental epilogue chronicling her rescue and final illness, the novel unmistakably dramatizes the drawbacks of the memoir as

---

[34] *The Victim of Prejudice*, ii. 85–6.

political manifesto.[35] Mary's narrative remains recalcitrantly personal rather than political, solipsistic rather than social, a problem which Wollstonecraft's final novel, *Maria; or, The Wrongs of Woman* (1798) attempts to tackle in its aim none the less to validate individual experience as an appropriate mode of political engagement. This novel, indeed, might well be read as a critical history of the radical experimental narrative strategies I have been detailing so far.

Maria; or The Wrongs of Woman contains only one very short letter and an implied series of letters, conspicuously eschewing epistolarity to the point where the narrator refuses 'to trace the progress of this passion' by eliding the passage of letters between Maria and her soon-to-be lover, an ex-American revolutionary, Henry Darnford.[36] Given that Maria's passion is structured very explicitly upon the model of *La Nouvelle Héloïse*, this erasure of epistolarity, and the marginalization of (forbidden) passion which seems to follow upon it, is intriguing. Incarcerated, like Williams's lovers, in an analogue to the Bastille, this time a madhouse, and (for much the same reason as Sibella) on a matter of inherited money, Maria exchanges not sentimental letters but a sentimental novel, *La Nouvelle Héloïse*, which comes to stand in for the love-letter itself as she and Darnford communicate through the erotic obliquities of marginalia; 'she read on the margin of an impassioned letter, written in the well-known hand—"Rousseau alone, the true Prometheus of sentiment, possessed the fire of genius necessary to portray the passion, the truth of which goes so directly to the heart" ' (38). This love affair thus takes place literally at the margins of Rousseau's text, mediated in positively Girardian

[35] Continuing this trajectory from the radical optimism of *Emma Courtney* to the sober despair of *Victim of Prejudice*, Hays herself, though remaining a close friend of other radicals such as Eliza Fenwick, seems to have toned down her own political views: indeed *The Victim of Prejudice* is already beginning to lose hope in even the possibility of political improvement, its heroine lamenting that 'Ignorance and despotism, combating frailty with cruelty, may go on to propose *partial* reform in one invariable, melancholy round; reason derides the weak effort; while the fabric of superstition and crime, extending its broad base, mocks the toil of the visionary projector' (ii. 232). In time Hays came increasingly to admire the more conservative Maria Edgeworth and Hannah More: More herself even published some of Hays's later work, the moral tales *The Brothers* (1815) and *Family Annals* (1817). See Todd, *DBAWW*, 157.

[36] Mary Wollstonecraft, *Maria; or, The Wrongs of Woman*, 49.

fashion by its seductive discourse.[37] The lovers desire, as it were, by the book, according to its letter, which triangulates and falsifies Maria's relation to Darnford to the point where she cannot perceive the man himself at all, preferring to rehearse the self-destructive story of excessive sensibility in the over-inflated (and by now worryingly hackneyed) terms of *La Nouvelle Héloïse*.[38] Perhaps 'rehearses' is the wrong word, for Maria is not content simply to look through Rousseau's lens. Like Sibella, she strives to edit the father's text, to appropriate it, above all to outdo it, while remaining fatally unaware that the fiction itself is not, and cannot be, owned by her. In the same way that the madhouse window imprisons and frames her view of the garden, so too does the partial eye of Rousseau's text control her fantasy pastorale as she tailors Darnford into her personalized St Preux:

She flew to Rousseau as her only refuge from the idea of him, who might prove a friend . . . still the personification of St Preux, or of an ideal lover far superior, was after this imperfect model, of which merely a glance had been caught, even to the coat and hat of the stranger. But if she lent St Preux, or the demi-god of her fancy, his form, she richly repaid him by the donation of all St Preux' sentiments and feelings culled to gratify her own . . . (38)

This exchange of epistolary novel and letters is after a time supplanted by an exchange of Rousseauistic memoirs, through which each illicit lover seduces the other. Initially addressed to her lost child (whom she actually believes to be dead), and written to beguile the time before she meets Darnford, Maria's memoirs are originally effectively self-addressed, functioning as a substitute novel once her library gives out:

Writing was then the only alternative, and she wrote some rhapsodies descriptive of the state of her mind; but the events of her past life pressing on her, she resolved circumstantially to relate them, with the sentiments that experience, and more matured reason would naturally suggest. (30–1)

---

[37] René Girard, *Deceit, Desire and the Novel: Self and Other in Literary Structure* (Baltimore, 1966).

[38] For a reading of Wollstonecraft's novel that is also interested in the ways that textuality is raised to thematic prominence, arguing in particular that the act of reading the various fictions produced within the novel is politicized as the potentially liberatory site of ideological critique, see Tillotama Rajan, 'Wollstonecraft and Godwin: Reading the Secrets of the Political Novel', *Studies in Romanticism*, 27 (1988), 221–51.

This progression, from 'rhapsodies' to a narrative moralized in retrospect, suggests the analogous movement from the epistolary, the immediate authentic effusion of the heart, to memoirs which moralize—or perhaps 'politicize' would be a better word—her narrative. This strategy relates *The Wrongs of Woman* to other formal experiments by English Jacobin novelists (notably Godwin), which exploit first-person memoirs as a variant on and development of sentimental form: such novels characteristically describe experience generating a political consciousness which is then validated in retrospective confessional narrative. Wollstonecraft's redeployment of this strategy, however, betrays considerable uncertainty over its power, for in writing (rather than plotting her escape in a more material fashion) Maria invents herself into sentimental impotence: '[s]he lived again in the revived emotions of youth, and forgot her present in the retrospect of sorrows that had assumed an unalterable character', writing (and reading) the novel of her own life (31). Maria's memoir is frankly novelistic throughout, and thus (despite the political rhetoric that laces it, reminiscent in many places of the tone of *A Vindication of the Rights of Woman*), the suffragette is transcribed as the seductive. Read by Darnford, Maria appears as the lovely captive heroine of sensibility, and can justly be accused of literary complicity in patriarchy.

Apparently more trustworthy, as it is told direct to Maria, avoiding the temptation of novelistic templates, Darnford's own story, strikingly similar to that of his prototype M. du Fossé in that Darnford too has been imprisoned by the machinations of his relatives over a question of inheritance,[39] nevertheless has a

---

[39] This is not to deny that Darnford has some relation to Wollstonecraft's lover between 1793 and 1796, Gilbert Imlay, who was himself American, and who wrote, possibly in collaboration with Wollstonecraft herself, an epistolary sentimental novel with confused radical overtones. The correspondents of *The Emigrants* (1793) debate the desirability of divorce, women's education, and sexual freedom, and noticeably criticize the British legislature: the novel is set partly in post-revolutionary America and partly (pointedly) in what one might call 'pre-revolutionary' Britain. Indeed this novel exactly delineates a discourse at once sentimental, radical, and, more ominously, sexually libertarian, a discourse that is also characteristic of Darnford; however, its plot allows a space to sentimental radical discourse in allowing the beleaguered heroine Eliza to escape to America, where this discourse can be publicly authorized and acknowledged. However, as I argue rather later in this chapter, it is clear that such fictional paradigms were also being lived out personally by their writers, and were also assimilated to them by their 'readers'; there is clearly a continuum between texts and personae.

similarly split personality, produced by its narration within the frame of the third person. The main narrative voice makes it plain that, so far as Maria is concerned, Darnford's story constructs him as analogous to herself, another victim of society, feminized by his imprisonment and powerlessness into the literary stereotype of the Man of Feeling by whom Maria allows herself to be seduced: 'A man of feeling thinks not of seducing, he is himself seduced by all the noblest emotions of his soul' (103). The reader, on the other hand, is meticulously sensitized to the text's ominous pointers to his future infidelity, most tellingly to his disgust at the prudishness of American women and his assertion that he was only able to save himself from boredom while in America 'by making downright love to them' (45). Maria's inadequate reading of this particular novelette, marked by her own lapses into sentimental jargon, will lead her to freight her hopes of personal liberation upon this hopelessly compromised revolutionary, a man as incapable of genuine commitment to the liberalism of post-revolutionary American society as to the sexual revolution associated with French revolutionary thinking.

Critics have regularly identified Wollstonecraft's political narrative antidote to this sentimental paradigm within the competing autobiographical account of the working-class woman, Maria's jailor, Jemima.[40] Jemima implicitly contrasts her oral narrative with Maria's novelistic memoir: 'I have since read in novels of the blandishments of seduction, but I had not even the pleasure of being enticed into vice' (59). Her 'plain tale' is indeed notably anti-novelistic; but things are not as simple as they might be, for Jemima and Maria are only able to establish any sort of common discourse by virtue of Jemima's extensive reading amongst the novels in the library of the man who first took her into keeping, and it is reading Maria's memoir, on top of her sentimental 'reading' of the tableau formed by Maria and Darnford (which prompts 'a tear of pleasure . . . the first tear that social enjoyment had ever drawn from her'—101), that softens Jemima's heart to the point where she agrees to aid Maria's escape. The sentimental is in fact conventionally displayed here as the means of sympathetic identification between different classes, a social mechanism wearisomely familiar from

---

[40] For an opposed reading, see Poovey, *The Proper Lady and the Woman Writer*, 103–4.

mainstream sentimental novels of the late eighteenth century such as Sterne's *Sentimental Journey* or Mackenzie's *Man of Feeling*.

In framing these competing styles of memoirs within a third-person narrative, Wollstonecraft is therefore not so much debunking the ideology of sensibility outright (as Mary Poovey argues), but rather trying to dissociate 'true' from 'false' sensibility: 'true' or '*active*' sensibility, 'the auxiliary of virtue and the soul of genius' (126), which is the foundation of fellow-feeling in Jemima and of moral independence in Maria (the justification, for example, of her self-proclaimed divorce), and 'false' sensibility, which Wollstonecraft regards as complicit with the debilitating patriarchal scripting of women, represented here by *La Nouvelle Héloïse*. Significantly, Jemima, linking this sort of 'feeling' with male libertinism, describes the man who kept her as both a disgusting libertine and as a writer whose aim in 'his writings was to touch the simple springs of the heart'—a writer who begins to sound very like a first cousin to Rousseau (62). Maria, in complementary contrast, links this sort of 'feeling' with the institution of marriage, within which a woman loses even the right to act upon her own desire, 'required to moralize, sentimentalize herself to stone' (102).

The novel endeavours valiantly to supersede this disempowering narrative of doomed sensibility. In an evident attempt to displace the value attached to the central consciousness of the sentimental heroine (or indeed of the author as sentimental heroine), Wollstonecraft repeatedly insists that her 'sketches' 'are not the abortion of a distempered fancy, or the strong delineations of a wounded heart' and that 'the history ought rather to be considered, as of woman, than of an individual' (21); that is to say, that she is writing not a novel of sensibility but a social realist novel 'exhibiting the misery of oppression, peculiar to women, that arises out of the partial laws and customs of society'. Assembling her social anatomy, Wollstonecraft resorts to the third person for social and moral authority beyond individual feeling, containing the subjective within a series of ever-larger box-narratives which isolate Maria's central first-person narrative, insulating the reader's sympathies. None the less, the novel as a whole remains radically unstable, teetering vertiginously between the general and the particular, as Janus-faced as the title itself. Despite Wollstonecraft's reservations over Maria's way of telling her own story and over her way of constructing yet another romantic fantasy within which to live, it is nevertheless clear that in *Maria; or, The Wrongs of Woman* experience is authenticized and validated by individual feeling. The problem played out in *Maria*, as in the other radical novels I have examined here, is how to claim public authority for a female narrative premised upon sensibility. It is neither possible to speak female subjectivity in its native language, the language of sensibility, and be heard, nor to speak as a female subject outside sentimental rhetoric altogether. As Mary Jacobus puts it, 'The prison of sensibility is created by patriarchy to contain women; thus they experience desire without law, language without power. Marginalized, the language of feeling can only ally itself with insanity . . .'[41] The 'lovely maniac' who, distressingly, interrupts the narrative of her song with a series of meaningless noises, is a living memento of the helplessness of sensibility; forcibly married to an elderly husband for the profit of her male relatives, she loses her mind as a consequence of losing control over her story. The dilemma is most forcibly dramatized in the law-court scene, in which Maria's written deposition, couched in the rhetoric of feeling, is sandwiched between the case for the prosecution, set out in dense legal jargon, and the judge's summing-up, which alludes to 'the fallacy of letting women plead their feelings', a practice that would promote 'new-fangled notions' and 'French principles' in public and in private life (149). The judge here reiterates Maria's husband's committal of her to the asylum in its description of her as mad—'indeed the conduct of the lady did not appear to be that of a person of sane mind' (150). By 1798 there seems to be no room for a woman's feelings except in the madhouse. This double-bind causes the distinction between 'true' and 'false' sensibility to collapse periodically, in part, as Poovey has pointed out, because

[41] 'The Difference of View', in Jacobus (ed.), *Women Writing and Writing About Women* (London, 1979), 15. In this passage Jacobus also recognizes 'a moment of imaginative and linguistic excess over-brimming the container of fiction, and swamping the distinction between author and character'—a moment of selective madness which she identifies as Utopian and revolutionary, pointing toward a new kind of feminist writing which rejects absorption into what she classes as a 'male' text and transgresses and disrupts the literary structures women's writing must none the less inhabit (16). While throughout this study I clearly read the figure of the letter as a place of resistance to precisely those plots the novel generally enforces, and while I recognize the pragmatic attractiveness of Jacobus's critical moves in instituting a practice of feminist criticism, I am inclined to agree here with Mary Poovey that the narrative collapse of this novel signals failure rather than the birth of a new form. See Poovey, *The Proper Lady and the Woman Writer*, 257 n.

'the narrator herself repeatedly lapses back into sentimental jargon and romantic idealism'; the net result is that *Maria; or, The Wrongs of Woman* 'threatens to lose sight of its political purpose and become just another sentimental novel'.[42] It threatens, indeed, to become a novel exhibiting an uncanny resemblance to Wollstonecraft's sarcastic 'receipt for a novel', which concludes scathingly that 'Sensibility is the never-failing theme, and sorrow torn to tatters, is exhibited in ... moping madness—tears that flow forever, and slow consuming death', and that the whole performance is more likely than not to culminate in 'a dismal catastrophe, and dying for love'.[43] Like Hays's heroine, who retains her kinship with 'refined, romantic, factitious, unfortunate beings' despite herself, and so frames her personal narrative in novelistic terms because she can 'find no substitute for the sentiment [she] regretted [romantic love] for that sentiment formed my character',[44] Maria is caught within the same sentimental terms of reference that compromise Emma's critique of 'the contradictory systems that have so long bewildered our principles and conduct' (ii. 39).

Critiquing the implications of sentimental fictions demanded a standpoint outside (patriarchal) ideology—a standpoint which could only be guaranteed by individual feeling. But as the novel of sensibility is also founded squarely upon acting out the tragic conflict of an individual woman's emotions with the social restrictions operating on those impulses, radical novels begin to look disturbingly like novels of sensibility, and prove prone to succumb to their built-in mechanisms of containment. Wollstonecraft's last attempt to unravel this conundrum appears in the fragment 'The Cave of Fancy' which was published posthumously, bound up with *Maria; or, The Wrongs of Woman*. In this 'oriental tale', as Godwin in his editorial capacity calls it, a daughter is

[42] Mary Poovey has suggested that the uncertainty of tone that marks the text, and, in particular, the wavering perspective of the omniscient narrator on the dangers and pleasures of 'romantic expectations', are related to the difficulty of attacking the ideology of sensibility within the genre of the sentimental novel, a position with which, as should be clear, I am in broad agreement. Poovey argues that the narrator is seduced in parallel to Maria, and seduced in the same way, via a sentimental story, which enables the heroine to 'novelize' first of all her husband, and then her lover, Darnford; *The Proper Lady and the Woman Writer*, 96–8, 105.

[43] Review of *The Exiles; or, Memoirs of the Count of Cronstadt* by Clara Reeve, *Analytical Review*, 4 (June 1789), 221; review of *Miscellaneous Poems*, by Anne Francis, *Analytical Review*, 7 (July 1790), 299–301.

[44] *Emma Courtney*, ii. 78, ii. 61.

fortunately orphaned in a shipwreck which frees her from the past, embodied by her mother (described as a standard heroine of sensibility), and the child is brought up instead by a convenient 'sage'. The result of this regenerate education by a revised Rousseau figure is that the plot of *La Nouvelle Héloïse* is borrowed once again; this time, however, to write out passion altogether. The daughter, although in love with a married man, marries a father-surrogate in response to the dictates of duty, virtue, and reason. Her lover dies, but she nourishes her passion as an integral part of her 'nature' (152). None the less, she eventually recants, recognizing that she 'saw through a false medium' (154), and resolves instead to become 'useful'. Wollstonecraft's alternative to the ideology of sensibility turns out to be not so very different from that of her impeccably respectable and politically more conservative contemporary, Hannah More, author of *Strictures on the Modern System of Female Education* (1799).

One final rewrite of *La Nouvelle Héloïse* may detain us: Charlotte Smith's late novel, *The Young Philosopher*, published in 1798, a novel which betrays the hopelessly beleaguered state of sentimental discourse at the end of the decade by systematically subjecting it to a simulacrum of conservative plotting which so nearly threatens its survival that Smith can only rescue it by recourse to drastic expedients. Although the central figure, George Delmont, is by now all too recognizable—a Rousseauistic philosopher, sympathizer with the principles of the French Revolution, a reader of *La Nouvelle Héloïse*, and a version of St Preux—and although he will accordingly dance the evolutions of the appropriate plot, the centre of gravity of the novel has significantly shifted, and the familiar sentimental syntax is materially modified by its insertion within an extensively realized and labyrinthine network of social convention: 'politics, and lawsuits, and old ladies finding out that we are people of bad character, and gossips repeating the malignant nonsense of other gossips'.[45] Rather than preoccupying itself with the involutions of sensibility, *The Young Philosopher* concerns itself instead with the tension between self-representation and the 'construction' that society puts upon appearances. The arrival in a small provincial neighbourhood (reminiscent of Austen's Highbury) of two strange women under

---

[45] *The Young Philosopher. A Novel* (4 vols., London, 1798), ii. 263.

the protection of the local freethinker, author, and pamphleteer on both the American and French Revolutions, inspires two intensely overdetermined plots; on the one hand an impeccably Rousseauistic affair between Delmont and Medora Glenmorris described from the inside in Delmont's letters, and on the other the fabrication and circulation by the local gossips of a miniature anti-Jacobin novel.[46] This discursive conflict between the scandalous and the sentimental, registered in Delmont's brother's remark to him that 'our delectable aunt has made a most terrible and terrific history of this, while your's is just fitted for the amiable young heroine of romance' (iii. 17), is worked out at some length. While the locals concoct and retail their outrageous accounts, Medora, to her astonishment and dismay, and in a mirror-image of her mother's own earlier fate, finds herself occupying first a diminutive Gothic novel, and then a pocket edition of a Richardsonian kidnap, both narrated in the first-person. The issue is whether first-person narration—persistently associated with madness throughout—will come to carry enough authority to discredit the web of second- and third-hand gossip. In the event the two discourses prove fundamentally incompatible, and in a remarkable denouement, denouncing the state of England and the social compact in effect there, Delmont, his new wife, Medora, and his parents-in-law depart for America. In 1798, in the context of a growing tide of reaction and patriotic fervour for the war against France, forms of discursive emigration seem to have been the only ways to validate sentimental experience.

III

Discursive and political power in these texts ultimately resides in the power to narrate others as heroines of sensibility. Recognizing this early in the decade in writing *A Vindication of the Rights of Woman*, Wollstonecraft (taking her cue from what might be regarded as Rousseau's own novelization of himself, the

---

[46] In the eyes of the local gossips, Delmont figures as a philosopher-rake, responsible for the sudden abduction of Medora—as one Mrs Grinsted insinuates, 'Mr. Delmont, perhaps, knowing the predilection of yourself and Mr. Glenmorris for the manners and morality of modern Gallia, may have conjectured that he acted not very injuriously to your principles, in appropriating for a short period your daughter to himself' (iii. 172).

Confessions) simply narrated Rousseau into the position of a senti-mental protagonist, victimized by his own passionate and over-active imagination. This treatment culminated in the unkindest cut of all, whereby Wollstonecraft edited Rousseau into a hapless heroine of sensibility:

Why was Rousseau's life divided between ecstasy and misery? Can any other answer be given but this, that the effervescence of his imagination produced both; but had his fancy been allowed to cool, it is possible that he might have acquired more strength of mind.[47]

As Patricia Yaeger has observed, Wollstonecraft in her dealings with Rousseau in this section of *A Vindication of the Rights of Woman* 'expropriates' his text, and treats it as a body: 'These embodied texts are mortal, penetrable, excitable; they become imperfect sites of that sometime thing we call "patriarchal discourse". Thus male bodies and texts can be made to circulate through women's texts—breaking that circuit of meaning in which women have been the objects of circulation.'[48] However, this strategy of re-circulation, despite Yaeger's optimism, could equally well be used on Wollstonecraft herself, and in the event she, for all her ultimate resistance to sentimentalism, came to occupy for her culture the position of the paradigmatic heroine of sensibility, a position by the end of the decade identified with 'a corrupt and vicious system of education' thought to fit women 'for revolutionary agents, for heroines, for Staëls, for Talliens, for Stones . . .'[49] This fate was hardly remarkable; her contemporaries, Helen Maria Williams (at whom the 'Stones' gibe is directed, defiantly living as she did with the married Stone in Paris) and Mary Hays (of whose *Memoirs of Emma Courtney* the *Anti-Jacobin* asked rhetorically, 'Does not this out-Helen even the wife or mistress of Stone?'),[50] were likewise assimilated to the model of 'senti-sensualism', via an equation between the female body and female writing. Williams's position as a novelist and politician of sensibility, played out in real life in her heroinical liaison, would eventually ensure her a reputation in the ever more conservative political climate of England in the 1790s as 'an intemperate advocate for Gallic

---

[47] *A Vindication of the Rights of Woman*, 146.
[48] Patricia Yaeger, *Honey-Mad Women: Emancipatory Strategies in Women's Writing* (New York, 1988), 161.   [49] *Anti-Jacobin*, 3 (1799), 55.
[50] Ibid.

licentiousness', to borrow Polwhele's characteristically florid phraseology,[51] appearing to the conservative Laetitia-Matilda Hawkins to be a living type of female Liberty and therefore of 'Eloisa' herself.[52] Writing of Hays after her death, Henry Crabb Robinson found her only defence to be in the denial of such an autobiographical connection between text and body: 'She confessed Mary Wollstonecraft's opinions with more zeal than discretion. This brought her into disrepute among the rigid, and her character suffered—but most undeservedly. Whatever her principles may have been, her conduct was perfectly correct'.[53] But if the construction of Wollstonecraft as a heroine of sensibility (a formation that continues to exert considerable influence even today) was by no means unique, it was remarkable for the sophistication with which the patterning was worked out, and for the extent of its subsequent influence.

It was William Godwin's ill-advised (however well-intentioned) *Memoirs of the Author of a Vindication of the Rights of Woman* (1798), published in the weeks following his wife's death, that set the terms for all subsequent biographies of Wollstonecraft, establishing in particular, as Catherine Parke notes, 'a marked and unusually active and exemplary relationship between her life and her work', and thereby making Wollstonecraft the heroine of her own life. With a certain truth to Wollstonecraft's well-documented propensity to dramatize herself, in the wake of reading Rousseau, as the stereotypical sentimental heroine, both in her private letters, her published *Letters from Sweden, Norway, and Denmark*, and in

[51] Richard Polwhele, *The Unsex'd Females; A Poem* [1798], ed. Gina Luria (New York, 1974), 19 n.

[52] Hawkins mounts an explicit attack on Williams's *Letters from France* in her *Letters on the Female Mind*, constructing Williams's career as an awful warning against female Liberty and connecting her radicalism with her affinities to 'Eloisa.' See Laetitia-Matilda Hawkins, *Letters on the Female Mind* (2 vols., London, 1793), i. 78–88.

[53] Henry Crabb Robinson, *Diaries, Reminiscences, and Correspondence*, ed. Thomas Sadler (Boston, 1869), i. 37. How necessary such a defence was is illustrated by the occasion in 1800 when Charles Lloyd, friend of Coleridge and author of the anti-Jacobin novel *Edmund Lloyd*, in perfect consonance with the structural logic of sentimental subjectivity, claimed that Hays had offered herself to him as 'Emma Courtney', a move that redoubled the original scandal of the real letters inset into that novel. See Mary Hays, *Appeal to the Men of Great Britain in Behalf of Women*, ed. Gina Luria (New York, 1974), 'Introduction'.

her first novel,[54] Godwin describes Wollstonecraft as a Rousseauistic heroine of sensibility who, in Parke's words, 'both as artist and
as political intelligence, is then defined primarily by her physical
and emotional capacity for feeling'.[55] This naïvely and perilously
out-of-date narrative patterning, an unwise throwback to the
uninflected celebration of radical sentimentalism characteristic of
Williams's early volumes, appears condensed and miniaturized in
the obituary by Mary Hays published in the *Annual Necrology for
1797–8* (composed before the publication of Godwin's *Memoirs*,
but according to Hays herself heavily based upon a reading of them
in manuscript), in which she says of Wollstonecraft by way of
preface that

persons of the finest and most exquisite genius have probably the greatest
sensibility, consequently the strongest passions, by the fervor of which they
are too often betrayed into error. . . . If by her quick feelings, prompt
judgements, and rapid decisions, she was sometimes betrayed into false
conclusions, her errors were expiated by sufferings, that, while they disarm
severity, awaken sympathy and seize irresistibly upon the heart.[56]

Hays describes *Mary* and *The Wrongs of Woman* as more or less
unadulterated autobiography, and quotes extensively from the
love-letters to Imlay. As this would suggest, Godwin's biography
neatly conflated the conventions of the sentimental novel with the

[54] See Ralph Wardle, *Mary Wollstonecraft: A Critical Biography* (Lawrence,
Kansas, 1951), 15, 66, 69,. 75, 86; Margaret George, *One Woman's 'Situation': A
Study of Mary Wollstonecraft* (Urbana, Ill., 1970), 41, 63–76; Margaret Walters,
'The Rights and Wrongs of Woman: Mary Wollstonecraft, Harriet Martineau,
Simone de Beauvoir', in Juliet Mitchell and Ann Oakley (eds.), *The Rights and
Wrongs of Women* (Harmondsworth, 1976), 312–13; Mitzi Myers, 'Mary
Wollstonecraft's *Letters Written . . . in Sweden*: Toward Romantic Autobiography'
Studies in Eighteenth-Century Culture, 8 (1979), 165–85.
[55] As Catherine N. Parke has remarked, Wollstonecraft's lifelong project might
be described as an attempt to fashion autobiography (especially entangled with the
politics of sensibility when the subject was a woman) 'into a suitably objective
context and resource for her work'. 'What Kind of Heroine is Mary Wollstonecraft?'
in Syndy McMillen Conger (ed.), *Sensibility in Transformation: Creative Resistance
to Sentiment from the Augustans to the Romantics* (London, 1990), 104–5, 107. For
an account of the history of the writing of the *Memoirs* which remarks on their
inflection by sentimental paradigms see Mitzi Myers, 'Godwin's *Memoirs* of
Wollstonecraft: The Shaping of Self and Subject', *Studies in Romanticism*, 20
(1981), 305, 312.
[56] Mary Hays, 'Memoirs of Mary Wollstonecraft', *Annual Necrology for
1797–8; Including Also, Various Articles on Neglected Biography* (London, 1800),
411–12.

tenets of the New Philosophy, mapping Wollstonecraft's life (including her liaison with Godwin himself) in terms of the sentimental novel of sexual transgression associated most notoriously with Rousseau. This enabled the subsequent wholesale fictionalization of the New Philosophers themselves, to the point where, as Godwin complained to Parr in 1800, 'not even a petty novel . . . now ventures to aspire to favour, unless it contains some expressions of dislike and abhorrence to the new philosophy, and its chief English adherent'.[57]

Godwin's narrative is underpinned by the characteristic and Rousseauistic premises of the sentimental novel that 'the sentiments of the heart cannot submit to be directed by the rule and the square'[58] and, further, that the minute delineation of such sentiments will induce the (morally desirable) sympathetic identification of the reader:

I cannot easily prevail on myself to doubt, that the more fully we are presented with the picture and story of such persons as the subject of the following narrative, the more generally shall we feel in ourselves an attachment to their fate, and a sympathy in their excellencies. (2–3)

Godwin's presentation of Wollstonecraft as moral exemplar relies upon a readerly endorsement of the validity of 'sentiments of the heart' over 'factitious rules of decorum', of individual feeling against social propriety—a construction of the reader that, as I have shown, is indebted to the characteristic mechanisms of the sentimental novel. Furthermore, Godwin's complicity with the ideology of sensibility leads him to appropriate the plot of *La Nouvelle Héloïse* to vindicate Wollstonecraft as a revolutionary heroine, an appropriation recognized by the hostile Polwhele, who was similarly unable to resist casting her as 'Eloisa' in *The Unsex'd Females*. This narrativization of Wollstonecraft as Julie, a woman led into sexual transgression through her deluded sensibility, eventually redeemed by love, and reinstated within the family as a paragon of avant-garde bourgeois conjugality, however it might be said to have blurred or 'misrepresented' the biographical 'truth', is nevertheless a generically appropriate transposition. Godwin

[57] William Godwin to Parr, 15 Apr. 1800. See B. Sprague Allen, 'The Reaction Against William Godwin', *Modern Philosophy*, 16 (1918), 57–75.
[58] William Godwin, *Memoirs of Mary Wollstonecraft Godwin, Author of a Vindication of the Rights of Woman* (Philadelphia, 1799), 156.

simply inserts Wollstonecraft into the plot of sensibility, hoping to authenticate through this perilous translation her revolutionary potential. Aligning his wife with the heroine of sensibility, Godwin mitigates the 'rigid and somewhat amazonian temper' of the published body of Wollstonecraft (*A Vindication of the Rights of Woman*) by emphasizing the susceptible femininity of its language; Wollstonecraft's words, according to him, convey 'a luxuriance of imagination and a trembling delicacy of sentiment, which would have done honour to a poet, burning with all the visions of an Armida and a Dido' (82). Separatist militancy is melted away into the passionate effusions of two powerful women who are nevertheless both deserted by their lovers and commit suicide in despair at their powerlessness, a powerlessness which is culturally eroticized. This transposition of the political onto the passional becomes even more pronounced when Godwin comes to deal with the *Letters Written During a Short Residence in Sweden, Norway and Denmark* (1796); Wollstonecraft figures this time as an explicitly epistolary seductress, whose letters detailing her abandonment by her lover Imlay serve to institute an erotic circuit between the body of the woman, exposed and vulnerable in the open circuit of her unanswered letters, and the reader, in this case Godwin, the next lover in the series:

If ever there was a book calculated to make a man in love with its author, this appears to me to be the book. She speaks of her sorrows, in a way that fills us with melancholy, and dissolves us in tenderness, at the same time that she displays a genius which commands all our admiration.   (129)

Concentrating on Wollstonecraft's love-affairs as at once evidence of her politics and of her sensibility, blending theory and practice, Godwin's novelization of her life extends to saturating the text with sentimental parallels, describing her at one point, for instance, as a 'female Werter'.[59] Exactly according to Rousseau's plot, individualism of feeling is privileged over a social decorum accused of insufficient delicacy:

We did not marry. It is difficult to recommend anything to indiscriminate adoption, contrary to the established rules and prejudices of mankind; but certainly nothing can be so ridiculous on the face of it, or so contrary to the

[59] Others also succumbed to the temptation of novelization; see also the *Monthly Mirror*, 5 (1798), whose review relates 'Letters to Imlay' both to *Werther* and to the inevitable *La Nouvelle Héloïse* (155).

genuine march of sentiment, as to require the overflowing of the soul to wait upon a ceremony, and that at which, wherever delicacy and imagination exist, is of all things most sacredly private, to blow a trumpet before it, and record the moment when it has arrived at its climax. (123–4)[60]

IV

Reviewing the sensational, not to say melodramatic, events of Wollstonecraft's life—an unsolicited avowal of passion for the artist Fuseli (a married man), an illicit love-affair in Paris at the height of the Terror with the American Imlay by whom she had an illegitimate child, two attempts at suicide, highly unconventional and widely published opinions on the status of women, another out-of-wedlock pregnancy, this time by Godwin (who was notorious for his own anti-marriage stance in *Political Justice*), and a final lingering death in childbed—it seems hardly surprising that conservatives during the 1790s and after reacted violently to Godwin's assertion that his account would serve as a 'source of animation and encouragement to those who would follow her in the same career' (6). The suggestion that the *Memoirs* could and should function as an exemplary tale is caustically picked up by the *Anti-Jacobin*'s reviewer, who, making the first of many similar uses of Godwin's reinvention of Wollstonecraft as a heroine of sensibility, reconceives the whole rather as a *cautionary* tale, a monitory display of the dreadful consequences of an erroneous education on a fatally 'ardent sensibility'.[61] Like Julie's, and indeed Maria's, effusions of sentiment, Wollstonecraft's political opinions could and would be henceforth dismissed by conservatives as the madness of a woman 'lost, utterly lost, in the track of an unbridled imagination'[62] and its corollary, uncontrollable sexuality: 'Fierce

[60] The logic of this sentimental fiction in the event overbore biographical 'truth' to the extent that Godwin discovered himself irresistibly reinvented by the public in the figure of the villain-seducer; consequently, in the 2nd edition he was obliged to recant his previously published views on marriage and to offer up a paean to the domestic affections in order to dissociate himself from this role. In like fashion he vainly insisted that Wollstonecraft's death, though courageous and admirable, was emphatically not to be read as the scenario of virtuous repentance familiar from, say, *La Nouvelle Héloïse*.   [61] *Anti-Jacobin*, 1 (1798), 94.

[62] *Dorothea; or a Ray of the New Light* (3 vols., London, 1801), i. 150.

passion's slave, she veer'd with every gust | Love, Rights and Wrongs, Philosophy and Lust,' as T. J. Mathias succinctly put it in 1798.[63]

Godwin's convenient textualization and publication of Wollstonecraft in the terms of a sentimental novel allowed for a systematic and punitive recirculation of her textual body, removing it from the subjective and private to an emphatically public sphere, a circuit analogous to that of gossip; hence the *Anti-Jacobin* implicitly suggests that Godwin is responsible, through his perverse publication/prostitution of his wife, for its analogous ability to publish Wollstonecraft as a whore:

> William hath penned a wagon-load of stuff,
> And Mary's life at last he needs must write,
> Thinking her whoredoms were not known enough,
> Till fairly printed off in black and white.
> With wondrous glee and pride, this simple wight
> Her brothel feats of wantonness sets down.
> Being her spouse, he tells, with huge delight,
> How oft she cuckolded the silly clown,
> And lent, O lovely piece! herself to half the town.[64]

Polwhele employs the same logic of recirculation, albeit in a less scurrilous and altogether more clerical register, when he reformulates her life story as follows:

I cannot but think that the hand of Providence is visible, in her life, in her death, and in the memoirs themselves. As she was given up to her 'heart's lusts,' and let 'to follow her own imaginations,' that the fallacy of her doctrines . . . might be manifested to all the world; and as she died a death that strongly marked the distinction of the sexes, by pointing out the destiny of woman, and the diseases to which they are liable, so her husband was permitted, in writing her memoirs, to labour under a temporary infatuation, that every incident might be seen without a gloss, every fact exposed without an apology.[65]

This refashioning of Wollstonecraft from sentimental heroine into public amenity in many respects previews and encapsulates the conservative strategies for rewriting the radicalism of the novel of

---

[63] T. J. Mathias, *The Shade of Alexander Pope on the Banks of the Thames* [1798] (2nd edn., Dublin, 1799), 48 n.

[64] *Anti-Jacobin*, 9 (1801), 518.

[65] *The Unsex'd Females*, 29–30.

sensibility that I shall be examining in my next chapter; it therefore seems useful here to notice in advance two important tactics which Wollstonecraft's critics use in their dealings with her posthumous reputation: reframing, and translation.

Critics of Wollstonecraft typically subject her individual voice to the verdict of public consensus by reframing sentimental first-person narration within a third-person structure, a ploy which allows her life to 'be seen without a gloss', or, more precisely, to be exposed to an alternative, more punitive gloss, to translation.[66] Such a technique of social reintegration is implicit in the *Anti-Jacobin*'s summary execution on the foolhardy anonymous *A Defence of the Character and Conduct of the late Mary Wollstonecraft Godwin* (1803):

> The defence of this part of Mary's conduct [her affair with Imlay], according to her advocate, is to be sought in the *exercise of her private judgement*. . . . If this were an apology for Mary Wollstonecraft, it would be an apology for every other young woman who, as Charlotte Smith would put it, erred from the susceptibility of too tender a heart. Suppose one of these susceptible spinsters, which is no improbable case, were brought before the magistrate for bastardy, and being charged with the crime, were to answer, please your worship, in my own private judgement I stand justified for what I have done, and therefore should be acquitted by you, should we not think the woman out of her senses?[67]

Borrowing almost wholesale Wollstonecraft's own closing court-room scene in *Maria; or, The Wrongs of Woman*,[68] this passage recapitulates subjective experience in the terms of social legislation, subordinating individual sentiment to a social verdict, a consensus

---

[66] Those novels that attempted a critique of the 'new philosophy' and its adherents without employing these tactics are strikingly unsuccessful. Charles Lloyd's conservative polemic, *Edmund Oliver* (1798), is notably sabotaged by its use of the epistolary mode which proved recalcitrantly inclined to subvert the overt moral by drawing the reader into sympathy with the self-inflicted sufferings of the Werther-like protagonist.

[67] *Anti-Jacobin*, 15 (1803), 186.

[68] The *Anti-Jacobin* regularly conflated Wollstonecraft with her heroine in a re-run of the trial scene: 'Mary Wollstonecraft could plead her feelings in justification of her concubinage and her attempted suicide. Most females who began their career in the same way, and who may have afterwards arrived at a more advanced stage of profligacy, might plead their feelings as a justification of their conduct. We doubt not, that even Newgate has considerable supplies from the *victims of sensibility* . . .'; 3 (1799), 40.

determined by recourse to Johnson's *Dictionary*, a socially and nationally prescriptive lexicon:

As such apologists cannot alter British sentiments, so neither can they alter the import and signification of the English language. If our author will turn over in Johnson's Dictionary to a word which the adventures of Miss Mary may very readily suggest, he will find the first sense annexed to the denomination in question—'*a woman who converses unlawfully with men*' . . .[69]

The reader is required to translate such apologists' 'French' into 'English' to affirm her 'British sentiments' (a process that makes explicit the politics of the similar strategic translation carried out in the plotting of *Desmond*); in providing the missing word ('prostitute', under which epithet Wollstonecraft is persistently indexed by the *Anti-Jacobin*), any female reader inscribes herself back into a public, not to say national, lexicon, and is jolted, if only momentarily, out of the erotic and unlawful 'French' circuits of the epistolary.

Such reframing and 'translation' was to prove a particularly effective weapon against the seductiveness of the literature of sensibility, epitomized by Rousseau's 'sentimental sorcery',[70] during the latter part of the revolutionary decade and into the new century. While the sentimental strain did not die out altogether, it amalgamated itself with the autobiographical voice of Rousseau's self-novelization, his *Confessions*, precipitating in a range of those novels now commonly lumped together under the shorthand 'Romantic' an uneasy and intriguing blend of Gothicism, first-person narration, and lingering revolutionary thematics that will be the subject of my last chapter. But the majority of novels produced over the next two and a half decades would be interested primarily in evacuating the erotics of the novel of sensibility in favour of a novel of social consensus, a collective endeavour that is represented in its most sophisticated form by the novels of Austen and Scott. Accordingly, my next chapter moves on to discuss the ways in which the anti-Jacobin novel and its descendants contain the letter of individual feeling in order to compel social consensus.

---

[69] Ibid.
[70] [Jane West], *The Advantages of Education, or, The History of Miss Williams. A Tale for Misses and their Mamas by Prudentia Homespun* (2 vols., London, 1793), ii. 26.

2

Redirecting the Letter:
Counter-Revolutionary Tactics,
1800–1819

Letters, the most intimate sign of the subject, [may be] waylaid, forged, stolen, lost, copied, cited, censored, parodied, misread, rewritten, submitted to mocking commentary, woven into other texts which alter their meaning, exploited for ends unforeseen by their authors. ... If letter-writing is in one sense free subjectivity, it is also the function of an ineluctable power system. Certainly no activity could be more minutely regulated. To 'correspond' is to implicate a set of political questions: Who may write to whom, under what conditions? Which parts may be cited to another, and which must be suppressed? Who has the authority to edit, censor, mediate, commentate?[1]

Terry Eagleton's meditation upon the perilous physicality of letters in Richardson's *Clarissa*, and, in particular, on their potential subjection to regulation, might also serve as a reflection on the fate of the letter within novels written to articulate and endorse broadly conservative viewpoints from the late 1790s onwards. Within such texts, the letter, construed throughout the 1770s and 1780s as primarily the transcription of authentic sentimental subjectivity, came to figure not only as duplicitous, but, by topical and logical extension, even as treasonous. In time of war and under the threat of French invasion, fictional representations of illicit correspondence resonated not only with the disruptive power of antisocial passion, but with the threatening activities of the Corresponding Societies (who maintained a correspondence with the French National Assembly), and the supposed despatches of an inferred network of spies in the pay of the French government (it is not irrelevant to note here that the correspondence of Helen Maria Williams and J. H. Stone was seized and used as evidence in

[1] *The Rape of Clarissa: Writing, Sexuality and Class Struggle in Samuel Richardson* (Oxford, 1982), 50.

goverment investigations into foreign espionage).[2] In the novels I shall be surveying in this chapter, the letter as double agent is accordingly unmasked by its subjection to a process of re-circulation, surveillance, edition, censorship, and commentary.

This public scrutiny of the letter is registered on the formal level by the subordination of the letter to centralized narrative authority modelled within variants of omniscient third-person narration, an aesthetic structure designed to enforce public circulation and a vocabulary of consensus, as opposed to the private circulation of the solipsistic language of feeling conventionally represented by the epistolary. On the thematic level, this redirection of the letter returns as the refraction of the heroine's desire through the lens of gossip; in Patricia Meyer Spacks's words, 'the voice of the "world"—the amorphous social organization that enforces its own standards and disciplines on those who go astray'.[3] Finally, on the level of plot, the redirection of the letter manifests itself as the redirection of the sentimental heroine back to the father, the patriarchal family, and its analogue, the Burkean nation.[4]

The majority of polemical conservative (or 'anti-Jacobin') novels written over the peak years of reaction, 1798–1801, can be relied upon to include at least one hostile reworking of the sentimental plot,[5] frequently featuring philosopher-villains who, in addition to

---

[2] Stone had already been indicted in England before 1794 for treason in connection with the projected French invasion; I am referring here to the supposed letters of Williams and Stone published in *Copies of Original Letters recently written by Persons in Paris to Dr. Priestley in America. Taken on Board a Neutral Vessel* (London, 1798), which, according to the (hostile) Editor's Preface, were seized as evidence in the legal proceedings against a Danish ship for spying, and which, according to the *Anti-Jacobin*, displayed 'every feature and lineament of the true Jacobin character' and of 'PROFLIGATE TRAITORS'. In a slightly hysterical but revealing fashion the *Anti-Jacobin* goes on to excavate by inference a whole train of treasonous correspondence. *Anti-Jacobin*, 1 (1798), 146–51.

[3] *Gossip* (New York, 1985), 7.

[4] The exemplary and specifically anti-Rousseauistic heroine, never, of course, left; as Julia, heroine of Robert Charles Dallas's *Percival, or, Nature Vindicated* (1801), laudably, if stiffly, remarks: 'Pleasing as the passion of your friend is to my heart, could a question arise between his felicity and that of my beloved parents, not a moment should I hesitate in deciding for the latter. Time and good sense might heal the disappointment of a lover, but what power but death could ever remove the stings of filial ingratitude from the lacerated heart of a father?' (quoted, with approval, by the *Anti-Jacobin*, 12 (1802), 54).

[5] I should emphasize that I am here only concerned with those satires that are primarily interested in evacuating the plot and form of the sentimental novel. There is a school of anti-Jacobin novels that owes much more to the tradition of the

being implicated in all manner of undesirable activities—from Irish rebellion to Illuminati meetings, from Methodism to methodical spying-for-the-French, from reading German literature to over-throwing Christianity—are notable for their strenuous seduction schedules.[6] Such novels are often, although not always, centrally concerned with letters as a genre of seduction;[7] I have chosen for

philosophic tale (of which the most celebrated were currently Johnson's *Rasselas* and Goldsmith's *Citizen of the World*). The anonymous *Massouf; or, The Philosophy of the Day* (London, 1802) is of this ilk, as is Elizabeth Hamilton's *Translation of the Letters of a Hindoo Rajah* (2 vols., London, 1796). D'Israeli's *Flim-Flams!* (3 vols., London, 1805) borrows from *Tristram Shandy*. Mary Anne Burges's *The Progress of the Pilgrim of Good Intent in Jacobinical Times* (London, 1800) is an entertaining allegory based on Bunyan. Such texts, however, are often explicitly anti-novelistic—as D'Israeli remarks, 'I have chosen the *form* rather than the *matter* of a novel', *Vaurien; or, Sketches of the Times* (2 vols., London, 1797), i. xvi—and characterized by a high proportion of political discussion, usually within the context of a group of satirized New Philosophers. Although these features make their appearance in the novels I am about to discuss, a crucial distinction between the two types can be made on the basis of the position accorded to the figure of the seduced woman, an index to the novel's interest in neutralizing the sentimental plot, a process which I argue is central to the important transition taking place at this time in the form of the novel. For further information regarding the anti-Jacobin novel, see B. Sprague Allen, 'The Reaction Against William Godwin', *Modern Philosophy*, 16 (1918), 57–75; also Peter H. Marshall, *William Godwin* (New Haven, Conn., 1984).

[6] Marauder of Charles Lucas's *The Infernal Quixote: A Tale of the Day* (4 vols., London, 1801) will serve as a representative example of such villainy; having seduced Emily Vasaley with the help of the rubric of *The Rights of Woman*, he abandons her to try his luck instead with her younger sister, Fanny. Leaving a trail of murders, he plots the Irish Rebellion, supports Catholic Emancipation, and eventually, kidnapping Fanny, offers her the alternatives of marriage or rape. She is rescued in the nick of time by the Christian hero, Wilson; Marauder throws himself over a precipice to escape. His philosopher tutor has already come to a bad end, executed for treason; his philosophical friend dies in the remorseful agonies of the atheist. See also Frederick in George Walker's *The Vagabond* (2 vols., London, 1799) who follows much the same course, even improving on it; he fails to rescue either his father or his pregnant lover from a fire while debating their relative claims to rescue in the manner of *Political Justice*, he incites the Gordon Riots and the assault on Newgate, and finally murders his mother while masquerading as a highwayman. I regret that for reasons of space it is not possible to analyse in depth a number of neglected, indeed hitherto unidentified anti-Jacobin novels that deploy sentimental seduction plots, esp. the anonymous *Men and Women: A Novel* (2nd edn., 3 vols., London, 1807) which features yet another heroine called Julia (inevitably seduced, by a philosopher villain by the name of Fitzowen) and is heavily based on a hostile reading of Mackenzie.

[7] Robert Charles Dallas's epistolary *Percival, or, Nature Vindicated* (4 vols., London, 1801) is an excellent example, which features, within an explicitly Revolutionary context, another heroine called Julia, opens as a regenerate revision of the epistolary sentimental novel, modulates into a hostile version of *Emma*

extended consideration here paradigmatic texts which, despite their authors' varying positions on the political spectrum,[8] make the implied connection between rewriting the sentimental plot and the erasure of the sentimental letter—between the politics of narrative and the politics of form—especially explicit.

In the first part of this chapter I shall be tracing three major strategies used to redirect the letter, all of them fictional devices interested in establishing a post-Revolutionary social consensus. I shall be illustrating the first, an attempt simply to shut down the letter (envisaged as a sentimental anarchist engaged in setting up forbidden circuits beyond the family) into the decorous silence of the private, by a reading of Jane West's three novels of the 1790s, *The Advantages of Education* (1793), *A Gossip's Story* (1796), and *A Tale of the Times* (1799). I shall be using Maria Edgeworth's belated *Leonora* (1805) to exemplify the second strategy, which, rather than erasing the letter altogether, attempts to return it to the authoritative rereading of public consensus, figured in its most extreme form as State officialdom. The third and most technically demanding of these strategies is the re-representation of the letter as pure artefact, a status that effaces the letter's content in favour of its potential for misdelivery, thus allowing the text to work towards a redirection of that letter back into the bosom of the patriarchal family, its appropriate (if not always its original) addressee. I shall be arguing that the errant sentimental letter can thereby mimic and substitute for the erring sentimental heroine—as it does in Maria Edgeworth's *Angelina* (1801), and especially in Eliza Hamilton's

Courtney, and ultimately ensures its status as an impeccably and self-consciously Richardsonian work through an elaborate system of recirculations of the letter. Dallas's subsequent *Sir Francis Darrell; or, the Vortex* (4 vols., London, 1820), which includes the attempted education of a young woman by her would-be seducer into another Julie, again contrasts the clandestine correspondences of sentimental fiction with a system represented as infinitely preferable, a system of 'open' letters. I might have included here also Mary Ann Hanway's *Ellinor; or, The World As It Is* (4 vols., London, 1798), which, featuring a scandalous feminist scapegoat (Lady Dareall), deploys a Burneyesque opposition of private identity (as constructed in first-person narration) to the circulation of scandalous stories based on circumstantial evidence.

[8] Jane West (1758–1852) can be regarded as well to the right (she published an elegy on Burke in 1797: see Todd, *DBAWW*, 319–20), whereas both Maria Edgeworth and Eliza Hamilton were notable for their comparatively liberal views, especially as regards education. Cf. Butler, *Jane Austen and the War of Ideas*, 108, 124–57.

Memoirs of Modern Philosophers (1800), a parody of Mary Hays's *Memoirs of Emma Courtney* which, I shall argue, provides the missing link between that notoriously radical novel and Austen's more famous, and considerably more conservative novel, *Emma*. In the final section of this chapter, I shall turn to examine the ways in which Austen herself reifies the letter in order to suspend the subversive power of sentiment, first of all in *Sense and Sensibility* (drafted in the 1790s),[9] then in *Mansfield Park* (1814), and finally in what I would regard as perhaps the last and certainly the most dazzling of these anti-Jacobin novels, *Emma* (1816). I shall be turning in conclusion to a brief consideration of *Persuasion* (1818) in order to analyse the startling tactics by which Austen ultimately succeeds in realigning the power of the sentimental letter with the interests of the nation state.

I

A short piece from Maria Edgeworth's *Letters for Literary Ladies* (1795) entitled 'Letters of Julia and Caroline', though hardly a novel, serves as a perfect paradigm in miniature for all three of the mechanisms for containing clandestine correspondence that I have been laying out—erasure, rereading, and redirection back to patriarchal authority.[10] With exquisite economy, Edgeworth outlines the structure of the conventional contrast plot, between the woman of excessive sensibility, inevitably called Julia, who professes 'only to *feel*',[11] and the woman of sense, Caroline, and traces Julia's progress from an ill-advised marriage to Lord V— (in preference to Caroline's sober middle-class brother) to separation and divorce, to disgrace with an unspecified lover, to lingering death in the depths of infamy and the final bequest of her daughter

---

[9] The letter-version of *Sense and Sensibility*, 'Elinor and Marianne', dates from 1795; the revised version was begun in 1797. See B. C. Southam, *Jane Austen's Literary Manuscripts* (Oxford, 1964), 62.

[10] For an argument to the effect that *Letters for Literary Ladies* may well have been written in direct response to *A Vindication of the Rights of Woman* see Iain Topliss, 'Mary Wollstonecraft and Maria Edgeworth's Modern Ladies', *Études irlandaises*, NS 6 (1981), 15.

[11] 'Letters of Julia and Caroline', in *Tales and Novels* (10 vols., 1833; New York, 1967), viii. 463.

Julia to Caroline's care. While this trajectory clearly echoes that of
Rousseau's heroine (albeit faintly), and while Edgeworth also
chooses the epistolary form for her story, the seductive language of
the heroine of sensibility is in the event suppressed by being literally
erased. Of the seven letters that comprise the whole text, only one,
the opening one, is Julia's; the remainder are Caroline's. Julia's
letters only appear in dismembered quotation (not even as
enclosures, as would be conventional); furthermore, she is only
quoted when she is repentantly acceding to the punitive rereading—
the second strategy outlined above—carried out by Caroline. Hence
Caroline's letter upon Julia's intended separation from her husband
includes the following passage:

> Five years have made then so great a change in your feelings and views of
> life, that a few days ago, when my letter to you on your marriage
> accidentally fell into your hands, '*you were struck with a species of
> astonishment at your choice, and you burst into tears in an agony of
> despair, on reading the wretched doom foretold to the wife of Lord V—. A
> doom,*' you add, '*which I feel hourly accomplishing, and which I see no
> possibility of averting . . .*' (viii. 474)

In a similar fashion Julia's dying letter of repentance enters the text
of Caroline's last letter shorn of the language of sensibility by
unsympathetic paraphrase; the condition of that entrance is the
sanitizing triangulation of the reading of that letter, for Caroline is
writing to inform Lord V— of his wife's last moments. In this way
Caroline fulfils her stated intention in her penultimate letter of
renouncing 'all further intercourse' with Julia on that heroine's exit
from the circuit of respectable society, an exit which, as Caroline
makes clear, is concomitantly a departure from social intelligibility
as a result of her seduction into the familiar discourse of sensibility,
here branded as solipsistic to the point of incomprehensibility:

> I observed a change in your conversation. . . . I perceived . . . an eloquence
> in your language when you began to declaim, which convinced me that
> from some secret cause the powers of your reason had been declining, and
> those of your imagination rapidly increasing; the boundaries of right and
> wrong seemed no longer to be marked in your mind. . . . some unknown
> power seemed to have taken possession of your understanding, and to have
> thrown everything into confusion.   (viii. 479)

The epistolary heroine of sensibility is finally erased by the
redirection of her final letter back to her husband, a redirection

which breaks the circuit of private correspondence extraneous to the marriage and subjects its language to social sanctions.

Turning to the novel proper, Jane West's anti-sentimental novels, which, rejecting the epistolary as a narrative alternative, take every opportunity of stigmatizing the letter as a fatal excess to proper social organization, serve as expanded examples of the campaign to cancel the letter by returning it to the private. But although in her earliest novel, *The Advantages of Education* (1793), the heroine, Maria Williams, is preserved from entering the compromising circuit of epistolary commerce by the submission of her correspondence to her mother's policing eye—her would-be seducer Sir Henry Neville is choked off by a letter dictated by Maria but written and signed by her mother—the letter none the less proves fatal to West's later heroines. The fate that the virtuous Maria escapes by relinquishing correspondence to the parental pen is neatly exemplified in that of Marianne Clermont, the sentimental sister in *A Gossip's Story* (1796). The letter proves to be a major factor in the undoing of Marianne's otherwise reasonably satisfactory marriage; her continued correspondence with her friend Miss Milton, represented as a leak in marital discretion, is magnified eventually into a complete rupture. Discovered writing to her friend, she throws the sheets into the fire so that her husband will not read them:

Mr Clermont's mind was not wholly free from the meanness of suspicion, and he felt deeply mortified at the idea of a wife's concealing secrets from him, which she implicitly confided in another. . . . his curiosity to penetrate into this interdicted correspondence was irresistible, [and] he determined to use *any* means to develope the mystery.[12]

The rift is healed only temporarily through the peremptory erasure of this subversive female correspondence by the father's death-bed letter, a letter which, in the best conduct-book tradition, condemns the Clermont/Milton correspondence for being non-publishable, and therefore culpable; 'could you without confusion see those sentiments publickly divulged, of which you have made her the unreserved depository[?]' (ii. 133). Marianne's indiscretion, initially expressed as a correspondence in excess of the marital, is eventually 'publickly divulged' as what appears to be an adulterous

---

[12] Jane West, *A Gossip's Story and a Legendary Tale* (2 vols., London, 1796–8), ii. 113.

relationship; private correspondence mutates into criminal conversation, the letter breaks into open scandal. Marianne, eventually separated from her husband as the final consequence of these epistolary indiscretions, is punished at the end of the novel by virtual exile from polite society.

Clandestine correspondence returns as the interdicted discourse that, before being finally shut down, destroys Lady Geraldine Monteith's ill-fated and ill-advised marriage in West's most hysterically anti-Jacobin novel, *A Tale of the Times* (1799). The virtuous Geraldine initially refuses the correspondence promoted by her maid with the lovelorn Monteith prior to their marriage on the grounds that her father would disapprove; the metaphor of Pandora's box makes it clear that a second Fall is thus, for the moment, averted:

Let the gentlemen . . . behold one of the sex whom they brand with the stigma of curiosity, sitting with a Pandora's box sealed before her, yet forbearing to lift the interdicted lid. She wrote a few lines which expressed her abhorrence of a clandestine correspondence . . . and, inclosing his lordship's letter, rung her bell, and ordered it to be delivered by the very first opportunity.[13]

After the marriage, the adulterous passion which Henry Powerscourt, the rejected suitor, seems perilously likely to nurse for Geraldine is neatly cauterized at the end of the first volume by a pair of letters prefaced thus:

As Henry Powerscourt will not for some time appear again upon the scene, I shall subjoin lady Monteith's first epistle to him, with his answer. They occasionally corresponded during his residence abroad; but the remainder of his letters were irrelevant to the subject of this history.   (i. 304)

West thus conscientiously evacuates the possibility of a correspondence that would generate plot by its dangerous excess to the marital. Geraldine's letter expresses her sense of her cousin Henry's noble sacrifice in resigning her to her preferred suitor, Monteith; his letter insists that his 'innocent attachment shall never degenerate into a guilty passion' and goes on further to distinguish him from his distant prototype, St Preux, freezing the potential for a Rousseauistic plot of adultery, by renouncing all further sentimental correspondence and the plot that it carries with it:

[13] Jane West, *A Tale of the Times* (3 vols., London, 1799), i. 135.

Eternal infamy light upon him who, under the pretence of pure sentimental attachment, seeks to excite an undue interest in a matron's heart! I will never return to England till I can see you without emotion in that character; and this is the last letter which shall express a thought inconsistent with the equanimity of an affectionate relation and a sincere friend. (i. 309–10)

These letters are further sanitized by the scrutiny of Monteith himself (ii. 3), but, despite this promising beginning to the marriage, it is ultimately shattered by a less benign incursion of the epistolary in the shape of a Jacobin philosopher-villain, Fitzosborne, who attempts with eventual success the seduction of Geraldine, a seduction which explicitly implicates her in Rousseau's plot as 'the third Eloisa' (ii. 263). Fitzosborne is a cunning manipulator of the letter, arranging for Geraldine to have sight (apparently accidentally) of a letter to Monteith from a mistress. On this occasion, disastrously, 'she could not resist her desire to peruse it' (iii. 36), an entry into the forbidden epistolary which is emphatically connected with a reading, or misreading, of Rousseau:

She perceived no preconcerted plan in the circumstance of her having been sent into the room by Fitzosborne to fetch a volume of Rousseau, from which he had just misquoted a well-known passage. (iii. 36)

One might speculate that the 'well-known passage', in the light of subsequent events, is probably Julie's refusal to countenance St Preux's adulterous passion after her marriage.[14] At all events, Fitzosborne's further misuse of Rousseau is of a piece with his Lovelacean perversion both of Rousseau's plot (he eventually rapes Geraldine) and of the perfect 'correspondence' between husband and wife. Geraldine's marriage is fatally triangulated by her correspondence with Fitzosborne, who, as her dissipated husband's friend, has offered to send her news of him (while encouraging Monteith's vices so as to further his designs on Geraldine), a correspondence which comes to displace her husband's—'More than once Lucy perceived her select the letter of this favoured correspondent, and retire to read it, while even her lord's lay unopened' (iii. 93). While Geraldine writes only formal letters to her husband, she 'write[s] at large to Mr Fitzosborne' (iii. 104). The fatal adulteration of the marriage that

[14] See Rousseau [tr. Kenrick], *Eloisa: or, a series of original letters . . .* (1761), ii. 231–2.

Fitzosborne introduces by his correspondence is paralleled by his adulteration of the letter itself, and finally, of course, by his literal adulteration of Geraldine's body; the culminating rape is, significantly, enabled not only by Fitzosborne's deliberate interception of a vital note from her husband but by his forgery of a series of letters (iii. 200–1, 230, 253).

West's novel thus argues for the necessity of closing down female sexuality—represented by the forbidden letter—to make it invisible within the private circle of the patriarchal family, by displaying the awful consequences of such correspondence. In this context, the fact that Geraldine refuses to seek public redress by telling the whole story may be read as her withdrawal from this semi-public circulation, adopting much the same strategy as Clarissa; her last letter evades public disgrace by assuring her husband that she is sinking into the inviolable privacy of a 'sentence' of death and requesting that he should ensure her future unreadability as a refuge from a form of textual prostitution:

You will soon be released from your disgraced wife by an irreversible sentence; and I would entreat your mercy to stop your proceedings in the courts of law, and to spare my yet remaining sense of shame the horror of having my story bandied about in the public papers, exposed to indecent raillery and merciless reproach.   (iii. 341)

Though Geraldine's story is in fact never published, the letters which convey the private story are superseded by a submission to the 'voice of the world'; as Geraldine finally insists, '[p]art of my story remains untold; but, judging of what is known, the world is right in its renunciation of me' (iii, 327–9).

II

If West is concerned above all with the desirability of eliminating the private letter entirely, Edgeworth's only major epistolary novel, *Leonora* (1805), seems primarily interested in subjecting the letter to authoritative rereading in order to neutralize it. *Leonora* opens with a letter from the Lady Olivia, an extravagant and Frenchified heroine of excessive sensibility and consciously unconventional principles, who loves according to the book, specifically Rousseau's book, and writes in much the same way, only rather more so: 'The events of my life shall be related or rather, the history of my sensations; for in a life like mine sensations become events' (Edgeworth, *Leonora*, in *Tales and Novels*, viii. 244). As Mr L—, the married man whom Olivia ensnares, ruefully remarks:

Rousseau, it has been said, never really loved any woman but his own Julie; I have lately been tempted to think that Olivia never really loved any man but St Preux. Werter, perhaps, and some other German heroes, might dispute her heart even with St Preux; but as for me, I begin to be aware that I am loved only as a feeble resemblance of those divine originals . . . (viii. 386).[15]

Remarkably, this opening letter is subjected to detailed and repeated exegesis, first of all by its recipient, the Lady Leonora (L—'s wife), who is inclined to take it at face value as a candid confession of past errors and is anxious to convince her mother, the Duchess, of its complete sincerity, and then by the Duchess, who is sent the original letter to facilitate her (hostile) commentary. This inaugural movement of the novel, which opens the closed dyad of correspondence to a rereading within a triangle of correspondents—which, in other words, subjects private correspondence to the verdict of public circulation—is replicated twice during the course of the novel. The first occasion of this triangulation occurs when the Duchess (in a fit of exasperation) forwards Leonora's letters to herself to Leonora's now estranged husband Mr L—, in order to prove that, contrary to his misguided belief, his wife has been tenderly in love with him all along; this stratagem proves highly efficacious, redirecting his affections from Olivia back to Leonora. The second occasion of triangulation also relies upon the truth-telling power of letters, when Olivia's self-incriminating letters to her French confidante, Madame de P—, fall simultaneously into the hands of Leonora and of her husband, thus promoting a final exorcism of marital infidelity and

---

[15] In order to retain her hold over this sceptical and reluctant St Preux, Olivia finally resorts to a full-blown Rousseauistic *mise-en-scène*, staged in a chamber full of flowers. The allusion is not lost on Mr L—: 'At this instant . . . a confused recollection of Rousseau's Héloïse, the dying scene, and her room ornamented with flowers, came into my imagination, and destroying the idea of reality, changed suddenly the whole course of my feelings.

'In a tone of raillery I represented to Olivia her resemblance to Julie, and observed that it was a pity she had not a lover whose temper was more similar than mine to that of the divine St Preux' (viii. 400). In response to this quip, Olivia stabs herself, and this apparent willingness to take the role of Julie/Werther as far as actual death succeeds in persuading Mr L— to remain, for the time being, a willing accomplice. See also the attempted suicide of Elinor in Frances Burney's *The Wanderer* (1814).

ensuring in future a perfect correspondence between the two. One beneficial triangulation (of letters) replaces the malign triangulation of lovers.

While the story so far manifests a clear (if inverted) family relationship to West's tactics, the eruption of Olivia's letters to France into public knowledge is peculiarly, and significantly, complicated. The *éclaircissement* is communicated in a letter from General B— (Mr L—'s friend) to the Duchess, which relates how Leonora received a packet of Olivia's letters but refused, an exemplary anti-Pandora, to open them as a matter of delicacy. Mr L—, breaking in upon this scene, was also debarred from reading them by considerations of decorum, but this apparently insurmountable problem of etiquette was resolved nevertheless; enigmatically, Mr L— claimed that he already knew their contents, without having compromised his honour. General B— is enabled to explain and verify this declaration when he reads 'a letter which Mr L— received by the same express that brought Olivia's letters' and which he then forwards to the Duchess. This letter, more than any other, carries the seal and *imprimatur* of authority: it comes from a private secretary to the Foreign Office, who writes as follows about the packet of Olivia's letters:

These letters were lately found in a French frigate, taken by one of our cruisers; and, as *intercepted correspondence* is the order of the day, these, with all the despatches on board, were transmitted to our office to be examined, in hope of making reprisals of state secrets. Some letters . . . led us to suppose that we should find some political manœuvres, and we examined further.   (viii. 421)

This letter at once makes clear the parallel between Olivia's subversive manœuvres against the family and the undermining of the state by 'spies' such as J. H. Stone: both can finally be unmasked by publicly producing their despatches against them. By deploying the Foreign Office to unmask Olivia, Edgeworth juxtaposes the threat to the family with the threat to the State, and resolves it by recourse to the authority of the State, which here excerpts and paraphrases Olivia's letters as 'evidence' against her; the private secretary summarizes Olivia's sentiments in relation to Mr L— as expressed in these contraband letters thus:

You will find yourself ridiculed as *a cold awkward Englishman*; one who will *hottentot again, whatever pains may be taken to civilize him; a man of* *ice,* to be taken as a lover from *pure charity,* or *pure curiosity,* or the pure *besoin d'aimer.* Here are many pure motives, of which you will, my dear sir, take your choice. You will farther observe in one of her letters, that Lady Olivia premeditated the design of prevailing with you to carry her to Russia, that she might show her power *to that proudest of earthly prudes,* the Duchess of * * * , and that she might *gratify her great revenge against Lady Leonora L—.* (viii. 421)

This (outrageously partial) rereading by an accredited office of public and political surveillance at once establishes an authoritative reading of Olivia's letters within an epistolary circuit set up with impeccable credentials between two men; it relieves the family of L— from having to conduct any more intimate reading of Olivia's letters, and furthermore, and most importantly, it pre-empts the need for further interpretation or further correspondence. The novel thus closes at the point where Leonora's original defence of the truth of Olivia's letter against the judgement of scandal:

[I]f you criticise letters, written in openness and confidence of heart to a private friend, as if they were set before the tribunal of the public, you are—may I say it?—not only severe, but unjust; for you try and condemn the subjects of one country by the laws of another (viii. 261)

has been fully gainsaid; in the end the 'truth' of the letter is used only to support the verdict of the public tribunal. Edgeworth's novel does indeed try 'the subjects of one country', those who inhabit the territory of the sentimental 'French' discourse of the letter, by an appeal to an emphatically English jury drawn from the realm of public affairs, and, as might be expected in time of war, finds them guilty.

Edgeworth's need to invoke the Foreign Office as *deus ex machina* points once more, however, to the difficulty of discrediting the letter within a framework which is itself epistolary. In resorting to State authority to rule upon the authenticity of the notoriously slippery discourse of the letter, she breaks open the postbag of the private to ensure national security, and effectively brands the epistolary as always potentially treasonous. The text of *Leonora* demands this outside arbitration to decide which of Olivia's letters are to be accredited as 'truthful' enough to convict her of heartlessness and thus to make it possible for L— to discard her honourably, for many of Olivia's letters to L— himself, which do appear in the text, suggest rather that Olivia is genuinely in the grip of feeling, however anarchic, and that she is not in fact completely and systematically duplicitous.

When the status of letters as 'truthtelling' was so radically suspect that only the State's counter-espionage system could unravel their duplicity, the epistolary novel was bound to disintegrate in favour of some more authoritative discourse. Thus Jane Austen's one major epistolary novel, *Lady Susan* (drafted 1793–4),[16] also interested in the potential for equivocation inherent in the epistolary form, chooses eventually to shut down the letter by recourse to third-person narrative.[17] In instituting third-

---

[16] Austen did, of course, make extensive use of letters both in her Juvenilia, and in a more nuanced fashion, as I shall be arguing later, in her mature novels. The first draft of *Sense and Sensibility* ('Elinor and Marianne') was epistolary, and it has been suggested that *First Impressions*, the original of *Pride and Prejudice*, was also in letters. Q. D. Leavis also argued, controversially and in the last analysis I think unconvincingly, that the first version of *Mansfield Park* was also epistolary: see 'A Critical Theory of Jane Austen's Writings: *Lady Susan* into *Mansfield Park*', *Scrutiny*, 10 (1941), 114–42, 272–94.

[17] The parallels, thematic and formal, between *Leonora* and *Lady Susan*, have been noticed also by David Jackel, '*Leonora* and *Lady Susan*: A Note on Maria Edgeworth and Jane Austen', *English Studies in Canada*, 3 (1977), 278–88. Critical interest in the related questions of why Austen initially experimented with the epistolary form and why she ultimately abandoned it has a long history. It has been argued on the one hand, that Austen was simply borrowing the available and dominant mode of narration, and subsequently abandoned it when she developed more versatility; e.g. Eva Figes, *Sex and Subterfuge: Woman Writers to 1850* (London, 1982), 41; Mary Lascelles, *Jane Austen and Her Art* (Oxford, 1939), 124. Alternatively, it has been argued that Austen was primarily interested in burlesquing a sentimental form which had come to seem merely stilted and out-dated; see e.g. esp. Julia Prewitt Brown, *Jane Austen's Novels: Social Change and Literary Form* (Cambridge, Mass., 1979), 50. Yet other critics have suggested that epistolary experimentation allowed Austen to develop a series of elaborately ironical voices in her subsequent novels: see in particular Butler, *Jane Austen and the War of Ideas*, 168. This discussion has currently been reactivated, especially in the context of the attempt on the part of some feminist critics to appropriate Austen as satisfactorily 'subversive': for variously sophisticated attempts at this see Deborah Kaplan, 'Female Friendship and Epistolary Form: *Lady Susan* and the Development of Jane Austen's Fiction', *Criticism*, 29 (Spring 1987), 163–78; Julia L. Epstein, 'Jane Austen's Juvenilia and the Female Epistolary Tradition', *Papers in Language and Literature*, 21 (1985), 399–416, offers an elaborate reading of the uses of the letter in Austen's Juvenilia. It should be clear from the following that my position is nearer the first two, though I would argue that Austen's narrative agenda was already effectively set by political events. Both Julia Epstein and Mary Poovey (*The Proper Lady and the Woman Writer*, 178) argue persuasively that in *Lady Susan* the epistolary form itself generates moral anarchy as a consequence of the lack of centralized narrative authority, postulating that the only way Austen can effectively censure Lady Susan's disruptive fictioneering is to shut down the exchange of letters by resorting to satirical third-person narrative in her 'Conclusion'.

person narrative, the official story, Austen resorts, like Edgeworth, to invoking a State institution:

This Correspondence, by a meeting between some of the Parties and a separation between the others, could not, to the great detriment of the Post office Revenue, be continued longer. Very little assistance to the State could be derived from the Epistolary Intercourse of Mrs. Vernon and her niece, for the former soon perceived by the stile of Frederica's Letters, that they were written under her Mother's inspection, and therefore deferring all particular enquiry till she could make it personally in Town, ceased writing minutely or often.[18]

Like Edgeworth, Austen secures a version of subjectivity by recourse to a State institution, while here at the same moment belittling the power of epistolary intercourse to do very much to undermine the State; unlike Edgeworth, however, Austen entirely collapses the epistolary framework, premised as it is upon absence, by bringing her characters into proximity, a proximity that is, in this early novel, reckoned as more transparent, less amenable to masquerade, than the letter. Throughout the novel, Austen assaults the sentimental idea that the letter is 'naturally' transparent, an unmediated expression of 'true feeling', by highlighting the letter as vulnerable to falsification. By definition divorced from the body,[19] the letter, Austen suggests, embodies only the deceitful differential between the actual feeling motivating the writer and the feeling expressed within her text.[20]

From representing the letter as (inevitably) a textual mediator between body and body, and thus, potentially at least, a fraudulent

---

[18] Jane Austen, *The Oxford Illustrated Jane Austen*, ed. R. W. Chapman (6 vols., Oxford, 1967), i.e. *The Novels of Jane Austen*, ed. R. W. Chapman (3rd edn., 5 vols., Oxford, 1933) with vol. vi, *Minor Works*, ed. R. W. Chapman (1954), rev. B. C. Southam (Oxford, 1967): vi. 311 (Austen, *Works* hereafter).

[19] On the desirably transparent correspondence between the inner and outer woman, see Mary Poovey, *The Proper Lady and the Woman Writer*, 24: 'As long as one postulates such a correspondence [between "genuine feelings" and "look and manner"] . . . the Proper Lady can presumably be read like an open book; she is (or should be) quite simply what she seems to be.' See also Janet Todd's comment on women's supposed 'bodily authenticity—their ready use of blushes, tears, palpitations, hysteria, and even death . . .' (Todd, *Sensibility: An Introduction*, 110). Though Todd deals here with women, the observation may be generalized to include the sentimental body, regardless of gender.

[20] For a reading also interested in the erasure of the letter by the State in *Lady Susan* see Favret, 'Idea of Correspondence', 219 ff.

counterfeit, it is a short step to imagining the letter solely as an alienated artefact. Thus in Charles Lloyd's novel *Edmund Oliver* (1798), for example, the philosophic seducer, Edward D'Oyley, 'one of your dashing modern democrats',[21] whose Godwinian sentiments against matrimony prove to stem from a prior marriage, is enabled to keep up the farce with the ruined Gertrude through the medium of the alienated—in the sense that it is all too transportable and transferrable—letter:

The letters which he transmitted to you [Gertrude], have been conveyed under cover to Bristol, and there put into the office, that the post-mark might not discover his treachery. (ii. 74)

This shifty swerve between sender and addressee, which relies upon the physical mediation of the letter, is exploited in comic mode by Edgeworth in her novella, *Angelina; or L'Amie Inconnue* (1801), which might serve as a fictional gloss upon the liberal-conservative Hannah More's ironical strictures upon the practice of female correspondence: 'to speak the language of sentiment, an intimate union of souls immediately takes place, which is wrought to the highest pitch by a secret and voluminous correspondence.'[22] The heroine, Anne Warwick, transformed by the alchemy of letter-writing into the romantic, textual 'Angelina', flees London to reside with her pen-friend, the novelist 'Araminta', known to Anne only by way of the quasi-Wollstonecraftian self-portrait contained in her novel *The Woman of Genius,* coupled with a perfect flood of sentimental correspondence, which regales her fascinated fan with melodramatic plots assembled out of Goethe, Mary Hays *et al.* As an enthusiatic and acute reader of sentimental fiction, Angelina makes the conventional identification between the female body and the sentimental letter; however, in this satire, the 'Frenchness' of sentimental letters (registered in the novella's subtitle) and of Araminta's inflated self-plotting, once meticulously translated into the good 'English' of third-person narrative, yields up only a salutary disappointment—in the shape of the unattractively stout and incongruously middle-aged body of one Rachael Hodges,

---

[21] Charles Lloyd, *Edmund Oliver* (2 vols., Bristol, 1798), i. 151.

[22] *Strictures on the Modern System of Education of Young Ladies,* in *The Works of Hannah More* (6 vols., London, 1834), ii. 359. For a similar and equally conventional conservative expression of the same view see Hawkins, *Letters on the Female Mind,* i. 125.

found drinking brandy out of a teapot with her dingy paramour, Nat.[23]

III

If both Edgeworth and the young Austen introduce a gap between the body of the text and the body of its sender, casting a sceptical eye, enabled by the structures of third-person narration, upon the letter's claim to sentimental authenticity, Eliza Hamilton widens yet further that fissure when she rewrites Hays's *Memoirs of Emma Courtney* as *Memoirs of Modern Philosophers* (1800). The deformed and squinting body of Hamilton's absurd heroine, Bridgetina Botherim, ironizes, to ludicrous effect, the conventional equation of the sentimental letter with the body of the sentimental heroine. Bridgetina conceives of herself as an emphatically epistolary heroine (she proposes to publish her correspondence under the title *The Sweet Sensations of Sensibility, or, The Force of Argument*), identifying herself (predictably) with both Wollstonecraft and Rousseau's Julie in her faithful parrotting of sentimental discourse;[24] however, the 'heart-moving history' of this version of Emma Courtney (quoted almost verbatim from Emma's letters), once relocated within the body of the heroine by courtesy of third-person narration, is satirically invalidated by its lack of 'correspondence' with the body that extrudes it:

It was almost impossible . . . to refrain from laughing at the figure of Bridgetina, as she pronounced these words. Every feature screwed into formality, and every distorted limb sprawling in affected agitation, she presented such an apparent antidote to the tender passion, that the mention of love from her lips had in it something irresistibly ridiculous.   (i. 227)

Bridgetina's attempt to live out the sentimental texts of *La*

---

[23] For a similar debunking of the sentimental heroine, see Elizabeth Hamilton's *The Cottagers of Glenburnie: A Tale for the Farmer's Inglenook* [1801] (2nd edn., Edinburgh, 1808) which castigates the vanity and ambition of the socially-aspiring Miss Bell, who indulges in a sentimental correspondence (pointedly not included) and, on the point of eloping, quotes *La Nouvelle Héloïse* (301). She is brought speedily down to earth with the revelation that she has married not a gentleman but the son of a village shoemaker.

[24] Elizabeth Hamilton, *Memoirs of Modern Philosophers* (3 vols., Dublin, 1800): see i. 105–7, 226, 229 ff., 236, 264.

Nouvelle Héloïse and *Emma Courtney* introduces social dysfunction, in much the same way as Emma Courtney's similar struggles are (although only apparently) the source of social breakdown. Like Emma Courtney, she selects for her St Preux a man already attached to another, and so perpetrates a mis-delivery or misappropriation, as it were, of the sentimental letter, a misappropriation comically literalized by her squint which allows her elected love, Henry Sydney, to remain largely unconscious that he is the object of her passion:

[T]hough her eyes were fixed upon him from the moment of his entrance, happily for Henry no one could possibly follow their oblique glances to the object on which they darted their most tender beams. (ii. 73)

Bridgetina's squint is only the most physical mark of her ability, through her privileging of the fiction of letters, to introduce ambiguity and pernicious triangulation into the novel as a whole. She systematically inserts herself between the two lovers, Henry Sydney and Harriet Orwell, causing maximum confusion by her misreading of Henry's declaration of love for Harriet (recited to Bridgetina in the mistaken belief that she knows all) as a declaration of love to herself. Her consequent compromising pursuit of Henry to London threatens to construct Henry as the familiar villain-seducer; only Henry's fortuitous ability to provide a third person, and indeed the reader, as impartial witness to the conversation exculpates him (ii. 83). Only recourse to the third person and to third-person narration can invalidate Bridgetina's version of the incident, and thus make it possible to return her, suitably chaste, if chastened, back to her mother.

If Bridgetina exemplifies the largely comic consequences of the letter's potential for misdirection, then her tragic double, Julia (as ever!) Delmond, suffers the conventionally fatal consequences. Induced to elope with a French New Philosopher-cum-hairdresser called Vallaton after a series of misunderstandings with her parents facilitated once more by the ambiguity of a letter (which seemed to give her parents' blessing to the courtship of Vallaton, while actually recommending another suitor entirely—ii. 28), Julia undergoes the fate of Clarissa in gruesome detail (ii. 29, 272) as Hamilton in effect, like West, returns *La Nouvelle Héloïse* back to its parent text for wholesome discipline.

IV

Hamilton's persistent identification of the letter with the introduction of destructive ambiguity into society is echoed in Austen's *Sense and Sensibility*.[25] *Sense and Sensibility* (1811) was redrafted around 1797, from its original epistolary format as *Elinor and Marianne* (1795) to something much nearer the text we are now familiar with, a decision on Austen's part which seems to reflect the increasingly problematic status of the letter in the 1790s. As the text now stands, the letter has, once again, largely been reduced to an artefact whose slippery doubleness and amenability to misreading threatens to destroy an appropriately transparent correspondence between lovers.[26]

The primary analogue to the letter-as-artefact here is Edward's ring, which, appearing before any other more conventional letter in the text, prefigures the subsequent failure of correspondence within the novel. Marianne notes Edward's ring 'with a plait of hair in the centre' and immediately 'reads' it as his sister's hair, though it seems strangely light-coloured. Elinor, on the contrary, reads it as her own hair, a reading which Marianne then immediately endorses. Their readings are consistent with the plot of the novel so far, in which a perfect correspondence of lovers (between Marianne and Willoughby, between Elinor and Edward) seems to subsist; but the ring introduces the problem of secret, not to say illicit correspondence, for 'what Marianne considered as a free gift from her sister, Elinor was conscious must have been procured by some theft or contrivance unknown to herself'.[27] In being capable of sustaining more than one reading, the ring signals its inauthenticity, an inauthenticity made possible by its status as artefact; Edward explains away the difference in colour between the hair in question and his sister Fanny's hair by suggesting that 'the setting always casts a different shade on it' (ibid.). It is no longer the content of the letter but its position or 'setting' within a nexus of relationships that will determine its meaning.

[25] For a general survey of Austen's use of letters in her novels see Ian Jack, 'The Epistolary Element in Jane Austen', in *English Studies Today*, ed. G. A. Bonnard (Berne, 1961), 173–86.

[26] Cf. Favret, 'Idea of Correspondence', 231 ff.

[27] Austen, *Works*, i (*Sense and Sensibility*), 98.

Indeed, the novel as a whole will favour the 'setting' of the letter over its content; that is to say, it will largely erase the expression of private feeling, and will do so by considering the letter solely as it physically enters social circulation. Underlining this similarity in status between the letter and the ring, the text neatly juxtaposes them; Lucy Steele provides as evidence to Elinor of her engagement to Edward, in addition to the ring, a largely unreadable letter, a letter reduced to its 'hand':

[T]aking a letter from her pocket and carelessly showing the direction to Elinor [she said], 'You know his hand, I dare say, a charming one it is; but that is not written so well as usual. He was tired, I dare say, for he had just filled the sheet to me as full as possible.' (134)

In a similar fashion, reduced to an address, its substance entirely repressed, the import of Marianne's letter to Willoughby is determined solely by a reading, focalized through Elinor's consciousness, of the way it is despatched:

Marianne's [letter] was finished in a very few minutes; in length it could be no more than a note: it was then folded up, sealed and directed with eager rapidity. Elinor thought she could distinguish a large W in the direction, and no sooner was it complete than Marianne, ringing the bell, requested the footman who answered it, to get that letter conveyed for her to the twopenny post. This decided the matter at once. (161)

The letter's entry into circulation is also an entry, however furtive, into a social system of surveillance, as Mrs Dashwood's earlier comment on the possible prior existence of a clandestine correspondence between Marianne and Willoughby would suggest:

'Remember, Elinor,' said she, 'how very often Sir John fetches our letters himself from the post, and carries them to it. We have already agreed that secrecy may be necessary, and we must acknowledge that it could not be maintained if their correspondence were to pass through Sir John's hands.' (84)

Elinor's reading of the epistolary transactions that finally do appear to ensue between Marianne and Willoughby is therefore of a piece with that of 'many—by some of whom you know nothing, by others with whom you are most intimate' (173), in that she views them as proof positive of the engagement between Marianne and Willoughby. But like the ring, the letter-as-artefact carries an unexpected and unwelcome meaning, which surfaces once the text of the letters emerges into full view; so far from setting the seal upon an engagement, this correspondence is entirely one-sided.

If the insistence on the letter as an artefact subject to social circulation neatly shears the sentimental letter of its seductiveness, Austen further diminishes its subversive power by insisting not merely on a punitive rereading of such letters but upon postponing that reading until after the letter has outlived its ability to generate plot. Thus the materialization of the substance of Marianne's letters seems rendered possible when, and only when, the original addressee has returned and repudiated them, when, in fact, the subversive power of Marianne's expressed desire has been destroyed and her imprudence already been 'most severely condemned by the event' (188). This timely abortion of the epistolary allows Marianne to escape replicating in her own person the miniaturized and conventionalized story of the two sentimental Elizas, whose fates are identified with the epistolary by the letter to Colonel Brandon that ruptures the apparent idyll at Barton and modelled upon those of more unfortunate heroines of anti-Jacobin novels.[28]

Removed from the dangerous circuit of the letter, Marianne survives to be integrated into society as Colonel Brandon's wife, a right-thinking substitute for the two Elizas. Effectively removed from the exogamous trajectory of the sentimental heroine, she is made to retrace her steps back into endogamy. Brandon is not Willoughby, not the anti-Jacobin villain-seducer, precisely because he is old enough to be her father, and because he is Elinor's and her mother's choice, rather than her own:

They each felt his sorrows and their own obligations, and Marianne, by general consent, was to be the reward of all. (378)

This delivery of the chastened Marianne to the paternal Brandon (himself the survivor of two tragic anti-Jacobin novels) closes down the possibility of that plot repeating itself.

Fittingly, the epistolary reverts to Lucy Steele, that efficient simulacrum of a sentimental heroine. Only Lucy remains in control

---

[28] The conventionality of the story of the two Elizas may be confirmed by a glance at the similar cautionary tale from Jens Wolff's *Sketches and Observations taken on a Tour through a Part of the South of Europe* (1801) excerpted by the *Anti-Jacobin*, which might be described as the sentimental story of the two Julias, told by a narrative persona not unlike that of Colonel Brandon. *Anti-Jacobin*, 13 (1802), 255–8.

of her letters; only her texts have any power to affect the action. Lucy's letter is the last to be read and the most powerful, for in it 'the substance made . . . amends for the defects of the style' (365). As writer of the only substantive letter in the novel, Lucy is surely entitled to the position of the epistolary heroine, a role for which she is peculiarly well-suited by virtue of her well-practised hypocrisy. In this she is like the letter itself in *Sense and Sensibility* which, the more it pretends to confidentiality, the more it aspires to publicity: consider Lucy's letter to Elinor which, announcing her engagement to Edward Ferrars, induces Elinor to perform 'what she concluded to be its writer's real design, by placing it in the hands of Mrs. Jennings who read it aloud with many comments of satisfaction and praise' (278). The covert doubling of readership here finds its parallel in a system of doubled authorship; Willoughby's wounding letter to Marianne, dictated by his wife, is thus exquisitely duplicitous. Lucy's virtuous double and antithesis, Elinor, who prudently refrains from any correspondence at all, repressing her sensibility into the private, may be said to embody, after that one little lapse over Edward's ring, the total suppression of the epistolary that *Sense and Sensibility* endeavours to institute.

This attitude to the potential duplicity of the letter is also reflected in *Mansfield Park*, which aims ultimately at establishing, in the person of Fanny Price, a virtuous and immutable transparency. If Austen, in this novel, translates the conventional senti- mental anti-Jacobin plot out of epistolary negotiations and into the body by staging Kotzebue's notoriously radical *Lovers' Vows*,[29] the letter, in spite of Sir Thomas Bertram's institution of a counter- revolutionary 'government' (196), returns as the vehicle for illicit manœuvres in the second part of the text, which is structured upon the model of the epistolary novel while resisting its form. The progressive dispersal of the party at Mansfield Park—Fanny to sojourn in Portsmouth, the Crawfords to London and a variety of

---

[29] In settling upon this choice of script, the company pick a notoriously immoral play (which gives sympathetic treatment to the figure of a seduced and abandoned woman to the extent of installing her in a happy ending), written by an author who had obtained amongst conservatives in the England of this period a reputation for licentiousness and immorality second only to Goethe; the play had been translated, moreover, by the liberal Elizabeth Inchbald, author of the 'Jacobinical' *Nature and Art* and friend of Godwin and Wollstonecraft. The play functions as a buried text of radicalism that leaks the 'infection'—Austen, *Works* iii (*Mansfield Park*), 184—of revolution through the house.

house-parties, Edmund to London, Maria Rushworth *née* Bertram
and her sister Julia to London, prompts a set of letters that
punctuate Fanny's exile. In the same way that Fanny had, by acting
as prompter and understudy in the amateur theatricals, served as a
clearing-house for the amatory negotiations being carried out under
cover of, and in the language of, play-acting, so too she serves in
this section of the novel as the sorting-office for a set of letters
ostensibly directed to her by Mary Crawford, but actually aimed at
someone else, Edmund Bertram. At the same time, she finds herself
also the unwilling recipient of letters apparently from one person,
Mary Crawford, which actually serve as a conduit for strictly
inappropriate, indeed faintly 'French' messages ('three or four lines
passionées', to borrow Mary's description) from Mary's brother,
Henry Crawford—a correspondence analogous to the affair of the
chain, apparently a gift to Fanny from Mary, but actually a gift
from Henry mediated by Mary:

She had heard repeatedly from [Henry Crawford's] sister within the three
weeks which had passed since their leaving Mansfield, and in each letter
there had been a few lines from himself, warm and determined like his
speeches. It was a correspondence which Fanny found quite as unpleasant
as she had feared. Miss Crawford's style of writing, lively and affectionate,
was itself an evil, independent of what she was thus forced into reading
from the brother's pen, for Edmund would never rest till she had read the
chief of the letter to him, and then she had to listen to his admiration of her
language, and the warmth of her attachments.—There had, in fact, been so
much of message, of allusion, of recollection, so much of Mansfield in
every letter, that Fanny could not but suppose it meant for him to hear; and
to find herself forced into a purpose of that kind, compelled into a
correspondence which was bringing her the addresses of the man she did
not love, and which obliged her to administer to the adverse passion of the
man she did, was cruelly mortifying. (375–6)

Correspondence is here infected by illicit, invisible correspondents
masquerading under the hands of Fanny and Mary; thus the letter
becomes literally duplicitous, indecorously multiple, subverting, by
functioning in this clandestine way, the apparently legitimate
correspondence it inhabits. In this trying situation, Fanny maintains
an obstinate disengagement from the business of correspondence (it
is telling that such letters as she is forced to write are only once
quoted—and then in third-person paraphrase, 436), despite Mary's
determined attempts to involve her in this game of circular letters:

'Adieu, my dear sweet Fanny, this is a long letter from London; write me a pretty one in reply to gladden Henry's eyes' (394). It is this disengagement that ultimately ensures her virtuous quarantine from the overdetermined *débâcle*, modelled, inevitably upon those novels that, in the words of the evangelical Andrew Reed, 'alienate the heart from domestic and retired duties—which convert every quiet home into a prison house. ... which ... become the apologists of ... fornication, adultery ... and suicide',[30] that inevitably overtakes all who are either involved in this epistolary game or who appear as characters within those despatches: the elopement of Maria Rushworth with Henry Crawford, and of Julia Bertram with Mr Yates.

These letters, far from representing authentic interiority in the way that they do, for example, in Charlotte Smith's *Desmond*, function instead as the ominous harbingers and allies of scandal and rumour, despite Mary Crawford's last-ditch attempt to use the letter to at once forestall and suppress such publicity:

'A most scandalous, ill-natured rumour has just reached me, and I write, dear Fanny, to warn you against giving the least credit to it, should it spread into the country. ... Say not a word of it—hear nothing, surmise nothing, whisper nothing, till I write again. I am sure it will be all hushed up and nothing proved ...' (437)

The letter, rather than bearing a meaning that in some sense contradicts the voice of the world, is both echoed by the newspaper report and echoes it: 'Miss Crawford's letter stampt it a fact' (441). The potential perversions of correspondence are ultimately suppressed altogether within the closure of the quasi-incestuous relation of Edmund and Fanny, 'brought up always together like brothers and sisters' (6). As in *Sense and Sensibility*, the radical potential of female sexuality can best be contained by keeping it within the family; only this near-sibling relationship can satisfactorily neutralize the revolutionary and disintegrative effects of female sexuality so as to preserve the father's house intact.[31] This

---

[30] Andrew Reed, *No Fiction* (2 vols., London, 1819), i. 196–7.

[31] It is interesting in this connection to recall some of the conservative family romance plots which the otherwise liberal Amelia Opie had been deploying since 1800, notably in the best-selling *The Father and Daughter*, which displaces the story of Agnes Fitzhenry's Rousseauistic seduction by the story of her repentant return to her father, deranged by her loss, and her incessant efforts to nurse him back to

pattern of the erasure of illicit correspondence in favour of familial transparency is repeated in its most successful and dazzling mode in the novel Austen published just two years later, *Emma*, a text concerned almost obsessively with arresting the mobility of meaning that the letter-as-artefact figures.

V

Although *Emma* has hitherto proved highly resistant to an explicitly political reading,[32] it is in fact an unusually successful (if perhaps belated) conservative novel in its insistent marginalization and miniaturization of radical plots and narrative form. The ostensible narrative of *Emma* effectively inhabits the earlier conspiratorial, potentially revolutionary Rousseauistic novel,[33] represented in this instance by the illicit and curiously 'feminine' correspondence between Jane Fairfax and Frank Churchill, whose epistolary manipulation of style, moreover, betrays him, according

---

sanity. Amelia Opie, *The Father and Daughter, A Tale in Prose* (London, 1801). This reworking of the Lear and Cordelia relationship is further politicized by the implicit reference to that other mad king, George III, whose son's scandalous adulteries themselves were read as a radical sentimental novel that undermined the State: see the *Anti-Jacobin*, 6 (1801), 208–9. *Mansfield Park* itself, of course, permeated by allusions to Shakespeare, casts Fanny as Cordelia to Sir Thomas Bertram's Lear (as well as Helena to Edmund's Bertram), pairing her with an 'Edmund' who in fact plays the role of the virtuous Edgar who marries Cordelia at the conclusion of Nahum Tate's acting version (still in use throughout Austen's lifetime). On Opie's novels see especially Gary Kelly, 'Amelia Opie, Lady Caroline Lamb, and Maria Edgeworth: Official and Unofficial Ideology', *Ariel* (1981), 1–24; also Gary Kelly, 'Discharging Debts: The Moral Economy of Amelia Opie's Fiction', *The Wordsworth Circle*, 11 (1980), 198–203, although I am less inclined than Kelly to find 'subversive' undercurrents in Opie's punitive fictions.

[32] See, for instance, Claudia L. Johnson's comments upon the problems of attempting to offer a 'political' reading of *Emma* in *Jane Austen: Women, Politics, and the Novel* (Chicago, 1988): 'The texture of *Emma* is remarkably spare . . . Austen does not allude to the tradition of political fiction as regularly in *Emma* as she does elsewhere, but such relative silence does not signify an abandonment of the political tradition . . . [S]he participates in the political tradition of fiction, not by qualifying or critiquing it from within, but rather by trying to write from its outsides' (126). As this chapter will make clear, I disagree radically with this position.

[33] There is evidence that Austen had in fact read *La Nouvelle Héloïse*: see Jean Hagstrum, *Sex and Sensibility: Ideal and Erotic Love from Milton to Mozart* (Chicago, 1980), 272.

to Mr Knightley, as 'amiable only in French, not in English'.[34] This
largely invisible narrative, that leaves only traces within the bulk of
the visible text—legible only to that morally regenerate detective,
Mr Knightley—is quintessentially a sentimental *epistolary* novel; it
is consequently perfectly in accord with generic conventions that
Emma should misread the symptoms of this epistolary plot as a
narrative of forbidden desire modelled upon *La Nouvelle Héloïse*,
with the hapless Jane Fairfax and her best friend's husband Mr
Dixon (currently in Ireland, not coincidentally a favourite home-
base for the Jacobinical villain) as its principal protagonists.
Coursing beneath the insistent banality of life in Highbury, creating
epistemological and moral anarchy, constantly disrupting proper
social circulation by its underground commerce in unpublishable
desire and secretly transmitted information, the buried Frank
Churchill–Jane Fairfax plot has something of the same revolutionary
charge as the prototype to which Emma rightly assimilates it; as
Emma remarks, horrified, once the story of their liaison is finally
revealed, '[w]hat has it been but a system of . . . espionage and
treachery? . . . with two people in the midst of us who may have
been carrying round, comparing and sitting in judgement on
sentiments and words that were never meant for both to hear'
(399).

This clandestine correspondence supplies the plot of *Emma* with
most of its potential for dangerous ambiguity, a potential amply
exploited by its heroine's well-documented (and ultimately re-
nounced) fictioneering. It is regularly remarked that the narrative of
Emma's 'education' depends upon disciplining Emma into right
reading; what is not recognized is that this education in close
reading is designed here, as in the earlier anti-Jacobin texts I have
been examining, to exorcize the epistolary novel of passion, and is

---

[34] Austen, *Works*, iv (*Emma*), 149. Cf. also Knightley's distaste for Frank's
handwriting: 'I do not admire it. . . . It is like a woman's writing', 297. For a general
survey of the letter in *Emma* and its thematic connection to Frank Churchill's 'moral
evasiveness' see U. C. Knoepflmacher, 'The Importance of Being Frank: Character
and Letter-writing in *Emma*', *Studies in English Literature*, 7 (1967), 639–58. For a
reading of Frank's letters and Emma's fictions as analogous sites of falsification
underwritten by a subjective perception undisciplined by the moral authority of the
omniscient author's voice, see Mack Smith, 'The Document of Falsimilitude: Frank's
Epistles and Misinterpretation in *Emma*', *Massachusetts Studies in English*, 9
(1984), 52–70.

therefore closely tied to a broadly conservative political agenda.

Austen's interest in the difficulties of deciphering the duplicities of written texts, and in particular in the social control of the equivocal nature of the letter, is first developed in the episode of the riddle-book, which introduces the written text as *double entendre*, prefiguring a series of similar ciphers which, successfully solved, will no longer obscure the right true happy ending.[35] Austen here attenuates the content of the letter to the point where it appears as an empty communication which is prostituted to the most successful bidder for its meaning, and whose meaning is, therefore, in very large part contingent upon its positioning between the characters.[36] The sentimental letter is debased to the status simply of riddle, anagram, and conundrum, littering the pages of *Emma* with sexual charades.[37]

The first riddle introduced, in a highly fragmented fashion, is Garrick's rather threadbare teaser, 'Kitty, a fair, but frozen maid', of which Mr Woodhouse fretfully attempts to remember more than the first two lines (a symptomatic failure of memory in an impotent valetudinarian, since the riddle as a whole is rather delightfully

[35] Unlike certain recent commentators, I would argue that it is Austen herself, rather than merely some of her wrong-thinking critics, who stigmatizes, in Joseph Litvak's words, 'linguistic playfulness, or merely a fondness for the written word, as a threat to moral well-being'. 'Reading Characters: Self, Society, and Text in *Emma*', *PMLA* 100 (1985), 763. As will become clear, I do indeed regard this as potentially repressive to certain forms of subjectivity associated with the feminine; but I would dispute any reading which tries to recuperate, as Litvak does, 'these linguistic residues' as 'traces of Austen's own rebellion against an overtly reassuring moral ideology' (763). On the contrary, Austen seems to me, particularly when read in context, to be peculiarly alive to the scandal of signs cut loose from their supposedly proper destinations, but to 'rehabilitate' her as a champion of anarchic free play by misreading or deliberately suppressing her own ideological choices seems both patronizing and dishonest.

[36] For an undeniably ingenious Girardian reading of this triangulation, which claims that the novel exhibits detours of desire supposedly facilitated by the breakdown of the French *ancien régime*, see Beatrice Marie, '*Emma* and the Democracy of Desire', *Studies in the Novel*, 17 (1985), 1–13.

[37] For a brilliant and delightful Lacanian reading of the charades in *Emma* as puns that resist closure, see Grant I. Holly, '*Emma*grammatology', *Studies in Eighteenth-Century Culture*, 19 (1989), 39–51. While I agree with Holly's interest in the gendering of such riddles as feminine, I would nonetheless insist that such puns and charades (however usefully productive of narrative, as D. A. Miller argues in his *Narrative and Its Discontents: Problems of Closure in the Traditional Novel*, New Haven, Conn., 1984), are ultimately closed down, systematically directed to their proper addresses on the basis of Austen's broadly conservative political agenda.

smutty).[38] Although only two lines appear in the text, I shall quote the whole, since the full text serves as a gloss upon the other riddles Austen poses. (The answer, incidentally, is 'chimney-sweep', itself an old chestnut of mild obscenity):

> Kitty, a fair, but frozen maid,
> Kindled a flame I still deplore;
> The hood-wink'd boy I call'd in aid,
> Much of his near approach afraid,
> So fatal to my suit before.
>
> At length, propitious to my pray'r,
> The little urchin came;
> At once he fought the midway air,
> And soon he clear'd with dextrous care,
> The bitter relicks of my flame.
>
> To Kitty, Fanny now succeeds,
> She kindles slow, but lasting fires:
> With care my appetite she feeds;
> Each day some willing victim bleeds,
> To satisfy my strange desires.
>
> Say, by what title, or what name,
> Must I this youth address?
> Cupid and he are not the same,
> 'Tho' both can raise, or quench a flame—
> I'll kiss you, if you can guess.   (489–90 n.)[39]

The meaning is double, and unstable, until it is guessed; but, as the rhyme is addressed to a woman, the slippage of the riddler's 'desires' from Kitty to Fanny will continue in series—'I'll kiss you if you can guess'—half punishment, half reward, resexualizing the 'straight' non-sexual meaning. By giving a name to the boy, the woman elects herself as the next named woman in the series. When we turn our attention to the function of Mr Elton's (very polite)

---

[38] Cf. Holly's remark on Mr Woodhouse's forgetfulness; Holly observes that it promotes 'the continual slippage that undermines [the symbolic order associated with the Name of the Father]. ... It is at this point, and with this disarming arbitrariness, that we learn the name of Emma's grandmother: "The name [Kitty]," says Mr Woodhouse, "makes me think of poor Isabella; for she was christened Catherine after her grandmama." The circulation of signifiers, here, is very rapid indeed, and we have the sense that such a train of associations could connect anybody with anybody—which is precisely the point.' ('*Emma*grammatology', 48).

[39] According to Chapman, from the fourth part of *The New Foundling Hospital for Wit* (London, 1771).

riddle—which Emma misreads as a compliment to Harriet rather than to herself—we see that the process of reading constructed by the Garrick riddle is as it were inverted; Harriet reads the riddle as 'Neptune?' 'a mermaid?' while Emma correctly decodes its sexual meaning ('courtship') but immediately transfers its sexual application to Harriet, reading the address as the riddle, filling in the blank in the title 'To Miss —'. Emma effectively re-riddles the riddle by supposedly solving it. Such perversions of proper application by the intended addressee recur constantly in the novel as a consequence of the obsessive triangulation of reception set up by Austen to subordinate the private to the public; there are very few scenes that concern the communication of two people unmediated by a third, the funniest example of this being the episode of the painting of Harriet's portrait, when Emma mistakenly assumes the portrait's importance to Elton to be its subject (Harriet), rather than understanding its significance as a transaction conducted between her and Elton, merely mediated by the figure of Harriet. This obsessive substitution of the 'figure' for the real thing, of the artefact for 'content', in the games of desire that Emma plays is characteristic of her social strategies until nearly the end of the novel. Thus she arranges for the recirculation of Mr Elton's riddle for fully social consumption by another operation of the shears upon the 'appropriation'; as Emma reassures Harriet,

The couplet does not cease to be, nor does its meaning change. But take it away, and all *appropriation* ceases, and a very pretty gallant charade remains, fit for any collection.   (77)

Emma is mistaken in her notion that the charade's meaning will not mutate, for until the riddle is properly (and privately) re-'appropriated'—readdressed, as it were—(as it is in the proposal scene between Emma and Elton), it continues to generate social confusion, remaining open to Emma's misinterpretation. Thus this charade functions in much the same way as Harriet's doubtful parentage, which allows Emma to justify her initial disruption of the alliance with Martin (on the grounds that Harriet must be a gentleman's daughter) and so to set off the game of substitution and reappropriation that she plays throughout the novel. 'I mention no names', she remarks after trying to encourage Harriet to transfer her affections to Emma's rejected suitor Frank Churchill, 'but happy the man who changes Emma for Harriet' (269). Emma, of course, gets more than she bargained for, as she has unwittingly sanctioned Harriet's new infatuation with Mr Knightley.

The riddle-book, 'ornamented with cyphers and trophies' and full of 'enigmas, charades and conundrums' (69, 70), is not the only riddle in the book; Emma soon finds Jane Fairfax 'a riddle, quite a riddle' and a much more interesting and insurrectionary one at that. Abandoning her excellent and improving reading-lists, Emma reads Jane Fairfax into a transgressive novel of passion, casting her as the other woman in an adulterous triangle of desire highly reminiscent of Helen Maria Williams's *Julia*.[40] The 'imaginist' is seized with 'an ingenious and animating suspicion'—that Mr Dixon, having made proposals to Jane's best friend, had fallen in love with Jane (160, 217); a narrative solution, designed to explain the enigma of the spectacular arrival of a piano for Jane from an anonymous donor, worthy of a Watson or a Hastings.

It is, however, Mr Knightley who reads aright, deciphering the 'bad hands', the texts to which Emma remains blind, by reading the double meaning circulating in the anagram game during which a 'letter' is delivered to Jane by Frank and then is 'carried wrong' to Harriet, who solves it:

The word was *blunder*; and as Harriet exultingly proclaimed it, there was a blush on Jane's cheek which gave it a meaning not otherwise ostensible. (348)

These private messages masquerading as public scramble the proper social circuits, while providing material both for 'the tittle-tattle of Highbury' and for alternative solutions such as Emma's.[41]

In general, more developed private messages such as letters are similarly subordinated by Austen to what I would call a socialized text; the body of the letter (with one notable exception, which I shall come to in a moment) is repressed, held out of sight, by paraphrase, in favour of the dramatization of its position in the

---

[40] See Ch. 1.

[41] I make no claim here to have exhausted all these 'messages'; e.g. for analysis of Austen's use of the song 'Robin Adair' as a musical clue or 'letter' in *Emma*, see Peter F. Alexander, ' "Robin Adair" as a Musical Clue in Jane Austen's *Emma*', *Review of English Studies*, NS, 39 (1988), 84–6. Alexander notes that the song is addressed by Jane to Frank, who secretly enjoys the ambiguity of a particular pronoun ('She is playing *Robin Adair* at this moment—*his* favourite', 243), while, for the benefit of Emma, allowing that pronoun to be misapplied to the absent Mr Dixon; the readdressing of the 'letter' in this way is typical of Austen's strategy as a whole.

system of circulatory gossip.[42] That famous moment in which Emma finally escapes Miss Bates, 'happy in this, that though much had been forced on her against her will; though she had, in fact, heard the whole substance of Jane Fairfax's letter, she had been able to escape the letter itself' (162), only underlines the fact that Frank Churchill's letters are similarly, and puzzlingly, absent even when they do arrive, appearing only, again, in the form of hearsay:

I suppose you have heard of the handsome letter Mr. Frank Churchill has written to Mrs. Weston? I understand it was a very handsome letter, indeed. Mr. Woodhouse told me of it. Mr. Woodhouse saw the letter, and he says he never saw a handsomer letter in his life. (18)

A clue to the reason for the absence of Frank's letters can be found in Mr Knightley's considerably crisper assessment:

He can sit down and write a fine flourishing letter, full of professions and falsehoods, and persuade himself that he has hit upon the very best method in the world of preserving peace at home, and preventing his father's having any right to complain. His letters disgust me. (148–9)

Mr Knightley, as the centre of moral authority in the novel, finds morally suspect precisely that which Emma finds seductive; while for Knightley only Churchill's presence could give substance to the style of the letter, for Emma the severance of the body from the letter ('there was something in the name, the idea, of Mr. Frank Churchill', 118) allows her to imagine him as a Grandisonian paragon (150), and thus to read his letters in a profoundly *literary* fashion:

Gratifying, however, and stimulative as was the letter in the material part, its sentiments, she yet found, when it was folded up and returned to Mrs. Weston, that it had not added any lasting warmth—that she could still do without the writer, and that he must learn to do without her. (266)

[42] Cf. Edgar Dryden's comments on gossip: 'Gossip . . . places [character] within the context of a shared morality. In some ways it may be regarded as the true voice of the community since it transcends self-interest by being associated with no identifiable source and by having existed prior to the involvement of any single individual. Moreover, it appears to be the channels of gossip rather than a dialogue between an I and a Thou which prompt communication and preserve communal unity. To participate in gossip, therefore, is to affirm one's membership in a community'; 'Hawthorne's Castle in the Air: Form and Theme in *The House of the Seven Gables*', *ELH* 38 (1971), 315; cited in Homer Obed Brown, 'The Errant Letter and the Whispering Gallery', *Genre*, 10 (1977), 578. Brown also notes the fundamental opposition between the letter and gossip. I am indebted here, too, to Patricia Meyer Spacks's discussion of *Emma* in *Gossip*.

This pattern of divergent response is repeated in a different key when Emma and Mr Knightley read the only letter that *does* appear in the text, that which bears Frank Churchill's confession, a letter that will invalidate Emma as the prime author (and indeed narrative authority) in the novel, necessitating another reading backwards of the text on the part of the reader, this time disengaged from Emma's narrative point of view. Churchill's letter will also position her as a pawn in his story, a humiliating come-down from her earlier happier fictionalizing of 'a thousand amusing schemes for the progress and close of their attachment, fancying interesting dialogues, and inventing elegant *letters*' [my italics] (264). Churchill's plot proves to have written Emma herself into a potentially sensational novel of seduction, betrayal, and abandonment by a glamorous stranger, a plot in fact that forms the staple of so many less adroit conservative novels (such as West's *Tale of the Times*) and which thus positions Frank as a residual philosopher-villain.

The reading of this letter is mediated for us three times, in a movement towards full social integration and social correction; the letter is addressed to Mrs Weston, 'ushered' into the text by her framing note of extenuation and read for the reader first by Emma and then by Mr Knightley, in a properly public and uncompromising fashion. Frank's letter itself is primarily preoccupied with con-structing a sympathetic audience for his narrative; perhaps I should say reconstructing his previous audience, this time as the willing rather than unwitting dupes of his spurious epistolary narratives. It is designed, furthermore, as a test of the reader's resistance to his blandishments. Exculpating himself, Frank retrospectively invents a fictitious circuit of communication with Emma—'we seemed to understand one another' (438)—which assigns blame not to his duplicity but to Emma's failure of reading. His 'confession' replicates the flow of the secret correspondence by including one of the only pieces of Jane's epistolary commerce to appear in the novel (tellingly, paraphrased): 'She felt the engagement to be a source of repentance and misery to each: she dissolved it' (442). The letter also includes a narrative of the uncertainty of epistolary intercourse itself, an uncertainty that has constantly ruptured the social fabric of Highbury—Frank's failure to post the crucial letter nearly destroys his chances of happiness permanently. 'Imagine the shock; imagine how, till I had actually detected my own blunder, I raved at the blunders of the post' (443), a blunder, as the insistent verbal repetition emphasises, which is akin to the anagram of 'blunder' that similarly goes astray. Only Jane's return of all his letters has put an effective end to the correspondence, forcing Churchill finally into *tête-à-tête*, and thus into what he hopes is a perfect and permanent communion of understanding—'no moment's uneasiness can ever occur between us again' (443).

Frank's unscrupulous rhetoric of feeling duly engages Emma's own sympathies, and '[s]he was obliged, in spite of her previous determination to the contrary, to do it all the justice that Mrs Weston foretold' (444), recommending it to the perusal of Mr Knightley in the fond persuasion that he will also be won over. Mr Knightley, as prosecuting counsel, then offers a running commentary-cum-explication for the edification of all concerned, a rereading of Churchill's rewriting of history. Though Emma begins to endorse Mr Knightley's fault-finding, his searching critique of Churchill's intriguing serves only to highlight the remaining reserves of Emma's own scheming:

'My Emma, does not everything serve to prove more and more the beauty of truth and sincerity in all our dealings with each other?'
    Emma agreed to it, and with a blush of sensibility on Harriet's account, which she could not give any sincere explanation of. (446)

The final rereading within the novel is the recirculation of the story concerning Mr Perry's carriage. The possibility of Perry's setting-up of his carriage (of which only the Bates household was aware) had been retailed to Frank by Jane in a letter, so that the illicit correspondence came perilously close to full exposure when Frank revealed his awareness of the scheme in general conversation. In the attempt to cover up, Frank resorts to the thin explanation that it must all have been a dream, a figure for human consciousness in its most unsocial form. In a last act of sanitization of the subtext, both the 'dream' and Jane's hitherto invisible letter are dragged into the surface layer of the text, made legible on the body of the transgressive woman, and thus brought into social intercourse; they are triangulated, appropriately enough, in a final image of a man inciting a woman's reading of another woman rereading a letter she had originally written to him:

'Such an extraordinary dream of mine!' he cried. 'I can never think of it without laughing. She hears us, she hears us, Miss Woodhouse. I see it in her cheek, her smile, her vain attempt to frown. Look at her. Do you not see that, at this instant, the very passage of her own letter, which sent me the report, is passing under her eye; that the whole blunder is spread before her; that she can attend to nothing else, though pretending to listen to the others?' (480)

Frank thus remains in some sense an epistolary villain, delighting until the last moment in the potential for social confusion provided by the *double entendre*, eager to negotiate a complicity with Emma to the last. The final scapegoat for his, and for Emma's, moral 'blunders' turns out to be Jane Fairfax, fulfilling Mrs Weston's early prediction that Emma herself would 'make no lasting blunder' (40).

The novel's final rerun of the social disorder caused by epistolary secrecy takes place in the rather squalid scene in which Mrs Elton plays one last vulgar game with Mrs Smallridge's letter. Believing Emma to be ignorant of the Churchill–Fairfax engagement, she directs all her efforts towards excluding Emma from this knowledge, conducting in her presence a conversation with Jane which is designed at once to hint at a double meaning and to withhold it. Significantly, Mrs Elton remains seduced by the flirtatious fascination of the riddle, by the severance of persons from names, happy in the erotics of the circulation and substitution of meaning that the novel as a whole has been straining to terminate:

You remember those lines—I forget the poem at this moment:—

> 'For when a lady's in the case,
> You know, all other things give place.'

Now I say, my dear, in *our* case, for *lady*, read—mum! a word to the wise. . . . I mentioned no *names*, you will observe. Oh no! cautious as a minister of state. I managed it extremely well. (454)

This scene underlines the latent vulgarity and the essential smuttiness of a text premised upon double meanings; the couplet is quoted from one of the more sexually forthright of Gay's *Fables*.

Austen's didactic programme is to bring the two discourses, the public and the private, onto a level, and to ensure a world of near-perfect, institutionalized intelligibility and legibility in which what Jane says of the postal system would be true of social intercourse in general:[43]

[43] See Litvak's comment on this passage that 'the postal service is merely a synecdoche for the much larger system of communication on which the novel

'The post office is a wonderful establishment!' said she.—The regularity and dispatch of it! If one thinks of all that it has to do, and all that it does so well, it is really astonishing!'

'It is certainly very well regulated.'

'So seldom that any negligence or blunder appears! So seldom that a letter, among the thousands that are constantly passing about the kingdom, is even carried wrong—and not one in a million, I suppose, actually lost! And when one considers the variety of hands, and of bad hands too, that are to be deciphered, it increases the wonder.' (296)[44]

Transparency, finally, is what this novel aims at; the rendering transparent of Emma's machinations to the point where she becomes marriageable, to the point, in fact, where Mr Weston's conundrum at the Box Hill picnic, 'M.A.' ('Emma') does indeed unproblematically translate as 'perfection':

High in the rank of her most serious and heartfelt felicities was the reflection that all necessity of concealment from Mr Knightley would soon be over. The disguise, equivocation, mystery, so hateful to her to practise, might soon be over. She could now look forward to giving him that full and perfect confidence which her disposition was most ready to welcome as a duty. (475)

In resettling open lines of communication and parameters of intelligibility (albeit with a faint smile at Emma's expense), Austen also resettles the lines of social hierarchy; the games of equivocation set in motion by Emma's wilful violation of the conventions of class by an importation of the conventions of romance (her romantic fantasies on Harriet's behalf) are replaced by an appropriate failure of intelligibility contingent upon the proper distances between classes. Thus Emma only partially understands Harriet's revived attachment to the lower-class Martin, '[b]eyond this, it

centers—namely, the social text in which the characters keep construing and misconstruing one another—so that any anxiety about mail deliveries may be taken as an anxiety about the semiotic efficiency or governability of society as a whole'; 'Reading Characters', 766.

[44] Mary Favret comments at some length on Austen's treatment of the post office in *Emma*, arguing that, as a receiver and distributor of letters, it is in competition with Austen as omniscient narrator. See Favret, 'Idea of Correspondence', 249 ff. Ironically, Jane's panegyric on the efficiency of the post office, a system of social communications in which 'blunders' (once again) do not occur (in pointed contrast to the prevailing state of affairs in Highbury) only confirms Emma's own pet blunder; she mischievously considers making 'an inquiry or two, as to the expedition and the expense of the Irish mails' (298).

must ever be unintelligible to Emma' (481). The same strategic unintelligibility as a mechanism for fortifying class boundaries is adumbrated by Mrs Elton's famous, final and scornful comment, 'Very little white satin, very few lace veils; a most pitiful business! Selina would stare when she heard of it' (484). Mrs Elton and Selina are here excluded from the inner circle of the upper classes, too *nouveau riche* to read their conventions aright. Moreover, the circulation of gossip is here differentiated into new and carefully defined levels based on class.[45] In the privacy of the final group, 'the small band of true friends', equivocation is finally exorcized by the exchange of marital vows. The last text on which Emma indulges in blank-filling is the Book of Common Prayer, which provides the novel's final riddle:

I will promise to call you once by your Christian name. I do not say when, but perhaps you may guess where—in the building in which N. takes M. for better, for worse. (463)

The conclusive ceremonial transaction in the church is rendered not only unequivocal, but fully visible to witnesses, a closing disclosure of the secret places of passion. In this transaction the circuit of the 'Highbury gossips', as the ground of the community, is finally fully institutionalized; this is the moment when the individual lovers are brought into a perfect 'correspondence' with both each other and their social world. The sentimental letter, figuring the vagaries of the female subject's desire, is finally subordinated to a system of gossip aligned with third-person narration, a system that takes the place of the father.[46]

[45] For a similar reading of the exclusionary system of gossip, see Casey Finch and Peter Bowen, ' "The Tittle-Tattle of Highbury": Gossip and the Free Indirect Style in *Emma*', *Representations*, 31 (1990), 1–18.

[46] For a sophisticated account of precisely what sort of third-person narrative authority Austen sets up, an authority analogous to that of gossip, see Finch and Bowen, 'The Tittle-Tattle of Highbury', esp. 13. For an alternative reading of gossip's role in Austen's fiction, diametrically at variance to my own, see Jan B. Gordon, 'A-filiative Families and Subversive Reproduction: Gossip in Jane Austen', *Genre*, 21 (Spring 1988), 5–46. The system of gossip is in the event so powerful that it can be imagined (although in this instance such confidence is rather premature) as pre-empting the privacy of the letter altogether, as Emma's complacent prefabrication of her 'flirtation' with Churchill for epistolary circulation suggests: '[I]n the judgement of most people looking on it must have had such an appearance as no English word but flirtation could very well describe. "Mr. Frank Churchill and Miss Woodhouse flirted together excessively." They were laying themselves open to that very phrase—and to having it sent off in a letter to Maple Grove by one lady, to Ireland by another' (368).

VI

If *Emma* ultimately subjects the letter's multiple meanings to public surveillance in order to render its seductions and slippages powerless, and so conforms to a broadly conservative model, *Persuasion* (1818), published only two years later, seems at first glance to reverse this strategy altogether in the famous scene of Captain Wentworth's declaration with which the novel reaches its climax. That scene, elaborately rewritten by Austen to replace the original draft, contains at its heart Wentworth's letter of proposal. In this revision, Austen effectively reverses the general thrust of *Emma*, prioritizing at the last moment the written over the oral, and this choice is the more surprising given that, up until this point, *Persuasion* has displayed a number of familiar features, notably the embedded and miniaturized anti-Jacobin seduction plot recognizably transliterated into the shape of Mr Elliot's melodramatically villainous seduction and abandonment to ruin (in this instance financial) of the imprudent but feeling husband of Mrs Smith.[47] Running true to form, this plot is again intimately associated with the secret circulation of information[48] and, in particular, with letters, which Mrs Smith produces as evidence against Mr Elliot. In this instance Austen chooses for the most part to withhold the letter from any public scrutiny, with the one exception of the letter which Mrs Smith shows to Anne, who, upset, was 'obliged to recollect that her seeing the letter was a violation ... that no private correspondence could bear the eye of others' (204). Instead, the content of the box of letters beneath Mrs Smith's sickbed is translated into Mrs Smith's retail of gossip, which displaces the letter's relatively confined itinerary with the more largely social:

[47] The new register that the novel slips into at the opening of Mrs Smith's disclosure is, despite a delicate sense of the melodramatic quality of Mrs Smith's rhetoric, authentically anti-Jacobin; Mrs Smith describes Elliot as 'a man without heart or conscience; a designing, wary, cold-blooded being, who thinks only of himself; who, for his own interest or ease, would be guilty of any cruelty, or any treachery, that could be perpetrated without risk of his general character. He has no feeling for others. Those whom he has been the chief cause of leading into ruin, he can neglect and desert without the smallest compunction. He is totally beyond the reach of any sentiment of justice or compassion. Oh! he is black at heart, hollow and black!'; Austen, *Works*, iii (*Persuasion*), 199.

[48] Anne Elliot, for example, discovers that Mr Elliot's inexplicable prior knowledge of her had been originally obtained from Mrs Smith (201).

[My information] . . . takes a bend or two, but nothing of consequence. The stream is as good as at first; the little rubbish it collects in the turnings, is easily moved away. Mr. Elliot talks unreservedly to Colonel Wallis of his views on you—which said Colonel Wallis I imagine to be in himself a sensible, careful, discerning character; but Colonel Wallis has a very pretty silly wife, to whom he tells things which he had better not, and he repeats it all to her. She, in the overflowing spirits of her recovery, repeats it all to her nurse; and the nurse, knowing my acquaintance with you, very naturally brings it all to me. (204–5)

Despite the familiarity of these moves, it is nevertheless true that, in this novel, the verdict of gossip, which confidently predicts the marriage of Anne with Mr Elliot, is actually mistaken; although Mrs Smith proves indeed to be well-informed on the heartless intentions of Mr Elliot and, indeed, of those of Mrs Clay, she, and her acquaintance, could not be further from the truth as regards the heart of Anne. In keeping with this conservation of the truth of private feeling, the letter, and the feeling associated with it, is ultimately salvaged in the unprecedented scene of letter-writing in which Captain Wentworth writes his love-letter to Anne while eavesdropping on her conversation with Captain Harville.

This scene is undoubtedly interested in evacuating some of the conventions of the sentimental letter; it should not be forgotten that the all-important conversation between Anne and Harville concerns the shortlived passion of the sentimental Captain Benwick for the recently-dead Fanny Harville. That conversation concerns what effectively functions as a sentimental letter in the same way as Edward Ferrars's ring does—the miniature of Captain Benwick, originally commissioned by Fanny, and now entrusted to Harville to procure a new setting, so that Benwick may give it to his new fiancée Louisa Musgrove. This manœuvre, that inauthenticates the sentimental letter by highlighting its potential for recycling, and thus insists on the divorce of text from interior emotional event, is familiar from Austen's other novels; what is unprecedented in Austen's *œuvre* is the way that compromised sentimental letter is then superseded by another, more genuine version. It is hardly irrelevant that the letter of business that Wentworth is supposedly writing concerns the resetting of the miniature, and that this letter of business gives place to a more fully sentimental letter—professing unabated and, importantly, undeflected love and constancy. This is, however, a sentimental letter with a difference; in dramatizing a speaking woman and a silent, writing man, Austen reverses the convention that allocates the writing and reactive position to a woman, and so relegates Wentworth to operating within a feminized discourse.[49] In keeping with this, his letter is radically contaminated and conditioned by the woman's discourse, forced helplessly (Wentworth describes himself as overpowered) into a correspondence with it, a correspondence that is, crucially and unconventionally, actually initiated by Anne. Wentworth's letter is intimately structured upon Anne's preceding conversation with Harville, taking as its entry-point her remark that '[w]e certainly do not forget you so soon as you forget us' (232), and answering her exclamation that 'I should deserve utter contempt if I dared suppose that true attachment and constancy were known only by woman' (235) with its own exit-line, 'You do believe that there is true attachment and constancy among men. Believe it to be most fervent, most undeviating in, F. W.' (237).

This letter, although written, delivered, and read in public, is covertly written, delivered by a ruse,[50] and as secretively read, and must, therefore, be regarded in some sense as clandestine correspondence, which for once seems to have had its revolutionary potential restored to it: 'the revolution which one instant had made in Anne, was almost beyond expression' (237). The letter eventually, indeed, effects a revolution, in the sense that Anne is at last enabled to marry the man originally regarded by her father as 'a very degrading alliance' (26). This salvage of epistolary feeling and the associated structures of private plot and private desire—a salvage signalled by *Persuasion*'s remarkable deployment of a narrative method inflected to an unprecedented degree by individual subjectivity—is therefore conducted more or less in the face of established social structures associated with the gentry and in flight from the patriarchal endogamy that marriage with Elliot would have represented.

[49] For my analysis of a roughly contemporaneous and more conventional treatment of this scene in Byron's *Don Juan* see Ch. 4.

[50] 'She had only time, however, to move closer to the table where he had been writing, when footsteps were heard returning; the door opened; it was himself. He begged their pardon, but he had forgotten his gloves, and instantly crossing the room to the writing table, and standing with his back towards Mrs Musgrove, he drew out a letter from under the scattered paper, placed it before Anne with eyes of glowing entreaty fixed on her for a moment, and hastily collecting his gloves, was again out of the room, almost before Mrs Musgrove was aware of his being in it . . .' (236).

In this move, Austen makes her most sophisticated manœuvre yet in relation to the structures of sentiment; rather than containing or erasing them, she recuperates them. In positioning Wentworth as the sentimental heroine, Austen reharnesses sentimentalism and the letter, for so long figured as inimical to the State, laundering them in the most striking fashion by the nationalism supremely exemplified by the profession that Wentworth follows, and underscored by the dating of the inception of the novel as the summer of 1814 (just after the abdication of Napoleon) and its climax in late February 1815 (just before Napoleon's comeback from Elba that was finally crushed at Waterloo). It is both fitting and prophetic that the novel's final sentence should celebrate a new marriage of the personal and the public, the sentimental and the national, as Austen declares the Royal Navy to be 'if possible, more distinguished in its domestic virtues than in its national importance' (252).[51] By the end of *Persuasion*, gossip, the expression of the twinned voices of social and paternal authority in *Emma*, is superseded by a discourse of elective nationalism.

After 1815 the letter appears only sporadically within the mainstream of the novel as a generic fossil. The related revolutionary plot of sensibility and seduction is still in evidence, but ever more faintly traced. These elements are still subject to regulatory discipline; indeed, I shall be arguing that this discipline (not coincidentally the title of an extremely successful novel published by Mary Brunton in 1814), by replacing the individualism of epistolary self-representation with communally accredited systems of right reading, was designed to produce both the ideal domestic subject and, by extension, the fully national subject. My next chapter will accordingly describe the various ways in which these residual elements were subordinated to an ever more powerful discourse of nationalism within the experimental and innovative national and historical tales of Lady Sydney Morgan, Jane Porter, Maria Edgeworth, and Sir Walter Scott.

---

[51] Cf. Mary Poovey's related argument that by granting the naval officers prominence 'Austen endows individual feeling with a new power', seeming to be less concerned with the problem of 'the *moral* authority of individual feeling'; *The Proper Lady and the Woman Writer*, 234.

3

Consigning the Heroine to History: National and Historical Tales, 1800–1825

1815, the year in which the battle of Waterloo was won, inaugurated a new mood of triumphant nationalism in Britain.[1] It is not coincidental that the years of Napoleon's defeat also saw the rapid development of the regional and historical novel, culminating in the appearance of a new and extraordinarily successful novelist, Sir Walter Scott, who published the first of his series of Waverley novels, *Waverley*, in 1814, the year of Napoleon's abdication. In this chapter I shall be detailing the ways in which Scott's immensely influential production of national history—a discourse that fundamentally conditioned fictional and historical consciousness for the remainder of the nineteenth century—is both the continuation and the logical culmination of the mainstream novel's attempt to discipline the literary forms of revolution in the shape of the letter and its reified surrogates.[2] (It is not irrelevant to note here that Scott wrote an admiring review of Austen's *Emma*, the parallel strategies of which I have already discussed.) I shall be exploring the nationalist inflections of this agenda as they become visible in a clutch of novels published between 1803 and 1824, novels by authors as diverse in their political sympathies as Lady Sydney Morgan, Charles Maturin, E. S. Barrett, Jane Porter, Maria Edgeworth, and Walter Scott himself. In reading these novels, Morgan's *The Wild Irish Girl* (1806), Maturin's *The Wild Irish*

---

[1] On British nationalism in the period 1790–1830, see Gerald Newman, *The Rise of English Nationalism: A Cultural History, 1740–1830* (New York, 1987); also Benedict Anderson, *Imagined Communities: Reflections on the Origin and Spread of Nationalism* (London, 1983).

[2] It is interesting to note, e.g., that one of the chief predecessors of *Waverley* among Scottish regional and historical novels is Robert Bisset's explicitly anti-Jacobin *Douglas: or, The Highlander* (4 vols., London, 1800). Bisset himself, however, did not pursue this avenue, turning instead to the mainstream anti-Jacobin novel with *Modern Literature* (3 vols., London, 1804).

Boy (1808), Barrett's *The Heroine* (1813), Porter's *Thaddeus of Warsaw* (1803), Edgeworth's *Ormond* (1817), and finally Scott's first series of three novels, *Waverley* (1814), *Guy Mannering* (1815), and *The Antiquary* (1816), I shall be displaying the various ways in which the sentimental plot, now embedded within an explicitly historical revolutionary setting (whether of the French Revolution itself or of analogues such as the Irish Rebellion of 1798, or the Jacobite rising of 1745),[3] mutates under the pressure of the yoked discourses of history and nationalism. In the light of the growing anxiety over domestic social unrest which came to a head with the Peterloo massacre of 1819, this project of disciplining revolutionary energy was by no means obsolete. I shall be showing in detail how the conventional plot of the education of the sentimental hero/ine is reworked by polemicists of various political shades, so as to extricate the sentimental protagonist from the plot of sensibility in order to instal her (or, increasingly, him) within an emergent genre of national romance; I shall also be considering, in tandem, the implications these developments had for novelistic form, by continuing to pursue the itinerary of the letter.

Although the letter itself progressively vanishes over these

---

[3] However muffled up in a wide variety of nostalgic period costume, these plots are all about the French Revolution, and would have been recognized as such by contemporaries. In the 1790s it was common to think of the French Revolution in terms of 17th- and early 18th-c. history, and in particular in terms of the Glorious Revolution of 1688 (often taken to be either its English analogue or antithesis, depending on one's political sympathies). As Jane West symptomatically remarks, introducing her own historical novel, her use of such history is informed by a particular stance on contemporary politics: 'The tale she now chooses as a vehicle, aims at conveying instruction to the present times, under the form of a chronicle of the past. The political and religious motives, which convulsed England in the middle of the seventeenth century, bear so striking a resemblance to those which are now attempted to be promulgated, that surely it must be salutary to remind the inconsiderate, that reformists introduced first anarchy and then despotism, and that a multitude of new religions gave birth to infidelity.' *The Loyalists: An Historical Novel* (2nd edn., 3 vols., London, 1812), i. 8–9. For an excellent discussion of the political uses made of 17th-c. history at this time and a little later see J. W. Burrow, *A Liberal Descent* (Cambridge, 1981), 1–36; on contemporary arguments over the significance of 1688, see especially Kathleen Wilson, 'Inventing Revolution: 1688 and Eighteenth-Century Popular Politics', *Journal of British Studies*, 28 (Oct. 1989), 349–88. For an extended discussion of the ways in which 1688 and its analogues are invoked in contemporary writing, see Joseph Nicholes, 'Revolutions Compared: The English Civil War as Political Touchstone in Romantic Literature', in Keith Henley and Raman Selden (eds.), *Revolution and English Romanticism: Politics and Rhetoric* (Hemel Hempstead, 1990), 261–76.

decades, serving as an increasingly ghostly symptom of those
narratives of self-authorized subjectivity that counter-revolutionary
forms are invested in suppressing (often appearing only in residual
form as a substitute token such as a signet ring, a seal, or a ring
containing hair, like those which circulate in Austen's novels), the
related thematics of reading, rereading, and misreading, traced out
in Chapter 2, survives in intimate syntactic relation to the plot of
revolution. Indeed, in the most sophisticated of these novels, Scott's
The Antiquary, the revolutionary plot is finally immobilized
entirely by the authority of a central authorial discourse invested
with the full competence of historical hindsight; revolution itself,
figured as Napoleonic invasion, is ultimately identified as merely an
effect of misreading.

The chapter concludes with a glance at *Redgauntlet*, published in
1824, the year the Combination Acts, originally enforced in 1799
in response to fear of domestic revolutionaries and especially of the
activities of the Corresponding Societies, were finally, after much
political agitation, repealed. *Redgauntlet* conveniently encodes in
miniature the entire shift in novelistic form and political sensibility
this study has so far charted: re-enacting the revolution and the
reaction to it at the level of narrative form, it metamorphoses from
letters to first-person narration, and thence to third-person narration, before dwindling altogether into simply a problem of
historiography, relegated to an impotent obsolescence figured by
the dusty historical chronicle of miscellaneous documents and
anecdotes researched by Scott's fictional amanuensis, the maunder-
ing antiquarian, Dr Dryasdust.

I

For the most controversially liberal among Scott's immediate
literary forebears, this emerging combination of romance, historic-
ism, and nationalism might not so much suppress the novel of
sensibility as offer a last chance of rehabilitating it. The hugely
successful *The Wild Irish Girl* (1806) by Sydney Owenson, later
Lady Sydney Morgan, like *Persuasion*, harnesses the energy of the
sentimental plot to underwrite national identity—indeed, it might
be described as an attempt to nationalize the sentimental heroine.
This late epistolary novel is given a historically specific setting, as

its title would suggest: Ireland at the time of the French-backed rebellion of 1798, an event considered both in England and in Ireland to be at once analogous to the French Revolution and a consequence of the spread of French revolutionary principles.[4] Thanks to the alliance between the United Irishmen and the French Revolutionary Government which produced this uprising (and not only the French government was involved; English radicals resident in Paris took an active part in planning the disturbances, amongst them Helen Maria Williams's lover, John Hurford Stone), Ireland could be imagined, paradoxically, as a locus at once of foreign and of domestic revolution—a perception which informs many anti-Jacobin novels, whose villains, generally French, are gleefully prone to involvement with the Irish disturbances. (The energetic Marauder of Charles Lucas's *The Infernal Quixote*, 1798, to take a particularly memorable example, includes in his catalogue of resourceful villainies the plotting of the entire Irish Rebellion.) The novelist's Ireland thus became a privileged site both for the residual revolutionary romance of sensibility, and for the most energetic and invasive narrative discipline, a region into which the struggle between Jacobin and anti-Jacobin narratives migrated rapidly and comfortably.

The Wild Irish Girl takes up this struggle with particular clarity and vigour: its action, conveyed in the letters of a young English libertine, Mortimer, concerns the self-inscription of both Mortimer himself and the heroine Glorvina within the structures of *La Nouvelle Héloïse* in the context of erupting revolution. Mortimer journeys towards his father's estate across the wilds of Ireland at a time when, as he puts it, Ireland is 'a country . . . shaken by the

---

[4] As one English officer serving in Ireland during the unrest of the late 1790s observed: 'If the Irish are in some respects a century behind us in point of civilization, they are at least 2 centuries before us in their Revolutionary principles; and if we are to be agitated hereafter by those doctrines which now shake Europe to her centre, we are as likely to have them imported from Ireland as from France'; National Library of Ireland, MS 54 A/111, [George Dallas] to Dundas, 20 Sept., 1797, cited by Marianne Elliott, *Partners in Revolution; The United Irishmen and France* (New Haven, Conn., 1982), 51–2. Wolfe Tone's account of Irish politics in the wake of 1789 underscores the point: 'We well knew what it was to be enslaved and sympathised most sincerely with the French people . . . In a little time the French Revolution became the test of every man's political creed, and the nation was fairly divided into two great parties, the Aristocrats and the Democrats.' Richard Hayes, *Ireland and Irishmen in the French Revolution* (London, 1932), 249.

convulsions of an anarchical spirit'.[5] As his journey continues, the jaded Mortimer (who opens the novel complaining that he is so *ennuyé* as to be unable to be roused even by 'the sentimental sorcery of *Rousseau*'—vol. i, p. xxxiii) is progressively seduced by the country into which he is travelling, a seduction strikingly characterized as an absorption into sentimental and romantic fiction (i. 156). At the furthest point of his trip, Mortimer eventually meets with the most ancient of all Ireland's inhabitants, a Milesian Chief and his daughter, the Princess of Inismore or Glorvina, making his final entry into this alternative fictional discourse by climbing up the walls of Inismore Castle to catch a glimpse of the patriotic harp-playing Glorvina. At the height of this romantic escapade he is so overcome by the spectacle of Glorvina's performance that he sustains a fall, recovering from unconsciousness to find himself safely within the walls. Passing himself off as an artistic tourist (rather than what he is, the son of the family who usurped the estate of Inismore during the Cromwellian Wars), he enters a full-blown novel of sensibility identified meticulously with *La Nouvelle Héloïse*, becoming Glorvina's drawing-master (a project pointedly described by Mortimer as worthy of 'the intriguing spirit of a French Abbé reared in the purlieus of the *Louvre*', i. 241). Although Mortimer is at first drawn only reluctantly into this narrative, he soon begins to direct it with relish. Glorvina is carefully coached in her role as heroine of sensibility by the books Mortimer imports for her delectation, including the inevitable 'Letters of the impassioned Héloïse' along with *Paul et Virginie*, *Werter*, and Chateaubriand's '*Attila*' (presumably *Atala*):

They were all precisely such books as Glorvina had *not*, yet *should* read, that she may know herself and the latent sensibility of her soul. . . . Let our English novels carry away the prize of morality from the romantic fictions of every other country; but you will find they rarely seize on the imagination through the medium of the heart; and, as for their heroines, I confess, that, though they are the most perfect of beings, they are also the most stupid.   (ii. 185)

This course of tutorials has the desired, overdetermined, effect:

Her abstracted air, her delicious melancholy, her unusual softness, betray the nature of the feelings by which she is overwhelmed—they are new to

---

[5] [Sydney] Owenson, *The Wild Irish Girl; A National Tale* [1806] (4th edn., 3 vols., London, 1808), i. 36.

herself; and sometimes I fancy, when she turns her melting eyes on me, it is to solicit their meaning. Oh! if I dared become the interpreter between her and her heart— (ii. 201)

Having rewritten Glorvina, Mortimer will now read her back to herself.[6] This collaborative sentimental epistolary novel is deftly identified as potentially political in that it both displaces and continues Mortimer's study of Irish history—'I fear my *Hiberniana* is closed, and a volume of more dangerous, more delightful tendency draws towards its bewitching subject every truant thought' (ii. 238).

This mutual rereading and rewriting of epistolary hero and sentimental heroine within the structures of the novel of sensibility, is, I should stress, represented as mutually beneficial, in striking contrast to the political anxiety usually centred on this plot for avowedly anti-Jacobin writers. Indeed, Owenson was already notorious in conservative circles for the sentiments given rein in her second novel, *St Clair; or, The Heiress of Desmond* (1803), which had wholeheartedly rehearsed a tragedy of sensibility by Rousseau out of *Werther*. None the less, because Owenson is interested in conscripting the power of the sentimental text into the service of Irish loyalist nationalism, *The Wild Irish Girl* completes a number of intricate manœuvres to close off some of its subversive and specifically revolutionary tendencies, figured at one point by Mortimer's unsettling dream concerning 'the princess of Inismore'; who 'approached my bed, drew aside the curtains, and raising her veil, discovered . . . the face, the head of a *Gorgon!*' (i. 185) To this end Morgan first rewrites the plot of *La Nouvelle Héloïse*, and then invokes the paradoxical figure of Jacobitism (paradoxical because while it encodes revolution, it is, unlike the Jacobinism it obliquely figures, a revolution legitimized by its determination to restore patrilineality) to underwrite her own Unionist version of Irish national identity.

The saving swerve from Rousseau is initiated in Glorvina's boudoir, where Mortimer discovers 'my own *Eloisa* . . . marked with a slip of paper in that page where the character of Wolmar is described' (iii. 3). That slip of paper, interleaved and interpolated within the secret correspondence between Julie and St Preux of the first part of Rousseau's novel, proves to be a love-letter to Glorvina

<hr />

[6] See also ii. 207–9, 219.

from an unknown, her father's friend and his choice of suitor to his daughter. It initiates a series of moments in which Glorvina, like Julie in the second half of *La Nouvelle Héloïse*, is portrayed as supportive of order and legitimacy, whether patriarchal, in the celebration of her filial feeling, or political, as when Mortimer borrows from Burke's panegyric on the Dauphiness to describe Glorvina's position among her people: 'I am sure there was not an individual among this crowd of ardent and affectionate people who would not have risked his life "to avenge a look that threatened her with danger" ' (iii. 60).

Nevertheless, the secretive correspondence in which Glorvina proves to be engaged is, with generic appropriateness, linked threateningly with revolution, for the correspondent and putative lover of Glorvina is a mysterious stranger who turns up in 'the spring of 17—', 'that fatal period when the scarcely cicatrised wounds of this unhappy country bled afresh beneath the uplifted sword of civil contention; when the bonds of human amity were rent asunder, and every man regarded his neighbour with suspicion or considered him with fear' (iii. 144). The stranger is sheltered on the apparently well-founded assumption that he is a fugitive rebel leader, a cousin in some sense to Lady Caroline Lamb's later villain-hero, Lord Glenarvon.[7] However, the revolutionary and sexual dangers of such clandestine correspondence are eventually averted in a surprise denouement, when Mortimer arrives back from Dublin in time to substitute for the mysterious stranger as Glorvina's bridegroom, the stranger proving, so far from being a rebel, to be his own father. In this way Owenson tidily conflates Wolmar and St Preux in Mortimer's own person, thus legitimizing the passion of Rousseau's lovers and excising the erotic conflict to which *La Nouvelle Héloïse* owes its political force. The crucially nationalist politics of this policing of sensibility are underscored in Mortimer's father's closing letter:

[B]e ever watchful to moderate that ardent impetuosity, which flows from the natural tone of the national character, which is the inseparable accompaniment of quick and acute feelings, which is the invariable concomitant of constitutional sensibility; and remember that the same ardour of disposition, the same vehemence of soul, which inflames their

---

[7] For a reading of *Glenarvon* (1816), see Ch. 4.

errors beyond the line of moderate failing, nurtures their better qualities beyond the growth of moderate excellence.   (iii. 262)

Ireland itself here becomes the heroine of sensibility, liable to error but ultimately as susceptible as Glorvina of being properly governed. The union of Mortimer and Glorvina within this regenerate sentimental plot is used to parallel the Union of England and Ireland of 1800, a union that came into being in direct response to the Irish Rebellion. This Union is rendered both legitimate and consensual by Owenson through a further appeal to Jacobitism: the Irish are represented as more legitimate and less revolutionary in their politics than the English:

The moment a Prince of the Royal line of Milesius placed the British diadem on his brow, the sword of resistance was sheathed, and those principles which force could not vanquish yielded to the mild empire of national and hereditary affection! the Irish of *English* origin from natural tenderness, and those of the *true old stock*, from the firm conviction that they were *then* governed by a *Prince* of their own blood. Nor is it now unknown to them, that in the veins of his present Majesty and his ancestors, from James the First, flows the royal blood of the *three* kingdoms united.   (iii. 68)[8]

This reading of *The Wild Irish Girl* may be usefully glossed by Charles Maturin's similar nationalization of the sentimental heroine in his opportunistic imitation of Owenson's novel, *The Wild Irish Boy* (1808). The heroine of the epistolary correspondence that opens the novel, which serves at once as a frame narrative

---

[8] Morgan repeats this move in *O'Donnel; a National Tale* (1814), representing the Irish as infinitely more devoted to any hereditary prince than to any revolution: O'Donnel himself, a legitimate but disinherited heir, treasures a diamond ring presented to him by Marie Antoinette, and boasts of the loyalty of the Irish to the *ancien régime* during the French Revolution: 'A devotion to hereditary monarchy has always been attributed to the Irish gentry, even by their enemies. To this of old they owe their misfortunes; to this in the present times they may look for the full restitution of their rights.' Lady Sydney Morgan, *O'Donnel; A National Tale* [1814] (London, 1835), 161. Morgan thus bases a claim to justice for the Irish on their hereditary Jacobitism—insisting they are legitimists rather than revolutionists. By contrast, Caroline Lamb maintains a simple equation between Jacobitism and Jacobinism, underlining her Irish villain-hero Glenarvon's innate revolutionary instincts by attributing to him a Jacobite heredity; Glenarvon's grandfather 'who, from the favourite of the lawful prince, had become the secret accomplice of a bloody conspiracy' had spawned a line in which 'the name of traitor was handed down with the coronet'; *Glenarvon* [1816] (2nd edn., 2 vols., Philadelphia, 1816), i. 194–5 (see Ch. 4).

and as a preview of what is to come, ultimately dies of her exquisite sensibility; however, her surrogate Ormsby, the wild Irish boy himself, dangerously addicted to the sublime in scenery, to *Werther*, and to *La Nouvelle Héloïse*, and infatuated with a married woman, Lady Montrevor (to whose daughter he himself is married), is rescued from this promisingly scandalous sentimental imbroglio alive and well. The potentially dangerous possibilities of this plot are hygienically truncated by the conversion of Lady Montrevor from siren to surrogate mother, which is accomplished just after a masquerade at which she appears first of all as the repentant courtesan of the *ancien régime*, La Vallière (recognized by contemporaries as yet another French version of Eloisa),[9] and then, metamorphosing, as Morgan's reclaimed Glorvina herself.

Despite these legitimizing tactics, Sydney Owenson's, or rather, at this juncture, Lady Sydney Morgan's novels were frequently indicted for their endorsement of the sentimental heroine, an endorsement that was recognized as 'Jacobinical'.[10] E. S. Barrett's *The Heroine* (1813) identified Morgan's brand of 'performing heroinism' as borrowed from Madame de Staël's celebration of desiring female subjectivity in her undesirably radical novel *Corinne* (Barrett, *The Heroine*, ii. 168–71)[11] and, worse, as thoroughly Rousseauistic: Barrett's 'heroine', Cherubina, to some large extent a parody of Glorvina, at one point describes herself as

---

[9] For a brief discussion of how the figure of La Vallière is assimilated to the figure of Julie in discourse associated with the French Revolution, see Nicola J. Watson, 'Novel Eloisas'.

[10] The *Quarterly Review*, for example, declares of her *Woman; or, Ida of Athens* (1809) that the 'sentiments . . . are mischievous in tendency and profligate in principle; licentious and irreverent in the highest degree'. *Quarterly Review* (Feb. 1809), 52. The same review conflates this subversiveness with her dangerous and marginal cultural status as an Irish national: 'The author like Caliban . . . "cannot endue her purpose with words that make it known" ' (50). Eight years later, Morgan is still being accused of 'Jacobinism . . . Licentiousness, and Impiety', *Quarterly Review* (Apr. 1817), 264. The *Edinburgh* commented caustically: 'Lady Morgan seems to think her heroines are "ne'er so sure our passions to create, As when they touch the brink of all we hate." ' *Edinburgh Review*, 1 (June 1819), 661. Finally, William Maginn lumps 'the filths of Lady Morgan' as undesirably Jacobin alongside the output of Byron, Mary Shelley, Hazlitt, Keats, Moore, Paine, Maturin, and Cobbett in *Blackwood's* (1819), reprinted in William Maginn, *The O'Doherty Papers* (2 vols., New York, 1855), 179–82.

[11] Barrett's novel is in fact closely modelled on an earlier anti-Jacobin text with a particular grudge against de Staël, Bayfield's *The Corinna of England; and a Heroine in the Shade* (2 vols., London, 1809), itself very much in the manner of Hamilton's *Memoirs of Modern Philosophers*.

'heroinized and Heloised' (iii. 174). The quasi-sentimental Cherubina's revolt against her father and subsequent setting of the fashionable world by the ears by occupying Monkton Castle and defending it against the local militia is envisioned as a thorough-going revolution—Cherubina's pre-battle speech to her retainers is notable for its garbled reformist rhetoric:

I will acknowledge the Majesty of the People;— ... I will institute a full, fair, and free Representation;— ... And I will establish a Radical Reform. ... I promise there shall be no ... degraded aristocracy, no oppressed people. ... Such is the constitution, such are the privileges, which I propose. (iii. 112–13)

This language accuses Morgan's narratives of Jacobinical tendencies; the point is hammered home when it appears that Cherubina's insurrectionist retainers include a large body of comically violent Irishmen. (iii. 115–18)[12]

II

Although Morgan's novels remained popular for the next fifteen years or so, fighting a rearguard action on behalf of what Gary Kelly has termed the 'novel of passion' in their attempts to conserve the politico-sentimental empowerment of the heroine (and thus, in this instance, of Ireland), the mainstream novel, more generally conservative, is interested primarily in writing its sentimental protagonists out of their native plot-structure, educating them into a social position entirely foreign to the 'heloised' romantic postures still favoured by Glorvina. Hence Jane Porter's best-selling early novel, *Thaddeus of Warsaw* (1803), rather than recruiting sentimental energy in the constitution of national identity, attempts instead simply to supersede the sentimental plot in favour of

[12] Intriguingly, Barrett was prepared to forgive Morgan's more emphatically legitimist *O'Donnel*, in which the performing heroine plays a much smaller role, recommending it as safe reading to his own reformed sentimental heroine, along with various novels of impeccable conservative pedigree—Goldsmith's *The Vicar of Wakefield*, Burney's *Cecilia*, Edgeworth's *The Fashionable Tales*, and More's *Coelebs in Search of a Wife* (iii. 233). For a more general conspectus of Barrett's satirical exploitation of anti-Jacobin conventions, see Gary Kelly, 'Unbecoming a Heroine: Novel-Reading, Romanticism, and Barrett's *The Heroine*', *Nineteenth-Century Literature*, 45 (1990), 220–41.

national romance. Like the novels discussed in Chapter 2, *Thaddeus of Warsaw* associates revolution with risky games of *double entendre* under the sign of *La Nouvelle Héloïse*; however, unlike them, it makes the context of revolution vividly explicit through taking as its central protagonist a real historical personage, Thaddeus Sobieski, still alive at the time of this novel's publication. Anticipating Morgan's strategies in a more hostile mode, the residual novel of sensibility is quelled by recourse to the romance plot of the lost father, which is paralleled on the conventionally historical level by a transposition of Jacobinism into Jacobitism, a move that, as I have already remarked, renders revolution not only improbably patrilineal, but also both romantically obsolete and a constitutive element of Britain's national past.[13]

Set in the 1790s, *Thaddeus of Warsaw* displaces the French Revolution into another region, in this case Poland;[14] in parallel, it similarly disciplines that other locus of transposed Revolution, the narrative of sensibility. *Thaddeus of Warsaw* falls into two sections, the first of which deals with the involvement of the young Thaddeus Sobieski in the ultimately unsuccessful war to defend the crown of Poland and preserve its territories from the partition between Russia, Austria, and Prussia that eventually took place in 1795. For Porter, Poland functions as a regional displacement of *ancien régime* France during the Revolution; Thaddeus's struggle to protect the crown is implicitly linked to the contemporaneous collapse of the monarchy in France in the preface, where Polish *émigrés* are conflated with French refugees:

[13] Porter's novel is in this respect, as I shall be arguing, an important influence on Scott: it is not irrelevant to note here that her next book, *The Scottish Chiefs*, is already transferring these narrative strategies to the Highlands four years before the publication of *Waverley*. See Jane Porter, *The Scottish Chiefs. A Romance* (5 vols., London, 1810).

[14] The contemporary political controversy over the partition of Poland attracted a more explicitly conservative commentary from Jane West, which amply illustrates both in content and context the political implications of Porter's choice of pre-partition Poland as a setting for her novel. West insists in her footnotes to her *Elegy on the Death of the Right Honourable Edmund Burke* (London, 1797)—a poem which devotes most of its energies to lamenting the disastrous effects of the French Revolution—that the partition proves that even lawful monarchs have become tainted with revolutionary ideology: 'Warmly attached to the cause of lawful Government, Subordination, and Property, she equally laments and reprobates the narrow Motives which induced Sovereign Princes to swell the Triumphs of Anarchy, and to undermine the principles by which their own thrones are supported by the forcible Dismemberment of Poland'; *Elegy*, 10.

I remember seeing many of those hapless [Polish] refugees wandering about in St. James's Park. They had sad companions in the like miseries, though from different enemies, in the emigrants from France; and memory can never forget the variety of wretched yet noble-looking visages I then contemplated . . .[15]

In addition to functioning as a displacement of *ancien régime* France, however, Poland figures, too, as a double for England, also under threat of invasion: Thaddeus's patriotic efforts are implicitly related to England's continuing war-effort. In particular, the Polish campaign is described in terms of the defence of 'the happy tendency of the glorious constitution of 1791' (41), a constitution which sounds like a first cousin to that which Burke maintained had been guaranteed for England by the Glorious Revolution of 1688. The war for Poland lost, and the country given up to the general ravage and rapine which claims Thaddeus's grandfather, mother, and ancestral home, Thaddeus makes his way as a penniless *émigré* to England, the setting for the second half of the novel.

Transposed into England, revolution is now represented in terms of a residual novel of sensibility. Nameless and penniless, Thaddeus, in a similar position to Frances Burney's later heroines, struggles to earn a living for himself, narrowly escaping insertion into a series of variously tragic and vulgar sentimental matrices. Employed as a tutor in German to a couple of spoiled *nouveau riche* misses, he is unfortunate enough to attract the affections of the younger, Euphemia; as a classic novel-reading feather-head, inflamed with ambition to emulate and inhabit the sentimental subjectivity of the heroines of Rousseau, Mackenzie, Radcliffe, Lee, Charlotte Smith, Goethe *et al.* (even, at one point, achieving a creditable impersonation of Burney's *Camilla*), she turns all her energies towards

---

[15] Jane Porter, *Thaddeus of Warsaw* [1803] (Chicago, n.d.), 5. See also the moment when Thaddeus as an *émigré* is confused with the French *émigrés* (126). Poland's defeat is in fact blamed ultimately upon the pernicious doctrines of Voltaire, who by promulgating infidelity and selfishness encouraged the nations to witness Poland's 'tragedy . . . without one attempt to stop or to delay its dreadful catastrophe!': 'Europe was then no longer what she was a century before. Almost all her nations [presumably excluding Britain!] had turned from the doctrines of 'sound things', and more or less drank deeply of the cup of infidelity, drugged for them by the flattering sophistries of Voltaire. The draught was inebriation, and the wild consequences burst asunder the responsibilities of man to man. The selfish principle ruled, and [the] balance of justice was then seen only aloft in the heavens!' (89).

inserting Thaddeus into a miniature Rousseauistic novel (a penchant tellingly attributed to her 'vile democratic ideas', 216). In pursuit of this end she dresses as Eloisa at a masquerade, successfully slotting Thaddeus into the unwelcome role of an Abelard or St Preux,[16] inveigles him into a reading of the more pathetic and passionate letters of Werther while casting herself as Charlotte, tempts him into the part of Romeo with herself as Juliet, and involves him in a complicated epistolary game of *double-entendre*,[17] in the course of which 'love-sick mottoes' give way to an episode involving a verse 'posy':

A few days prior . . . she had presented to him another of her posies, which ran thus: 'Frighted love, like a wild beast, shakes the wood in which it hides.' . . . 'Do, dear Mr. Constantine [the name under which Thaddeus is currently known],' cried she, 'translate it into the sweetest French you can; for I mean to have it put into a medallion, and give it to the person whom I most value on earth!'   (200)

Complying unwillingly, he partially mistranslates this sentiment as 'L'amour tel qu'une biche blessée, se trahit lui-même par sa crainte, qui fait remuer le feuillage qui le couvre'; and 'this unlucky addition of the words *se trahit lui-même*' (201), an addition which appears to Euphemia to initiate a covert correspondence, prompts her to send him secretly a packet which includes 'a gold medallion with the words he had altered for Miss Euphemia engraved on blue enamel' and some verses headed ' "To him who will apply them" ' (201). In reply Thaddeus pretends to misunderstand and translates the verses, already a translation from the Greek, into Italian, maintaining the 'letter' in circulation, and so avoiding, like Emma, the appropriation. Nevertheless, as this quick-witted evasion of Euphemia's advances might suggest, these episodes, in the upshot, prove no more than a financial embarrassment from which he is

---

[16] For a reading that would implicitly identify the masquerade itself as a figure for revolution in the shape of female sexual transgression, see Terry Castle, *Masquerade and Civilization* (Stanford, Calif., 1986), especially her chapter on Elizabeth Inchbald's *A Simple Story* (1791). Mary Ann Hanway's conservative novel *Elinor; or, The World As It Is* (4 vols., London, 1798) also features a masquerade imagined quite explicitly as a version of the French Revolution; for a brief account of how that revolution is policed by the emphatically British and paternalistic figure of Shakespeare's Prospero, see Michael Dobson, 'Remember/First to possess his books: the appropriation of *The Tempest*, 1700–1800', *Shakespeare Survey*, 43 (1991), 99–108.

[17] *Thaddeus of Warsaw*, 187, 191, 193, 196–7, 200–1, 205, 234.

quickly extricated. A similar sedative is applied to the other threatening seductress, Lady Sara Ross, whose adulterous passion for the hero, modelled explicitly on de Staël's *Delphine*, again threatens to overturn the social order, and indeed, her husband being on active service in the navy, the national order: unconventionally repenting without the aid of a fatal illness, she voluntarily removes herself from the action. These revolutionary scripts of social subversion (analogues to the historical carnage on the continent described earlier in the novel) being cleared away, Porter accelerates the process of restoring social equilibrium, which, for her as for her successor, Scott, involves the rediscovery of the lost past in the shape of a lost father for the (only apparently illegitimate) hero.

In this closing section of the novel, Porter laces up the tear in history represented as the missing link between father and son by seaming up the rents in fictional consciousness, figured earlier in the novel by the letters in which Thaddeus's mother confessed to him the true circumstances of his parentage, by the inserted letters from the mysterious father, and by the letters from the disobedient son, Somerset, Thaddeus's English ally, to his father in England. The discourse of history here functions as that inquisitorial narrative mode within which it is possible to resolve the discrepancies performed by the fragmented narrative of letters. Furthermore, having collected all her dramatis personae in one place, Porter proceeds, in a series of exquisitely convoluted gyrations which baffle plot-summary, to relate her hero to every character whom the novel endorses, and to disentangle him meticulously from certain supposed relationships with the villain of the piece. The threatened repetition, a generation later, of the initial betrayal of Thaddeus's mother is averted, and in a last burst of virtuosity Porter inserts Thaddeus into a regenerate England as not only the legitimate son of the elder Lord Somerset, but also, extraordinarily, in a move that reveals history as romance, as a legitimate descendant of the Young Pretender. Jacobitical legitimacy is thus imported into present-day Britain, as a guarantee of Thaddeus's nobility. Porter makes very clear the relation between the Jacobitical past and the revolutionary present; beginning with a parallel drawn between the Glorious Revolution and the contemporaneous 'deeprooted conspiracy in certain neighbouring states [to Poland] . . . to undermine the accession of [the Sobieski] family to the throne' by 'foreign and domestic revolutionists', Porter goes on to chronicle the retreat of both families into domestic tranquillity symbolized by the marriage of Lady Clementine Sobieski (who, incidentally, will feature in *Waverley* as the source of Flora MacIvor's pension) with the Young Pretender (434–6). This movement from revolution to domestic retirement is replicated on a larger scale in Thaddeus's enviable fate. His political lineage, at once legitimate and yet, by virtue of that legitimacy, revolutionary, is safely domesticated in the interests of national security.

A similar move is evident in Maria Edgeworth's novel, *Ormond* (1817), which also works to supersede sentimental revolutionary identity in favour of a new national identity articulated as regenerate domesticity. Edgeworth's novel depicts the re-education of a stand-in for the heroine of sensibility, a young Irish gentleman, Ormond, spoilt 'by the most injudicious indulgence, and by neglect of all instruction or discipline' and consequently displaying 'all the faults that were incident to his natural violence of passions' (Edgeworth, *Tales and Novels*, ix. 235)—the perfect example of sensibility in need of proper control. Ormond is associated with the narrative of domestic insurrection, but is enabled to evade some of the more serious consequences of his peccadilloes—although residual Rousseauistic narratives duly make their appearance, they are carefully contained, reduced to mere episodes in the hero's travels.

Journeying (in the steps of Owenson's Mortimer) to the furthest western part of Ireland, the Black Islands, his uncle 'King' Corny's domains, Ormond falls straight into the stock Rousseauistic plot, becoming briefly infatuated with Corny's already-betrothed Frenchified daughter, Dora, an affair which eventually makes its way onto the epistolary gossip-circuit 'through various circuitous channels of female correspondents' as a fully-fledged, if entirely unfounded, miniature anti-Jacobin novel, modelled inevitably upon a debased version of *La Nouvelle Héloïse*:

This Harry Ormond had gained the affections of his benefactor's daughter, though, as he had been warned by her father, she was betrothed to another man. The young lady was afterward, by her father's anger, and by Ormond's desertion of her, thrown into the arms of a French adventurer, whom Ormond brought into the house under pretence of learning French from him. Immediately after the daughter's elopement with the French master, the poor father died suddenly . . . (ix. 491)

Needless to say, Edgeworth does not endorse any such melodrama in her plot proper, discrediting this erroneous account at her first opportunity; in fact, the 'benefactor's daughter', Dora, has been persuaded (by appeals to her vanity) to abandon Ormond and to marry her original fiancé's brother, M. de Connal, and is subsequently whisked off to pre-revolutionary Paris.

Ormond next graduates to an imbroglio with the sentimental Lady Millicent, 'all for sensibility and enthusiasm', purveying a 'female metaphysics' of which Edgeworth comments:

Her ideas of virtue were carried to such extremes that they touched the opposite vices—in truth, there was nothing to prevent them; for the line between right and wrong, that line which should be strongly marked, was effaced: so delicately had sentiment shaded off its boundaries.   (ix. 403)

This heroine of sensibility is, like Lady Sara Ross, a Julie *manquée*, married but unhappy, and of compromised reputation, 'a very imprudent, though . . . still an innocent woman' (184), from whom Ormond is ultimately saved by his own good principles.

These two episodes in Ormond's progress towards the perfect marriage with Florence Annaly are mounted upon a backing of rebellion and revolution, making clear what is at stake in such an education. Ormond's first appearance, hideously bloodstained in the ballroom, a violent anomaly who reduces to utter confusion a highly sophisticated social ritual, is occasioned by an 'Irish disturbance'; Ormond and his illegitimate half-brother Marcus have involved themselves in a brawl with some of the tenantry, which is sparked by accusations of tyranny on one side and epithets of 'rebel' upon the other (ix. 241). Although Edgeworth charac-teristically cauterizes this rebellion by representing it largely as a regrettable misunderstanding between the warm-hearted Ormond and his devoted dependants, that rebellion later appears, writ much larger, in the setting for the last and most serious mix-up which threatens him.

This final trial takes place, pointedly, in pre-revolutionary Paris and Versailles, where Ormond is once more tempted to implicate himself in the revolutionary plot of sensibility; as his attachment to the now-married Dora revives, Dora, associated now with the affected, not to say decadent, material stylistics of the sentimental letter—writing 'on green paper, with a border of cupids and roses, and store of sentimental devices in the corners. The turn of every phrase, the style . . . was quite French' (ix. 457)—is also led astray by 'the fashionable *cant* of sensibility' (ix. 484). The plot of potential adultery is carefully articulated with the plot of impending revolution—Dora's social position is insistently paralleled to that of Marie Antoinette, as described by Edgeworth's respectable abbé:

[T]hese flattering courtiers will do no good to our young dauphiness, on whom so much of the future happiness or misery of France will depend. . . . [W]hat head of a young beauty and a young queen will be able to withstand perpetual flattery? They will lead her wrong, and then will be the first to desert her. . . . [B]ut I will not trouble you with forebodings perhaps never to be realized.   (ix. 490)

The flattery to which the abbé refers is an exaggerated display of 'French sensibility, that eagerness to feel and to excite *a sensation*; that desire to *produce an effect*, to have a scene; that half real, half theatric enthusiasm, by which the French character is peculiarly distinguished from the English' (489), a display occasioned by a portrait of the queen. The ominous and reiterated quotations from Burke's *Reflections* buried throughout this episode (489 ff.), coupled with the deliberately anachronistic references of the post-revolutionary narrator, insist that sensibility, whether deployed within a political or a sexual narrative, is always, at least in Paris, a threat to the social fabric. For the time being, however, revolution is averted, Dora preserving her virtue and her reputation at the very last moment as a result of a providential intervention in the shape of a 'letter' from her father:

[Ormond] seemed to be suddenly shocked by the sight of one of the rings on her finger . . .
   'Dora, whose grey hair is this?'
   'My father's,' said Dora in a tremulous voice . . .
   'And is this the return I make!' cried Ormond.   (500–1)

Ormond being reminded at a convenient moment of the superior virtue of Florence Annaly, a rediscovery that is staged scrupulously in England and in terms of the proper delivery of a letter that had earlier gone astray, the novel culminates in the entirely suitable marriage of the regenerate Ormond, now 'reigning' over the Black Islands; his marriage thus symbolizes the appropriate union of native Irish with Anglo-Irish within the structures of a new, post-sentimental, post-revolutionary national identity.
   Ormond was not only written by an author whom Scott admired

and cited as an influence upon *Waverley* in its 'Postscript which Should Have Been a Preface', but was apparently written actually in response to *Waverley*. Viewed as a reworking of the sophistications of Scott's novel which translates them back into strategies that bear a striking resemblance to those deployed in *Thaddeus of Warsaw*, *Ormond* confirms that Scott is in fact operating within and against familiar political structures of fictional polemic.[18] Indeed, the first closed sequence of the Waverley novels, *Waverley* (1814), *Guy Mannering* (1815), and *The Antiquary* (1816),[19] read as meditations upon and extensions of the projects of Morgan, Porter, and Edgeworth. (The debt to Porter and Edgeworth was acknowledged openly in the closing chapter of *Waverley*, that to Morgan more covertly and with some hostility: invited to choose a name for one of his daughter Sophia's pet donkeys, Scott christened it 'Lady Morgan'.) The compromised opposition of the sentimental to both Jacobitism and the related romance of the lost father which I have been detailing reappears as the core of Scott's meditation upon the nature of revolution in his early novels, under the guise of a thematic preoccupation with a process of reading and misreading. Revolutionary narrative modes make their appearance as figures of textuality, sometimes explicitly in the form of letters, sometimes appearing in the guise of cryptic texts or reified riddles; such 'texts' of revolution, characteristically duplicitous, either in that they carry more than one latent meaning or in that their styling conceals their

---

[18] The similarities between *Waverley* and *Ormond* have been noticed by Pamela Reilly, who nevertheless argues, bafflingly, that *Ormond* has no political content. 'The Influence of *Waverley* on Maria Edgeworth's *Ormond*', in J. H. Alexander and David Hewitt (eds.), *Scott and His Influence: Papers of the Aberdeen Scott Conference 1982* (Aberdeen, 1983), 290–7. In regarding *Waverley* as an elaborate suppression of prior narrative models I shall be taking that whimsical and self-deprecating opening chapter to *Waverley*, in which Scott declares that his novel will neither be sentimental, Gothic, nor concerned with high society, in good earnest. Although one commentator has at least flirted with the possibility of this kind of reading—namely George Levine, who remarks that '[i]f we were to take the first chapter seriously, we would have to read *Waverley* as an evasive action among competing romance conventions or at least as an attempt to define his kind of historical fiction against them' (*The Realistic Imagination* (Chicago, 1981), 88) the success of Scott's attempt to exorcise the sentimental, to produce an 'uncontaminated' space for a new form of realism, has diverted attention from the productive pollution of Scott's novels by older forms.

[19] It will be recalled that Scott takes the first of many leaves of the reader in the preface to *The Antiquary*, and in his next publication, *Tales of my Landlord*, presents himself in the persona of Jedediah Cleishbotham rather than as 'The Author of Waverley'.

true import, challenge both protagonists and reader to decipher them accurately, in much the same fashion as the letter and its analogues serve as moral and political cyphers in Austen's contemporaneous novels. The novels reframe and so close down the threatening vagaries of sentimental reading by recourse to the authoritative discourse of history, represented by Scott as aligned with the authorial third-person voice which is characteristically scarred with oblique allusions to the Revolution in France; in so doing, Scott's novels succeed at once in containing the French Revolution and in transforming its historical significance, carrying out an essentially counter-revolutionary remaking of the national past.[20]

III

Edward Waverley (like his sisters under the skin, such as Arabella, the heroine of Charlotte Lennox's *The Female Quixote* (1752), Angelina, Cherubina, Catherine Morland, and Emma herself)[21]

---

[20] In this I am following Hazlitt, who with pointed irony neatly spitted Scott's novels ('a relief to the mind, rarefied as it has been with modern philosophy, and heated with ultra-radicalism') as ultra-conservative: 'it is thus he administers charms and philtres to our love of legitimacy, makes us conceive a horror of all reform, civil, political, or religious, and would fain put down the *Spirit of the Age*'; 'Sir Walter Scott', *The Spirit of the Age* (1825), *The Complete Works of William Hazlitt*, ed. P. P. Howe (21 vols., London, 1930–4), xi. 65, 66. Byron reputedly remarked apropos of *Waverley* that he 'lamented that its author had not carried back the story nearer the time of the Revolution', a comment that suggests strongly that Byron had decoded Scott's cover story. Ioan Williams (ed.), *Sir Walter Scott on Novelists and Fiction* (London, 1968), 419. The cover seems perilously close to being blown by Scott's own review of *Waverley*; discussing the author's 'judicious' choice of 'the era of the Rebellion in 1745' he comments that 'when [the English] saw the array of West country Whigs, they might imagine themselves transported to the age of Cromwell'; *Edinburgh Review*, 24 (Nov. 1814), 209. As late as 1824 (the year Scott published *Redgauntlet*), Scott seems to have mentioned to Southey the possibility of a comparison of 'the Great Rebellion and the French Revolution', of which Southey comments, 'Very interesting it would be, and very important are the warnings which it would convey, if nations ever were warned by experience'; Kenneth Curry (ed.), *New Letters of Robert Southey* (New York, 1965), Southey to Scott, 7 Oct. 1824, ii. 268. The two pieces that Scott seems to have completed in its lieu were of course his *Life of Napoleon* (1827), prefaced by a lengthy account of the French Revolution, and *Redgauntlet* itself.

[21] Catherine Morland is an especially pertinent example here (particularly in the light of Scott's celebrated admiration for Austen): cf. the famous misunderstanding between her and Eleanor Tilney, in which Catherine's description of a forthcoming

derives his dangerous predilection for misreading, in the usual fashion, from an over-indulgence in romance; cultivating an effeminized 'dainty, squeamish, and fastidious taste',[22] he is ever ready to read his experience in terms of novelistic conventions. In conceiving his hero, Scott states his intention of describing 'that . . . aberration from sound judgement, which apprehends occurrences indeed in their reality, but communicates to them a tincture of its own romantic tone and colouring' (i. 55). Like Austen, Scott depicts his hero's education in order to close down the destabilizing oscillation in perspective between the dangerous and seductive lens of unbridled individual imagination and a more appropriate consensual and nationalistic aesthetic, represented here by the narrative of history.

Despite these thematic similarities to *Emma*, however, the nature of the protagonist's misreading in *Waverley* is, as it were, inverted. Rather than wilfully misreading the real in sentimental terms only to discover that the real is, by and large, more banal, if more hurtful—the punitive trajectory of *Emma*—Waverley misreads the real as sentimental only to find that the real is decidedly more dangerous, not to say revolutionary.[23] Accordingly, the historically real, as it precipitates in the opening third of *Waverley*, is presented as a set of primarily decorative fragments of multiple and competing genres, overlaid upon the 'sober prose' (i. 40) of the third-person historian. These fragments are variously deceptive— mediated either in tone, such as the reportage of 'the cool and procrastinating alembic of Dyer's Weekly Letter' (i. 10), or through

Gothic novel is understood as relating to a projected uprising. In thus dramatizing the danger (and perhaps inevitability?) of confusing the discourses of contemporary fiction and contemporary politics, Austen seems to identify the collapse of the aesthetic into the real and vice versa as a function of female sensibility and language. Austen, *Works* v (*Northanger Abbey*), 112–13.

[22] Sir Walter Scott, *Waverley Novels* [1814–32], (1830–3; 48 vols., Boston, 1893–4), i. 32.

[23] Cf. Waverley's response to Rose Bradwardine's account of Highland raids: 'It seemed like a dream to Waverley that these deeds of violence should be familiar to men's minds, and currently talked of, as falling within the common order of things, and happening daily in the immediate vicinity, without his having crossed the seas, and while he was yet in the otherwise well-ordered island of Great Britain.' (i. 37–8). Scotland can hereby function as the home at once of romance (like Morgan's Ireland) but also of a history here disturbingly akin to recent events in France. On Scotland as the locus of both romance and history in this novel see esp. Jane Millgate, *Walter Scott: The Making of the Novelist* (Toronto, 1984), 38, 40.

the lens of family history (the family tradition and genealogy of the hero's uncle, Sir Everard Waverley, the family 'legends' of his aunt Mrs Rachel, the litter of family portraits of Lady Alice Waverley, of Sir Hildebrand, of the Baron of Bradwardine, his wife, and his ancestors), or through sentimental aesthetics (the ruins of the Queen's Standing and the Strength of Waverley), or, finally, through sentimental narratives in the shape of a liberal sprinkling of literary set-pieces (Waverley's poetic effusions on leaving Waverley-Honour, the idiot Gellatley's curiously apposite fragments, Rose Bradwardine's legend of St Swithin's Chair, and last, and most important of all, Flora MacIvor's famous showpiece, the translation of the clan-bard's call to battle and her verses on Captain Wogan). What all these artefacts or narratives have in common is a certain sort of foregrounded textual styling, akin to that of the letter in *Emma*, a styling that conceals the actual violence of the history that they memorialize or invoke.[24] The history of Waverley's education in right reading will centrally dramatize the vexed relation between style and meaning (supposedly organic but in practice subject to dismaying slippage) and the kindred problem of the relation between text and context.

This destabilizing doubleness of textuality appears first, and most elaborately, in the episode of Edward Waverley's visit to the stronghold of Fergus MacIvor, manifesting itself as a fascination with the problematics of translation. Flora's translations and transcriptions of history act as revolving doors both into and out of revolution, metamorphosing back and forth between elegant 'letters' and proscribed politics. Flora MacIvor occupies a position of some importance in being the translator of the first major text Waverley is unable to read at all, the 'Celtic verses' chanted at the clan-feast, in which an obscure mention is made of Waverley himself (i. 188). As is appropriate to a revolutionary translator, she is described as an exotic hybrid of French and Scottish in both her manners and her dress; as translator she consciously manipulates

---

[24] The discussion that follows is thus a distant cousin to readings of *Waverley* in terms of the picturesque and the sublime, although these readings have rarely been directed towards examining the politics of the novel. I am none the less indebted to the following discussions: Millgate, *Walter Scott: The Making of the Novelist*, 44–52; P. D. Garside, '*Waverley*'s Pictures of the Past', *ELH* 44 (1977), 659–82; Alexander M. Ross, *The Imprint of the Picturesque on Nineteenth-Century British Fiction* (Waterloo, Ont., 1986), 46–72.

the conventions of representation, however primitive the effect she represents might initially appear to be. Thus her Highland songs are not so much the effusions of a native sensibility as the accomplishment of a highly-cultivated taste, fashionably, if anachronistically, tinctured with the late eighteenth-century fad for the sentimental Ossian (i. 193). Flora's translation of the bard's verses that have named Waverley as a participant in the coming uprising is therefore similarly filtered through the conventions of polite literature, a styling and recontextualization that conceals the true nature of the story from both Waverley and the reader. Flora prettifies 'the measured and monotonous recitative of the bard' by substituting for it 'a lofty and uncommon Highland air, which had been a battle-song in former ages' (i. 205); an example of stylistic transposition which effectively obscures, while paradoxically revealing, the import of the verses. Constructing them as romantic relics of a bygone age, aestheticized by the passage of time, the translation fails to convey the fact that these verses do indeed operate as a battle-song in the here-and-now, that for true appreciation or effect they must be sung in the Chief's hall amongst the clansmen, more truly their 'wild and appropriate accompaniments' than Flora's sublimed landscape. The transposition of place, tune, and language aestheticizes, most inappropriately and perilously, revolution-in-the-making. Revolution is, in effect, what is lost in translation. In this context, Scott's insistence upon Waverley's inadequacies as a translator of the classics takes on a new importance: he would 'make himself master of the style so far as to understand the story, and if that pleased or interested him, he finished the volume. But it was in vain to attempt fixing his attention on critical distinctions of philology, upon the difference of idiom, the beauty of felicitous expression, or the artificial combinations of syntax' (i. 20). Assuming sentimental style to be transparent, that it neither generates nor essentially inflects the 'story', Waverley misses the syntax of revolution, and so is fatally susceptible to the fictions that Fergus and Flora weave around him.

The issue of translation serves as a turnstile into the central section of the novel, in which Waverley finds himself precipitated into the exigencies of real history. This section is characterized by the disconcerting tendency of what had appeared to be purely figurative, even overly literary, to metamorphose into the literal. Thus the Highland hunt, which in retrospect proves to have been a secret war-conference, is initially presented as a well-researched exercise in antiquarianism (featuring the author solemnly leafing through the number of existing literary and historical accounts at his disposal) and is then described in a series of persistently militaristic metaphors ('small army', 'bivouacked', 'desperate stand', 'battle-array'; i. 219–21), which ostensibly remain, nevertheless, metaphors. This doubleness of language gives way abruptly to a total failure of translation on Waverley's part:

The word was given in Gaelic to fling themselves on their faces; but Waverley, on whose English ears the signal was lost, had almost fallen a sacrifice to his ignorance of the ancient language in which it was communicated. (i. 221)

Waverley's inability to 'read' here, presaged in comic mode by Cathleen's 'little Gaelic song', 'the comic tones of which, though he did not understand the language, made Waverley laugh more than once' (i. 211), is a failing that will culminate in the most dramatic of his 'translations' when on the battlefield; 'looking around him, he saw the wild dress and appearance of his Highland associates, heard their whispers in an uncouth and unknown language, looked upon his own dress, so unlike that which he had worn from his infancy, and wished to awake from what seemed at the moment a dream, strange, horrible, and unnatural' (ii. 139–40).

Waverley's successive 'translations' show him to be functioning in the same way as the letter is made to do in the classic anti-Jacobin text; he is insistently recirculated and misappropriated. Under the auspices of revolution, which, as the Shakespearean epigraph ('Under which king, Bezonian?') makes clear, takes place under the radically ambiguous and ever-slipping sign of 'king', signs detach themselves from identities; this movement is inaugurated, significantly, when Waverley's signet ring is filched by the rogue Donald Bean-Lean, who uses it, so we learn later, to forge the letters which convince Waverley's troop to defect to the Stuarts, thereby convincing the world that Waverley has himself joined the Jacobites. The orphaning of signature from body, of style from meaning, results in the production of an alternative textual and revolutionary identity for Waverley; only when he regains his ring does he finally escape that circuit of misappropriation, hitherto dramatized only locally, in terms of the letter. This ominous slippage is amplified by the ways that the terms of reading change;

hence 'elegant literature . . . designed for a lady's perusal' becomes 'treasonable tracts and pamphlets' (ii. 16); Flora's lines on Captain Wogan, originally read by Waverley as love poetry, metamorphose into verses describing 'the very counterpart of his own plot—and summed up with a "go thou and do likewise", from that loyal subject, and most safe and peaceable character, Fergus Mac-Ivor of Glennaquoich' (ii. 29); and the letters of Waverley's relatives, initially read as expressive of their outdated and therefore lovable hobby-horses, spring into new and violent meaning as expressing actively contemporary sedition. At the intersection of the irreconcilable clash between the two reading practices, at the central point of the novel, during his delirious imprisonment in what later proves to be Janet Gellatley's cottage near Tully-Veolan, Waverley is reduced to precisely the predicament of the sentimental/Gothic heroine, for whom nothing remains intelligible; Rose appears as Flora, Janet Gellatley as 'an old Highland sibyl', and the Gaelic remains resolutely impenetrable (ii. 60, 57).

The first major crisis of the novel comes at the moment when individual sentimental statement is most starkly at odds with State truth—when private history diverges sharply from public. Arrested for treason, and subjected to an informal trial, Waverley, like Wollstonecraft's Maria, is depicted as powerless in the face of an alternative official narrative: 'Waverley almost gave up his life and honour for lost, and leaning his head upon his hand, resolutely refused to answer any further questions, since the fair and candid statement he had already made had only served to furnish arms against him' (ii. 20). The novel will only reach resolution when Waverley's personal narrative can be squared with the official version of events and the two reconverge. (For a measure of how conservative a move this is in the light of the radical stories Scott is interested in suppressing, one need only turn to Godwin's *Caleb Williams* (1794), which resolutely destabilizes all possible official narratives by having Caleb refuse to acquiesce in any.) Those persons who refuse to assimilate their personal histories to the State's account of events are necessarily expelled; Fergus MacIvor, refusing the verdict of the court, insists upon the incommensurability of the Jacobite and the Hanoverian narratives, which finally leaps unnegotiably out of the polite ambiguity of the word 'king'— 'what I have to say, you would not bear to hear, for my defence would be your condemnation' (ii. 325). The excoriated body of

Fergus is deported from the novel in the place of the violated bodies of all those unfortunate heroines I have been chronicling elsewhere in the tradition of Clarissa, allowing for the survival of Waverley: this consummation is in part made possible by the biological gender of Scott's sentimental protagonist, who, though seduced indeed by the machinations of the residual Jacobinical philosopher-villain in the shape of Fergus, does not experience irretrievable and inescapably physical 'ruin' in the manner of the heroines whose position he occupies.

Despite the untrustworthiness of texts in the first half of the novel, Scott none the less eventually promotes textuality as a way of effectively freezing the slippages of revolution. In the closing movements a series of regenerate texts rehistoricize, and thus mute and mediate, revolution, just as the letter Waverley sends to his soon-to-be wife Rose Bradwardine describing Fergus MacIvor's execution for treason sets out to do:

The impression of horror with which Waverley left Carlisle softened by degrees into melancholy—a gradation which was accelerated by the painful, yet soothing task of writing to Rose; . . . he endeavoured to place it in a light which might grieve her without shocking her imagination. The picture which he drew for her benefit he gradually familiarised to his own mind . . . (ii. 344)

This 'picture' is paralleled by the reincarnation and re-articulation of Fergus's shattered and dispersed body in the famous portrait 'representing Fergus Mac-Ivor and Waverley in their Highland dress; the scene a wild, rocky, and mountainous pass, down which the clan were descending in the background' (ii. 359–60). This is revolution reduced, with some relief, again to styling; the security this picture depends upon is that this particular Highland Chief, however brilliantly depicted, will indeed 'do all but walk out of the canvas' (ii. 360).[25] Now at liberty to indulge

---

[25] For a reading of this picture as 'a painting rendered by an artist in London from a sketch drawn by an artist in Edinburgh', that is to say, as a clear 'misrepresentation' of events in the service of a domestication of Scotland within Britain, see James Kerr, *Fiction Against History: Scott as Storyteller* (Cambridge, 1989), 19–20. While I agree that the portrait aestheticizes, and most importantly, domesticizes, the historical event, I do not think, with Kerr, that Scott includes this episode merely to draw attention to the inevitable falsifications of historiography; rather, as I argue below, I would relate this to a project of closing down revolutionary energy within a revised aesthetics.

himself 'in the quiet circle of domestic happiness, lettered indolence, and elegant enjoyments, of Waverley-Honour', Flora's delightful predictions for Waverley have come true by virtue of the exclusion of revolution; he will be at leisure to:

refit the old library in the most exquisite Gothic taste, and garnish its shelves with the rarest and most valuable volumes; and he will draw plans and landscapes, and write verses and rear temples, and dig grottoes; and he will stand in a clear summer night in the colonnade before the hall, and gaze on the deer as they stray in the moonlight, or lie shadowed by the boughs of the huge old fantastic oaks;—and he will repeat verses to his beautiful wife, who will hang upon his arm;—and he will be a happy man. (ii. 190)

In short, Waverley becomes a model of the literary dabbler in antiquarian books, of the picturesque gardener, of the sentimental versifier. History is reabsorbed into old books, the Highland landscape metamorphoses into the cultivated space of the park, and the violence of the hunt and its analogue, war, is figured only by the decorative deer.

Waverley thus opens the cavity of revolution only in order to close it down more finally. The imaginative violence of the novel is concentrated at that moment when private sentimental texts are rescripted by the sudden incursion of a historical date, 1745, ominously concrete after the vague nostalgia of 'sixty years since' (i. 6), which had suggested that private time operates within an ahistorical continuum; the thrust of Waverley, like that of Emma, is to embed and police the mistaken individual reading within a socially sanctioned version of the real, dramatizing the failure of individual reading in the face of an 'official' quasi-historical rereading of past events, ultimately subsuming all voices within an authorial discourse judiciously scarred by the post-revolutionary experience it registers by strategic anachronism.[26] Through transposing the French Revolution onto the Jacobite uprising, Scott constructs even revolution as profoundly counter-revolutionary: as William Hazlitt remarked caustically, '[t]hrough some odd process of *servile* logic, it should seem, that in restoring the claims of the Stuarts by the courtesy of romance, the House of Brunswick are more firmly seated in point of fact, and the Bourbons, by collateral reasoning, become legitimate. . . . [T]his loyalty is founded on

[26] See e.g. i. 77; i. 124; ii. 43, and ii. 80.

would-be treason: he props the actual throne by the shadow of rebellion.'[27] *Waverley*, like its predecessors, reconstrues revolution within the structures of national romance.

IV

Heaven first, in its mercy, taught mortals their letters,
For ladies in limbo, and lovers in fetters,
Or some author, who, placing his persons before ye,
Ungallantly leaves them to write their own story.

(Scott, *Guy Mannering; or, The Astrologer: Waverley Novels*, iii. 152.)

If *Waverley* is interested at once in demonstrating the revolutionary implications of a sentimental reading of history and in disciplining the reading practices of the sentimental hero/ine to extricate him from complicity in that revolution, *Guy Mannering* is altogether less covert, applying itself openly to disciplining the original of Edward Waverley, the letter-writing sentimental heroine. Indeed, *Guy Mannering* is virtually unique in Scott's *œuvre* in so extensively incorporating the epistolary, the only other novel to do so being *Redgauntlet* (1824). The preoccupation of this second of the Waverley Novels with the evacuation of the letter, almost to the exclusion of anything one might immediately dub historical, reinforces the argument that *Waverley*'s foregrounded historicity can be read as an expansion of the third-person narrative which here so conspicuously supersedes the epistolary. *Guy Mannering*, however, goes one step further than *Waverley* in instituting the paradigm of full-blown romance, borrowed here from the impeccably British texts of Shakespeare,[28] superseding the ('French') narrative of female disobedience with the reinstatement of the broken link between father and son and thus of the proper lines of patriarchal inheritance.

Scott's flippant, doggerel version of Pope's well-known lines in

---

[27] Hazlitt, *Works*, xi. 65.
[28] On Scott's political uses of Shakespeare see Nicola J. Watson, 'Kemble, Scott and the Mantle of the Bard', in Jean Marsden (ed.), *The Appropriation of Shakespeare: Post-Renaissance Reconstructions of the Works and the Myth* (Hemel Hempstead, 1991), 73–92.

'Eloisa to Abelard'[29] laconically signals the beginning of a process of denaturalization of the letter as a mode of narrative, and the concomitant displacement of the narrative paradigm of *La Nouvelle Héloïse*. Underscoring the final metamorphosis of the fiction of private epistolary passion into publisher's commodity, and so destroying its characteristic immediacy and its voyeuristic frisson, Scott suggests that the epistolary is essentially a hackneyed amateur mode (it was, of course, this very amateurishness, its status as unmediated effusion of the heart, that had originally guaranteed its authenticity). This lofty dismissal of the epistolary is intimately involved with Scott's other project, the hushing-up of revolution (figured in *Guy Mannering* by the 1756 mutiny in India, the backdrop employed to mark this novel as historical), a revolution which is, unsurprisingly, superimposed upon a sentimental plot; the exorcism of the revolutionary sentimental redeems the past through the reunion of father (Guy Mannering) and (surrogate) son (Vanbeest Brown/Harry Bertram), originally separated by a duplicitous woman (Sophia, Mannering's wife). That original separation and fragmentation enter the text in the form of conflicting epistolary narratives; the remainder of the novel labours to resolve the discrepancies between these very different constructions of events, subordinating them eventually to the fiat of third-person authority. That authority socializes, relativizes, and contextualizes the reader, who, no longer the privileged, secret voyeur of intimate passions constructed by the epistolary, becomes instead the acquiescent spectator of critical readings performed by an omniscient narrator on a series of transfixed embedded texts.

It is Mannering's voice which opens the central section of the

---

[29] On other uses of Pope's poem as an antidote to *La Nouvelle Héloïse*, see Nicola J. Watson, 'Novel Eloisas'. Scott's debunking of the power of the epistolary here is extended by his remarks on Rousseau's novel: 'The enthusiasm expressed by Lord Byron is no small tribute to the power possessed by Jean Jacques over the passions; and, to say truth, we need some such evidence, for, though almost ashamed to avow the truth, which is probably very much to our own discredit . . . we have never been able to feel the interest, or discover the merit, of this far-famed performance. . . . we can see little in the loves of these two tiresome pedants to interest our feelings for either of them . . . and, upon the whole, consider the dulness of the story as the best apology for its exquisite immorality.' Scott goes on to quote Burke's verdict on the novel in *Letters to a Member of the National Assembly* (quoted in my Introduction) before, by association, considering Rousseau's role as 'a primary apostle of the French revolution'; *The Miscellaneous Prose Works of Sir Walter Scott Bart.* (28 vols., Edinburgh, 1848), 384–5. For Byron's own reworking of both Pope and *La Nouvelle Héloïse* see Ch. 4.

novel in a letter which recounts the past tragedy of his marriage, a tragedy set in India during the rebellion, where white colonial troops are beleaguered and attacked on all sides. The domestic insurrection that leads to the breakup of the marriage is thus already to be construed in the context of revolution. Mannering recapitulates, appropriately enough in the terms of *Othello*, his belief that he has killed his subaltern Brown in a duel provoked by Mannering's suspicion that Brown was paying attentions to his wife, Sophia; Sophia, after Brown's supposed death, dies of shock. However, Brown's account, also given in a retrospective letter, reveals that he had actually been courting Mannering's daughter, Julia, with the full encouragement of her mother; given this daughter's first name, Brown's nameless and penniless state and Mannering's high ideas of family pride, this alternative narrative looks a good deal like yet another version of *La Nouvelle Héloïse* in the making. Indeed, the narrator, recapitulating the story one more time in judgemental mode, is at pains to lay the blame for the catastrophe upon Sophia Wellwood's fictioneering, her passion for writing her own little 'family novel', condemning it as:

the folly of a misjudging mother, who called her husband in her heart a tyrant until she feared him as such, and read romances until she became so enamoured of the complicated intrigues which they contain, as to assume the management of a little family novel of her own, and constitute her daughter, a girl of sixteen, the principal heroine. She delighted in petty mystery, and intrigue, and secrets, and yet trembled at the indignation which these paltry manœuvres excited in her husband's mind. Thus she frequently entered upon a scheme merely for pleasure, or perhaps for the love of contradiction—plunged deeper into it than she was aware— endeavoured to extract herself by new arts, to cover her error by dissimulation . . . (iii. 159)

In the main body of the novel, Mannering, as one who covered himself with glory in quelling the rebellion of 'our black dependants', turns his attention towards applying a similar damper to the domestic rebellion represented and instigated by his dead wife's fatal predilection for fictioneering. His settling in Scotland is designed as an explicit parallel, his rationale a quest for order, to be 'commandant' in 'my own family at least'. This involves a rooting out of deceitful languages; as he says to Julia, 'there is a little too much of this universal spirit of submission, an excellent disposition in action, but your constantly repeating the jargon of it puts me in mind of the eternal salaams of our black dependants in the East' (iii. 166). The story of the daughter's rebellion against the father and its crippling threat to the proper transmission of property cannot be allowed another foothold in this text if the novel's counter-revolutionary project is not to be sabotaged. Consequently, Julia's letters, her written insurrection, are ultimately transmuted into silence. The new Eloisa plays herself out in little in the margins of this novel; and she plays herself out too, in that she is finally erased.

Julia herself is quintessentially an epistolary heroine of sensibility, 'generous and romantic', given to exercising both her feelings and her pen in tandem to produce 'formidable quires' (iii. 150, 152) for the eyes of a sentimental friend, Matilda. These 'quires' constitute, in fact, Julia's own embryonic novel, a sequel to her mother's fiction; as she puts it to Matilda, 'I remember, in our stolen voyages to the world of fiction . . . I was partial to the involved intrigues of private life;' (iii. 271). In fact, she tries her hand briefly at 'involved intrigues' by attempting to matchmake her father with the orphan Lucy Bertram—a short-lived attempt cut off by stern paternal edict, 'so here I am,' she complains, 'neutralized again;' (iii. 270). This novel—unlike her mother's, which ran out of her husband's control—is aborted, paralleling the fate of her letters themselves.

Julia's letters not only stand out as an anomaly in themselves, set as they are into a primarily third-person narrative, but are marked out even more pointedly as letters which are never used for exposition. Their action—both the action described and the clandestine action of writing them—is always pre-empted; more-over, the letter mode itself, which classically depends on a number of conventional fictions that vouch for its authenticity (the discovery of letters in a chest, the bequest of Clarissa's letters) is frankly ridiculed as a creakily obsolete and artificial device. Prefacing an extract from one of Brown's letters, the narrator simply announces that 'we have assumed already the privilege of acting *a secretis* to this gentleman, and therefore shall present the reader with an extract from this epistle' (iii. 145). This invasive narrative eye is also privy to Julia's correspondence, which, so far from being presented as valuable documentary evidence of the genuine effusions of her tender heart, is reduced to a mere narrative convenience—or, at least, that is all the significance the narrator is prepared to allow it: 'the perusal of a few short extracts from these may be necessary to render our story intelligible' (iii. 154).

This selective evisceration and curator-like display of letters refuses to respect their secrecy, while floodlighting the gap between individual, partial perception and the true state of affairs. Furthermore, as the account Julia gives in this letter of her strange meeting with Brown at the dead of night has already been anticipated by a letter from the eavesdropping Mervyn (to whose care she has been entrusted) to her father, which describes the same incident nearly as fully, her first letters are pruned of the power to describe action, their value inhering purely in the rendition of her reaction. (In deploying this strategy Scott is strikingly close to the tactics by which Austen neutralizes the letter in *Sense and Sensibility*, described in Chapter 2.) Julia's sentimental language is framed by Mervyn in his letter, in a voice which mimics it but which clearly subscribes to other values; 'you know how I have jested with her about her soft melancholy, and lonely walks at morning before anyone is up, and in the moonlight when all should be gone to bed, or sat down to cards, which is the same thing' (iii. 148).

Mervyn's framing of Julia's language is, however, largely redundant, as her own language regularly self-destructs, illustrating, as the narrator smugly points out, 'natural good sense, principle, and feelings, blemished by an imperfect education and the folly of a misjudging mother . . .' (iii. 159). In fact she personally nips the whole Rousseauistic narrative in the bud early in the novel by refusing Brown's clandestine proposal, citing 'the madness of a union without any father's sanction', continuing, 'I have resisted, I have subdued, the rebellious feelings which arose to aid his plea' (iii. 160–1). She thus reverses her mother Sophia's earlier actions, and throughout the text continues thus to substitute confession for secrecy, domestic reintegration for rebellion.

Julia's presumption in wishing to write her own story is none the less punished by the novel's narrative action (an action which includes a smugglers' raid on the Mannerings' house, effectively a miniature riot), the shock of which reduces Julia to a sickbed, threatening to relegate her to a corner of that literary mortuary set aside for the sole use of sentimental heroines bearing her name. From being the progenitor of the story she is now caught up in a narrative which she characterizes as quite beyond her control. Furthermore, as Julia is absorbed more and more into the new Scottish household, removed from both her friend Matilda and her lover Brown, her letters grow less frequent and more 'transparent'—

that is to say, it is less and less important that it is Julia writing them. Their language begins to reflect uncritically the value-judgements towards the instatement of which the novel as a whole is projected; her point of view becomes less important as the potential locus of a competing script of rebellion. Consequently her letters begin to be presented whole, rather than in extracts, dramatic dialogue ousts sentimental reflection, and her voice eventually fades out entirely into a dramatic presentation almost indistinguishable from the narrator's. This cancellation of Julia and her letters is finally ratified by the little scene in which she gives up her mother's casket of letters to her father, subordinating her mother's subversive fiction and its mechanics to his policing eye. The casket's textual secrets are rendered harmless by the reading father, a scene analogous to the pivotal moment in *La Nouvelle Héloïse* when the father strikes the errant daughter, precipitating a miscarriage and thus deleting the consequences of Julie's forbidden desire. The retrospective clearing of the mother's name (for these letters prove to Mannering that she never had an affair with Brown, while documenting her rebellious, offended concealment of this from her husband) perfectly exemplifies Peggy Kamuf's description of 'the mechanism of social legitimacy' as 'the inspection of a woman's interior, that hidden contradictory space where things may not be what they appear'.[30] In this case, it is the casket of secret letters which is broken open, allowing the woman's potential for deception and disruption to be both acknowledged and obliterated. Nothing of the text of Sophia's letters is permitted to materialize within this text. They are visible only as already-read artefacts, rather than as active agents.

This scene, fittingly, is written in the third person. Paralleling the earlier scene between Julia and her father where she is frightened out of making the confession she has determined upon by his sternness (a scene, incidentally, narrated within one of her letters), this scene, by contrast, succeeds in exorcizing the past (in a deliberate reference to Rousseau's famous reunion scene between Julie and her father), and this cleansing, full and final, is crucially marked by the change in narrative mode. The primary relationship here, set up by the third person mode, is that between the narrator and the reader; it effectively screens the heroine, blocking further

---

[30] *Fictions of Feminine Desire*, 106.

identification, and positions the reader as audience rather than addressee. Moreover, it is clear that the heroine has once again become part of her father, that they are no longer separable: 'let me not lose the confidence of a child who ought to love me if she really loves herself' (iv. 263). Precisely reversing the radical scenario of Fenwick's *Secresy*, the tyrannous father is revealed as the benevolent father, and the face of patriarchy gets a facelift.

Julia's dutiful submission to the status of mere extension of her father is duly rewarded by marriage with her lover, Brown. As Brown, however, proves to have been the lost Harry Bertram all along, a much less embarrassing prospect than the generality of Rousseauistic lovers, and Mannering's surrogate son into the bargain, even the daughter's earlier rebellion is finally revealed as nothing of the kind, defused by a happy ending virtually as incestuous as that enjoyed within another family of Bertrams in Austen's *Mansfield Park*. With Julia's marriage, moreover, what was an affair of passion becomes an affair of inheritance—the father inherits his surrogate son, the surrogate son inherits his 'father's' Indian wealth, and the old feudal order is re-established with this laundered money. Whatever there was initially of Julia's passion is buried in the final chapter within the oblique account given of the successful culmination of the affair. The last conversation we hear, that which informs the reader that Bertram and Julia are to marry, involves neither fiancé nor fiancée, but instead takes place between Mannering and his lawyer, Pleydell:

'But what is all this' added Pleydell, taking up the plans;—'tower in the centre to be an imitation of the Eagle Tower at Caernarvon—*corps de logis*—the devil!—wings—wings? Why, the house will take the estate of Ellangowan on its back and fly away with it!'

'Why then, we must ballast it with a few bags of Sicca rupees', replied the Colonel.

'Aha! sits the wind there? Then I suppose the young dog carries off my mistress Julia?' (iv. 330)

The sentimental plot of passion here undergoes its final decentring in which Julia is metamorphosed into rupees, and Harry Bertram (or Ellangowan) is turned literally into the House of Ellangowan, topped off by an imitation of a tower that functions as an image at once of national empire and of legitimate male inheritance— Caernarvon Castle, site of the investiture of the Princes of Wales.

V

If the letter is debased and displaced as it appears in *Guy Mannering*, in *The Antiquary* it becomes ever more vestigial, so vestigial that when the crucial letter does make its belated appearance, it is not so much a question of its substance as of its addressee. However, it makes its presence felt in a persistent thematics of decipherment, for, like its two predecessors, *The Antiquary* is concerned with issues of legibility and legitimacy, and the relation of the one to the other. Generally viewed as a text obsessed with the laborious necessity of distinguishing 'the genuine and the fraudulent past' from each another,[31] an endeavour which has, however, not been recognized as crucially implicated with its very precise setting within the 1790s, *The Antiquary* occupies a quirky status as supposedly the least political or historical of all Scott's novels.

Yet for all that it deliberately eschews the French Revolution as subject-matter, it is, perhaps, the most telling example of Scott's counter-revolutionary narrative strategies.[32] That the critical gaze has so often been deflected from the historico-political to the historiographical in reading *The Antiquary* is, so far from being fortuitous, the inevitable result of Scott's political project, for it is by collapsing revolutionary history into self-reflexive historio-graphy—the business of reading evidence and constructing adequate

---

[31] Francis R. Hart, *Scott's Novels: The Plotting of Historic Survival* (Charlottesville, Va., 1966), 249.

[32] George Levine comments upon this anti-historicity without allowing that this is the novel's conscious project: '*The Antiquary* dismisses the past from the living present without, as it were, knowing that this dismissal is its central subject' (*The Realistic Imagination*, 123). Harry Shaw recognizes the imbrication of both *Guy Mannering* and *The Antiquary* in 'contemporary political and social concerns' in that they both explore 'a range of social concerns that the French Revolution and its aftermath had brought vividly to light for Scott and his contemporaries' (the problem of constructing social cohesion and patriotic unity in the face of the Napoleonic Wars) but perversely relegates both novels to his category of 'history as pastoral', which is as much as to say that they are exceptions to Scott's general run of 'properly' historical novels. *The Forms of Historical Fiction; Sir Walter Scott and his Successors* (Ithaca, NY, 1983), 72. Avrom Fleishman simply states flatly that *The Antiquary* is 'not a historical novel', although it 'has the makings of a historical vision of the present, and almost survives its meanderings of plot.' *The English Historical Novel* (Baltimore, 1971), 75.

narratives—that Scott succeeds in detoxifying the plots of Revolution. The perilous discrepancies between the sentimental and the historical, the letter and third-person narration, the individual and the social, that both *Waverley* and *Guy Mannering* labour to delete, are here in this most accomplished novel safely reduced simply to comical discrepancies in reading: either within historiographical discourse itself (purely a matter for the amiable wranglings of the Antiquary himself, Mr Jonathan Oldbuck, and his neighbour Sir Arthur Wardour, over the correct interpretations, translations, etymologies, and genealogies to be given to the texts and artefacts that are the remaining traces of history), or within the various plots that all hinge upon the discovery and interpretation of textual evidence of various kinds. Episodes of decipherment weave in and out of the fabric of the novel: but what eventually emerges is that right reading always proves that revolution is simply an effect of misreading.

The preoccupation with legibility and intelligibility which dominates *The Antiquary* is introduced at the entrance to that worthy's house in the shape of an inscription so effaced as to be hospitable to any number of random interpretations, an amenability which points towards the similarly playful disjunctions of history into unintelligibility displayed in Oldbuck's den: 'numberless' books 'amid a chaos of maps, engravings, scraps of parchment, bundles of papers, pieces of old armour, swords, dirks, helmets, and Highland targets', 'busts and Roman lamps and paterae, intermingled with one or two bronze figures', a 'wreck of ancient books and utensils', 'portraits in armour, being characters in Scottish history', 'a profusion of papers, parchments, books, and nondescript trinkets and gewgaws'—in short, a *bricolage* of 'miscellaneous trumpery where it would have been as impossible to find any individual article wanted, as to put it to any use when discovered' (v. 28–9). The simultaneous incoherence and profound uselessness of this version of history guarantees its harmlessness; the worst damage that might befall the hero, Lovel, within this discourse is to sit down on a pair of antique spurs. In an audacious reversal of the scheme of *Waverley*, Quixotic misreading (Oldbuck is specifically compared to Don Quixote as a fellow bibliomaniac) is here regarded as merely comic. While the antiquary's regular failure to discriminate between the genuine and the fraudulent signs of history has certain embarrassing consequences (as illustrated in the famous discomfiture at the supposed Kaim of Kinprunes, when his triumphant interpretation of yet another inscription is disproven without a doubt), these consequences are nevertheless always laughable.

None the less, at the level of plot *The Antiquary* remains seriously concerned with the business of making the past legible, a legibility that will produce legitimacy. The main plot of the novel, which revolves around the mysterious Lovel's identity, accordingly opens with a set of figures of illegibility, associated, as ever, with the sentimental letter. In the post-master's house at Fairport, his wife Mrs Mailsetter and some female friends sort letters for delivery:

This is very often in country towns the period of the day when gossips find it particularly agreeable to call on the man or woman of letters, in order, from the outside of the epistles, and, if they are not belied, occasionally from the inside also, to amuse themselves with gleaning information, or forming conjectures about the correspondence and affairs of their neighbours. (v. 179)

This comprehensive surveillance (of the mail of Jonathan Oldbuck, Sir Arthur Wardour, Lovel, and two local lovers, Jenny Caxon and Richard Taffril) ranges over the tell-tale appearance of the letter: how it is folded and sealed ('faulded unco' square, and sealed at the tae side' means 'protested bills', a wafer rather than wax means impatient creditors), what its genre is (the 'ship-letter'), where it came from (evident by its post-mark), and who it came from (deduced from its seal—'see, the seal has an anchor on't—he's done it wi' ane o' his buttons'—or from its frank). The waylaid loveletter is, of course, subjected to particular, if misplaced, disciplinary scrutiny; held up to the light, not only does the signature become visible, but also some of the clichéd text—'there's something about a needle and a pole'—an observation explained variously by the town gossips by the theory that Taffril has 'cast up to her that her father's a barber and has a pole at his door, and that she's but a manty-maker hersel' ', as well as by the threadbare nautical lover's trope. Notable for its rather pathetic transparency, the amorous letter here poses so little threat to the national interest that Mrs Mailsetter can describe it as eminently loyal to the interests of a State institution: 'it's a great advantage to the revenue of the postoffice thae love-letters'—an appropriate enough loyalty since Jenny Caxon's lover is, like Anne Elliot's, in the navy. (v. 180–4)

If the sentimental letter is here stripped of any secrecy or subversiveness, that enigmatic status is taken on by the official letter addressed to Lovel that arrives in the same postbag. Largely unreadable due to its thick, opaque paper, protected by a tamper-proof seal and a daunting message from the Secretary of State, this letter gives rise to a good deal of local speculation, in part clearly erroneous, prompted by an atmosphere of tension over local political factions and by the fear of an impending French invasion. The plots invented around this letter are notably politically unstable, belonging to a variety of competing genres:

Some said Lovel was an emigrant noble, summoned to head an insurrection that had broken out in La Vendée—others that he was a spy—others that he was a general officer, who was visiting the coast privately—others that he was a prince of the blood, who was travelling incognito.   (v. 185)

The illegibility of this letter and its liability to misconstruction are of a piece with the impenetrable Lovel himself, travelling under an assumed name that Scott slyly identifies as stereotypically novelistic. In so doing, Lovel renders the letter double: in a confrontation with Captain M'Intyre, the antiquary's nephew, that leads to a duel, Lovel is challenged to provide evidence of his identity and produces a letter of credential from his general; it is guaranteed by the general's 'hand', but lacks its crucial component, the envelope bearing the address, Lovel's real name (v. 248). For once, the substance of the letter is actually on the envelope, and the inside of the letter is less revelatory than its outside would have been; this paradoxical concealment marks Lovel 'a very dubious character' (v. 187).

Lovel's position, as a 'dubious character', connects him indubitably in the minds of the local gossips with revolution; his supposed illegitimacy, which forces him to maintain this ambiguous position, is equally figured as being implicated in the force-field of revolutionary politics, as his account of the way in which he discovers a doubt of his supposed parentage reveals:

[L]ast year, while we occupied a small town in French Flanders, I found in a convent near which I was quartered a woman who spoke remarkably good English. . . . in the process of our acquaintance she discovered who I was, and made herself known to me as the person who had charge of my infancy. She dropped more than one hint of rank to which I was entitled, and of injustice done to me, promising a more full disclosure in case of the death of a lady in Scotland. . . . We were attacked by the enemy and driven from the town, which was pillaged with savage ferocity by the republicans. The religious orders were the particular object of their hate and cruelty. The convent was burned, and several nuns perished, among others Teresa, and with her all chance of knowing the story of my birth. (vi. 302–3)[33]

Lovel's understanding of himself as illegitimate, here tantalizingly gainsaid by the hints of his old nurse, is ratified, if only temporarily, by those agents of all that is illegitimate, the *sans-culottes*, who repeat the fracture of the patrilineal narrative through their murder of Teresa.

Encoded and elided in this yoking of Lovel's illegitimacy with revolution is the familiar equation of the duplicitous woman with the production of social chaos, brought to consciousness in this novel, albeit in comical and shrunken form, in the shape of Oldbuck's absurdly misogynistic characterizations of his niece and the maid, Jenny, as inimical to the order of his den, as productive of the loss and failure of history (v. 27), as adulterous Eves, liable to overturn the social order (v. 37–8), and as generally resistant 'to lawful rule and right supremacy' (v. 53). This association is borne out parenthetically by the inset legend of Lovel's apparent double, Malcolm Misticot; the illegitimate Misticot, son of a disobedient daughter and adulterous wife, turns out to be a proto-revolutionary: 'he threeps the castle and the lands are his ain as his mother's eldest son, and turns a' the Wardours out to the hill' (vi. 38).

The questions surrounding Lovel's birth are eventually referred back to the body of his mother, the (long-dead) sentimental heroine Eveline Neville, together with that which substitutes for her and eventually clears her name, the letter. Lovel's mother makes her first appearance embodied within a letter delivered many years late to her one-time husband, the Earl of Glenallan, which contains another characteristic epistolary token, a ring 'in which was set a braid of hair, composed of two different colours, black and light brown' (vi. 72). This letter is delivered by a messenger, the wandering Edie Ochiltree, who, despite his initial apparent status as a quintessential figure of errancy, proves to hold impeccably counter-revolutionary credentials; his delivery of the letter is only

---

[33] Scott's relegation of the sadistic sacking of a convent by French republicans (ultimately derived from Lewis's *The Monk*) to a mildly Gothic moment in an inset narrative is symptomatic at once of his interest in such conventional narratives of revolution and of his Austenian technique of compressing and displacing them.

made possible by his status as a veteran of the wars against the American revolutionaries, a status which allows him to claim comradeship with a member of the Earl's household, and so gain admittance. What the letters that come to light subsequently prove, however, is that the supposedly illegitimate liaison between Lord Glenallan and Eveline Neville was not, in fact, despite the Countess of Glenallan's asseverations, either extra-marital or incestuous. Their evidence actually produces the legitimacy of Lovel, a.k.a. Major Neville, confers upon him a name, and allows him both to marry Isabella Wardour and to save the fortunes of her father, Sir Arthur Wardour. Letters are, most uncharacteristically, made to uphold 'loyalty' and 'legitimacy'; locked in escritoires, in caskets, in ebony cabinets, in sealed packets in the care of stewards, and in the collections of antiquarians, they yield up secrets long buried, by virtue of their status as evidence. If 'falsification and forgery', not to mention simple misinterpretation, is the dominant mood of the discourse of the Antiquary and his circle, letters themselves, once read in their entirety, never lie.[34] In keeping with this turn, in a last sly *tour de force*, the policies of the Revolution itself are shown to have contributed to the reinstatement of legitimacy: further evidence proving the legality of the marriage between Lovel's parents is provided by Glenallan's tutor 'who solemnized the marriage' and who, having been granted a living in France by the machinations of the Countess, covering her tracks, is enabled to present his evidence only because he 'has lately returned to this country as an emigrant, a victim of his zeal for loyalty, legitimacy, and religion' (vi. 232). 'That's one lucky consequence of the French Revolution, my lord—you must allow that at least', comments Oldbuck.

In much the same way as the full and proper reading of the lost letters ensures legitimacy, so, too, in other sections of this novel, it erases revolution. True interpretation of texts and events always proves them, in direct antithesis to the case in *Waverley*, to be less revolutionary, and more loyally British, than at first appeared; to read something as revolution in this text is always to misread. The residual Jacobinical villain, Dousterswivel, 'tramping philosopher'

---

[34] The caveat is rendered necessary by the interpretative machinations of the Countess of Glenallan, who managed to convince her son that Eveline Neville was his sister, by extracting certain parts of her husband's letters to give a misleading impression.

(v. 164), *illuminé*, Rosicrucian, and swindler, who competently undermines the fortunes of the indigenous gentry as represented by the Wardour family, is for once not guilty (unlike his more flamboyant colleagues) of what he is accused of, namely 'a plot against the state', 'treason' or 'sedition at least' (v. 358). Similarly, the gossip sparked by the visit of Glenallan to the Antiquary, which reported it variously as a conspiracy to put down the Friends of the People or as espionage for the French, is equally unfounded.

The most remarkable instance of this slippage informs the denouement of the entire novel, in which the bonfire of the charlatan Dousterswivel's mining equipment is misread as a signal beacon warning of impending French invasion. In all these instances the rhetoric of revolution and invasion has been wrongly applied. Revolutionary violence imported into this text automatically shape-shifts from the political to the farcically accidental, allowing the reintegration of British society both at the level of romance (the legitimate heir is found, the house of Wardour is rescued) and at the level of national politics (the beggar and the gentry—Oldbuck armed with 'the sword which my father wore in forty-five', vi. 295—unite in defending the country on the alarm of French invasion). *The Antiquary* works very like the poem that it in some sense replaces, Jonathan Oldbuck's cherished project of the epic 'grand old-fashioned historical poem' (v. 174), to be entitled *The Caledoniad; or, Invasion Repelled*, and to come complete with a heavy-duty apparatus of antiquarian notes (the only portion of the poem that does get written, as the closing sentences of the novel point out with affectionate irony). The narrative of invasion is conspicuously absent: only the scattered bric-à-brac of musty textual and historiographical notes remains to indicate where revolution and invasion might have been lodged. *The Antiquary* finally suggests that the phenomenon of Napoleon, and its analogue, the breakage of the legitimate paternal line, were both in some sense unfortunate accidents of misreading and misappropriation, rectifiable by the romance of Restoration.

VI

The Antiquary clearly reworks *Waverley*: if *Waverley* at first takes seriously the conventional ideological equation between revolution and the vagaries of textuality, it also takes that equation seriously in another sense—if revolution may be equated with textuality, then it can be safely reimprisoned within it, either aestheticized, as in *Waverley*, or, in *The Antiquary*'s even more sophisticated formulation, converted into historiographical knick-knacks. *Redgauntlet* takes this strategy a stage further. If, in order to censor revolution, *The Antiquary* flirts with the possible radical inauthenticity of the discourse of history, *Redgauntlet* (1824) unabashedly metamorphoses history, in the shape of revolution, into a pure fiction,[35] thus underscoring its utter illegitimacy. In pursuit of this end, *Redgauntlet* effectively recapitulates the formal metamorphoses of the mainstream novel from the 1780s to the 1820s, neatly correlating successive narrative modes and motifs with the stages in its hero Darsie Latimer's development from a close cousin to the sentimental heroine[36] to a man of such substance that 'the progress or arrest of important political events were likely to depend upon his resolution' (xxxvi. 229). At first, Darsie is associated above all with the letter, and then with the epistolary Journal. It is, in fact, a letter concerning Darsie's mysterious disappearance in the Solway Firth that disrupts the due process of law, sending his dear friend, the lawyer Alan Fairford, haring after him to the rescue, in preference to continuing to pursue the legal case upon which he was engaged.[37] That important letter, however, is not in fact written by Darsie, and indeed the remainder of his letters are reduced to complete impotence, as they are never sent, forming instead a journal of his imprisonment at the hands of his fanatical Jacobite uncle Redgauntlet.

It is no accident that the inadvertent delivery of this crucial letter to Alan Fairford should coincide with the novel's change to third-person narration. Shuffled by accident among a legal correspondence, the letter switches from a transparent narrative medium to a

[35] For another reading of *Redgauntlet* that is interested in its explicit and flirtatious elision of historical referent in favour of fiction, arguing that its correspondent fascination with a thematics of decipherment betrays it as an elaborate metafictional meditation upon the processes of producing historical fiction, see James Kerr, *Fiction Against History*, 102–23.

[36] Darsie, as a version of Waverley, is even more explicitly assigned the position of heroine of sensibility, since he spends a good portion of the novel cross-dressed: Scott, *Redgauntlet: Waverley Novels*, xxxvi. 189. At one point he is even equated with the novel-reading Lydia Languish; xxxvi. 200.

[37] Cf. Favret, 'Idea of Correspondence', 358–65.

mislaid object. This shift is signalled by Scott's mischievous introduction' to the episode; discussing the relative merits of the epistolary and 'narrative', the text, by denying any such intention, slyly underlines the sophistication or adulteration of the sentimental authenticity of the letter which it begins to carry out:

The advantage of laying before the reader, in the words of the actors themselves, the adventures which we must otherwise have narrated in our own, has given great popularity to the publication of epistolary corres-pondence, as practised by various great authors, and by ourselves in the preceding chapters. Nevertheless, a genuine correspondence of this kind (and Heaven forbid it should be in any respect sophisticated by interpolations of our own!) can seldom be found to contain all in which it is necessary to instruct the reader for his full comprehension of the story ... (xxxv. 211)

If for Darsie as heroine of sensibility the letter eventually becomes impotent, translated into the solipsistic medium of a Journal, for Alan Fairford (the hero of sense) the letter, reduced to its last vestiges of an envelope and an address, takes on all too much potency, an excess of meaning which threatens to rewrite him, like Waverley, into political conspiracy. The possibilities for mis-appropriation and for misreading explored in *Emma* are here again, as in *Waverley*, given a visibly political dimension. Carrying (unwittingly) a letter of introduction from one notable Jacobite to another (with which he hopes to effect Darsie's release), Alan is inevitably construed as a messenger with inside knowledge, knowledge, in fact, of the inside of the letter. So far is this from the truth that Alan is twice warned that the letter might bear a double meaning, one for its carrier and the other for its recipient. That doubleness is reflected in its palimpsestic qualities; thus the envelope is reinscribed by the sea-captain, Nanty Ewart, out of pity on Alan—though only Father Buonaventure (the disguised Pretender), to whom the letter is misdelivered, perceives, presumably by sympathy, its masquerading doubleness:

Having turned it round ... and ... having examined the address with much minuteness, he asked whether he had observed these words, pointing to a pencil-writing upon the under side of the letter. Fairford answered in the negative, and, looking at the letter, read with surprise, '*Cave ne literas Bellerophontis adferres*' ... (xxxvi. 172)

The unpleasant consequences of assuming a letter's transparency are here suggestively linked with the plot of sexual misdemeanour;

in Greek mythology Anteia, wife of Proitos, King of Argos, falsely accused Bellerophon of seducing her, and as a result Proitos sent Bellerophon to his father-in-law carrying a letter requesting the bearer's death, a sentence Bellerophon only narrowly escaped.[38] The parallel is reiterated by a reference to 'the letters of Uriah' (xxxvi. 181), the not-so-lucky husband of Bathsheba. Nevertheless, even broken open by Father Buonaventure with its text exposed plainly to view—a text designed to betray Fairford into captivity— the letter is only momentarily unequivocal; it quickly acquires a second (and equally equivocal) meaning once enclosed within a letter from the Pretender himself, a letter which itself carries certain information relative to the planned Jacobite uprising in cypher.

The dangers of the letter are only superseded by the failure of the Jacobite attempt, a failure which itself is signalled by the fortunate misdelivery of a letter. The traitorous correspondence between Campbell and Cristal Nixon falls into the hands of a less trusting Alan, who, this time, has no scruples about opening it. In effect, the opening of the letter finishes the novel, for that violation, in revealing that the letter has finally been co-opted for the purposes of betraying the traitors themselves, signals the uselessness of the Jacobite attempt which has up till now been heavily associated with the letter. Moreover, the text simply aborts the expected violent climax at this point; to be subjected to official scrutiny seems tantamount to being defeated.

With the Pretender safely shipped off back to France, deserted by all his supporters save Redgauntlet himself, the novel slides out of revolutionary fiction into the discourse of historiography; the Conclusion presses the letter into the service of an antiquarian, Dr Dryasdust, a close acquaintance, not coincidentally, of Jonathan Oldbuck, the Antiquary himself. Invoking the familar fragmenting discourse of antiquarianism, the novel allows historical fiction to fall apart into its skeletal components: textual artefacts (an old newspaper, a marriage contract—xxxvi. 338) and anecdotal traces. As one might perhaps suspect from the reference to *The Antiquary*, the conclusion, under the guise of fusty authentication, is really interested in de-authentication; thus it offers a series of archaeo-logical problems and uncertainties relating to the events presented

---

[38] I am indebted here to Kathryn Sutherland's explanatory note in her 1985 Oxford edn.: *Redgauntlet*, 455 n.

as having really happened in the main body of the narrative (xxxvi. 340). In particular, these relate to the subsequent subjectivity of Redgauntlet himself, who, entering a monastery, only narrowly escapes (posthumous) canonization, a canonization that is on the one hand prompted by a misreading of the man, and on the other stalled by the recognition of a nagging discrepancy, a discrepancy once again embodied by an enigmatic textual artefact:

There was a circumstance which threw a doubt over the subject. . . . Under his habit, and secured in a small silver box, he had worn perpetually around his neck a lock of hair, which the fathers avouched to be a relic. But the Avocato del Diablo . . . made it at least equally probable that the supposed relic was taken from the head of a brother of the deceased Prior, who had been executed for adherence to the Stewart family in 1745–6; and the motto, *Haud obliviscendum*, seemed to intimate a tone of mundane feeling and recollection of injuries, which made it at least doubtful whether, even in the quiet and gloom of the cloister, Father Hugo had forgotten the sufferings and injuries of the House of Redgauntlet. (xxxvi. 341)

This 'relic' is the last duplicitous letter to make its appearance; coupled as it is with the last Jacobite, himself consistently associated with, as I have shown, the duplicities of the letter, it records the last vestige of revolution within the text. Yet the rather bewildering joke is that this last splutter of sentimental Jacobitism has no more actual historical foundation than the whole of this particular fiction—for there was, of course, no Jacobite agitation in the 1760s at all; in this novel the discourse of history is thus revealed simply as another form of fiction, but now the dominant one, executing a final flourish over the grave of the letter. Such virtuosity prompts speculation that by this late date, the business of disciplining the sentimental by way of historico-national discourse was complete and could itself be quietly burlesqued as a fictional convention. As Scott's remarks apropos of his relatives in the preface would suggest, *Redgauntlet* ultimately domesticizes history, reducing it to the display of souvenirs within the respectable privacy of the family:

Their love of past time, their tales of bloody battles fought against romantic odds, were all dear to the imagination, and their idolatry of locks of hair, pictures, rings, ribbons, and other memorials of the time in which they still seemed to live, was an interesting enthusiasm; and although their political principles, had they existed in the relation of fathers, might have rendered them dangerous to the existing dynasty, yet as we now recollect them, there could not be on earth supposed to exist persons better qualified to sustain the capacity of innocuous and respectable grandsires. (vol. xxxv, p. xxxv).

Constructing revolution as at once ridiculously obsolete and as romantic national inheritance, Scott is able to domesticate it, however improbably, within the family, in much the same way as, in *The Antiquary*, Sir Arthur Wardour's nostalgic Jacobitism is consecrated as one of his most attractive, because ultra-loyal, traits as a father.[39]

For contemporaries, Scott, appropriately, became identified extensively with a similar taming of fiction, a domesticization that was read as the guarantee of a secure national identity. As early as 1820, the *Monthly* was celebrating Scott's successful policing of the unruly novel. The reviewer announces that 'the mob of fictitious productions which over-ran our circulating libraries [and which] demanded the constant inspection of a literary master of ceremonies to keep order and decorum amongst them' has been replaced by 'one family of fictions, descended from one progenitor'; in this scaled-down rendition of Scott's national romance, the sentimental belles of Bath, perhaps amongst them Catherine Morland, have been suitably chastened into patriarchal domesticity, the novel has successfully been weaned from female sexual promiscuity and disciplined into virtuous filial piety, the revolutionary mob has been returned to the paternal authority of the king (*Monthly Review*, 2nd ser., 93 (1820), 259–61).[40] In the chapter that follows, however, I shall be examining a number of contemporaneous texts that construct themselves as deliberate commentaries on and

---

[39] I do not regard all of Scott's novels as unproblematically underwriting such fictions of social and national order (*Old Mortality*, 1816, for instance, is a peculiarly compromised example); none the less, for contemporaries, Scott's novels were most characteristic of his output when they promoted this sort of national health.

[40] For a similar view of Scott's immediate (if ultimately ambiguous) 'masculinization' of the novel, a 'masculinization' carried out by an appropriation both of the female romance and the moral tale, see Ina Ferris, *The Achievement of Literary Authority: Gender, History, and the Waverley Novels* (Ithaca, NY, 1991). For further discussion of the signs under which Scott was canonized see Nicola J. Watson, 'Purloined Letters: Revolution, Reaction and the Form of the Novel, 1790–1825', D.Phil. thesis (Oxford, 1990), 325–47.

counter-fictions to this history of family law and national order, by reinstating the semiotic and social restlessness of the sentimental—a restlessness which makes itself felt in continually erupting instances of illegible and illegitimate texts, opening unresolved ellipses within the fictional fabric.

4

Compromising Letters:
Shades of the Sentimental,
1812–1825

From 1814 onwards, the Waverley novels exerted such a far-reaching influence over the field of fictional possibilities that it is tempting to assume that *Redgauntlet* gave the *coup de grâce* to the power of the letter by the mid-1820s. Nevertheless, the residue of the letter survived, albeit in ever more attenuated and oddly miscellaneous forms that, betraying a particular affinity with the Gothic, would haunt the edges of the fictional spectrum throughout the later nineteenth century. It is, therefore, the project of this final chapter to survey the varied ways in which this residue appears in a number of texts that postdate the initial sensation surrounding the Waverley novels, a sensation which peaked with the publication of *Ivanhoe* in 1819: the event, as I suggested at the end of my last chapter, that firmly established their author within the canon. If Sir Walter Scott can be seen to be reprocessing the epistolary insurrections of *La Nouvelle Héloïse* within a disciplinary structure intended, through invocation of the discourse of history, to reassert patrilineal romance, the same knot of problems is tackled by a rival constellation of contemporary publications in ways which, instead, maintain the sentimental letter (albeit conspicuously debased and compromised) as a threat to the stability of genre, generally figured as guaranteed by the paternal. Moreover, the destabilization of codes of reading achieved by the residual presence of the letter in these texts threatens to undermine, by analogy, personal identity, social stability, and national security. The preoccupation with the legibility or otherwise of inset texts, displayed so insistently by Scott's early fiction and traceable ultimately to the struggle over the status of the epistolary within the post-revolutionary novel, appears, in these oddly belated examples, reinflected through a set of formal procedures which privilege or retain a strategic illegibility.

   This discussion of some of the disturbing remainders of

sentiment in the writing of the 1820s falls into two parts, the first of which offers a conspectus of three fictions, bound together by their investment in de-authorized narration, all of which conspicuously retain a quasi-sentimental textuality as radically illegible, in-decipherable, or downright duplicitous—Charles Maturin's *Melmoth the Wanderer* (1820), William Hazlitt's *Liber Amoris* (1823), and James Hogg's *Private Memoirs and Confessions of a Justified Sinner* (1825). Taking up many of the meanings assigned to the letter—in particular, its errancy and unreliability—in more formally conservative texts, these fictions actually encourage its disruptive latitude. While Maturin here constructs the sentimental as inimical to the paternal will and only very uncertainly controlled by it, and Hazlitt displays a version of *La Nouvelle Héloïse* in which the sentimental heroine's body escapes his scripting into promiscuity, Hogg produces a Jacobinical textuality that consist-ently scrambles the editorial apparatus of state surveillance, offering a counter-genealogy of the sentimental which explicitly revises and reverses Scott's deployment of the twinned disciplinary discourses of patrilineal romance and national history.[1] These fictions thus read as adversarial counterpoints to Scott's achieve-ment, and, indeed, as amplifications of the real-life correspondences that both Maturin and Hogg, as his protégés and rivals, conducted with the Wizard of the North.

Perhaps the most startling feature of *Confessions of a Justified Sinner* is its insistence that the sentimental—tying, as it does, the letter to the body—so far from being inevitably inimical to Scott's romance, teeters on the very edge of complicity with its investment

---

[1] In tandem, they may be said to transgress what Jacques Derrida has called 'the law of genre', a law which these fictions specifically locate within patrilineal political systems, to the extent that *Liber Amoris*, in particular, has consistently defied generic categorization, floating ambiguously between the novelistic and the autobiographical. 'La Loi du Genre/The Law of Genre', *Glyph*, 7 (1980), 221. If, as Mary Jacobus has suggested, building upon Derrida's insights, the legibility of genre depends upon the notion of family resemblance, then a lapse in the family, such as an eloping or adulterous text, will promote generic incoherence. *Romanticism, Writing, and Sexual Difference: Essays on* The Prelude (Oxford, 1989), 202. Jacobus's remark (tellingly, in the context of a discussion of the ways in which another version of the story of Julia troubles the genre of *The Prelude*) that 'an unbroken line of descent' is essential to generic purity is especially suggestive when taken in conjunction with April Alliston's formulation of the 'fiction of patrimony' as 'the fiction of transmission of value along readable lines'. 'The Value of a Literary Legacy: Retracing the Transmission of Value through Female Lines', *Yale Journal of Criticism*, 4 (1990), 123.

in aligning lineal bodies with paternal wills. Hogg's destabilizing counterfiction accordingly displays the sentimental letter as intrinsically alienated from its originating body; and it is in pursuit of this politics of estrangement that the second section of the chapter takes up, by way of conclusion to this entire study, a reading of a composite 'text', the production of which spanned the years between 1812 and 1824: namely, the peculiar exchange of competing epistolary forgeries and appropriations carried out between George Gordon, Lord Byron, and his sometime mistress Lady Caroline Lamb, within not only their private amatory correspondence, but Lamb's novel *Glenarvon* (1816), and Byron's 'metrical novel', *Don Juan* (1818–24). I shall be reading this amplified 'correspondence'—occupying as it does in turn all the possible orientations of the sentimental letter available in the post-revolutionary period—as a generically unstable site upon which the conflicting strategies applied to Rousseau's plot within the novel proper over this period flagrantly and mischievously undo one another, in the process unravelling and ironizing the politics of the letter. In the course of reading these quasi-autobiographical writings, I hope not only to offer a recapitulation of the generic mutations and negotiations I have been detailing throughout this study, but also (amplifying my readings of *Liber Amoris* and *Confessions of a Justified Sinner*) to suggest some of the ways in which contemporary subjects were able to emplot their own identities through readings of the sentimental, and its detours through the anti-Jacobinical, the national, the Gothic, and its ultimate metamorphosis into commodity and travesty.

I

Whereas *The Wild Irish Boy* seems comparatively untroubled by the vagaries of the sentimental, following Morgan in assimilating it comfortably to an Ascendancy version of national romance, Maturin's last and most ambitious novel seems not only to describe but to perform a pervasive unease visibly related to sentimental textuality. Published the year after Peterloo, and the same year that the Cato Street Conspiracy (to assassinate the Cabinet, seize vantage-points in London, and set up a new government) was detected and punished, *Melmoth the Wanderer* is understandably preoccupied with revolutionary thematics, a thematics that seems, on whatever level it emerges, to translate into an anxiety about the readability of inset texts—very much as it does for Scott. Indeed, it is, above all, the novel's extraordinary formal extravagance, disintegrative excess, and bewildering multiplicity of narrative authority—its extremely elaborate frame structure, incorporating no fewer than nine inset narratives, some embedded within each other to the extent that they are buried up to three levels below the outer frame narrative, making it virtually impossible to remember any story's provenance—that captures the reader's attention.[2] This general sense of disorientation is thematized by Maturin's insistent presentation of an ever-proliferating constellation of intermittently illegible texts connected with revolution—whether registered as real historical events (such as the Civil Wars, the persecution of the Covenanters terminated by the Glorious Revolution, or the troubles in the Ireland of the 1790s) or whether registered, with equal familiarity, as a series of female sexual transgressions against domestic and national patriarchy.

This excess that confounds disciplinary reading is initiated, appropriately enough, by a flaw in the will that makes over the dead John Melmoth's property to his nephew and surrogate son, also called John Melmoth, the proving of which is conducted in Ireland in the outermost frame narrative. More precisely, it is inaugurated by an unsigned and therefore unauthorized and legally inadmissible supplement to the paternal will proper, 'in the handwriting of the deceased':

'I enjoin my nephew and heir, John Melmoth, to remove, destroy, or cause to be destroyed, the portrait inscribed J. Melmoth, 1646, hanging in my

---

[2] Maturin seems to have identified even the non-epistolary texts within his novel as functioning analogously to letters: cf. the description of the transmission of the first manuscript in series (the autobiographical substance of which is actually transcribed only in paraphrase) that '[Stanton] seems, in fact, to have acted like men, who, in distress at sea, intrust their letters and dispatches to a bottle sealed, and commit it to the waves'. *Melmoth the Wanderer* [1820], ed. Alethea Hayter (Harmondsworth, 1977), 105. Although not all the embedded narratives are strictly describable as 'writing'—since some are told stories, or even paraphrases of manuscripts, rather than found manuscripts—I am, none the less, going to treat them all as quasi-epistolary texts, taking my cue from Beth Newman's observation in another context that such inlaid tales have characteristically broken loose both from their original teller and their subsequent retailer (the frame being the mark of that severance) and, being thus portable, function like transmitted manuscripts; 'Narratives of Seduction and the Seductions of Narrative: The Frame Structure of *Frankenstein*', *ELH* 53 (1986), 147.

closet. I also enjoin him to search for a manuscript . . . ; he will distinguish it by its being tied round with a black tape, and the paper being very mouldy and discoloured. He may read it if he will; I think he had better not. At all events, I adjure him, if there be any power in the adjuration of a dying man, to burn it.' (58)

Part of the young John Melmoth's legacy is this teasing and ambivalent instruction to destroy the narrative part of his inheritance, that which comes to him from the earlier, seventeenth-century John Melmoth, who, according to local legend, is still wandering the earth thanks to a contract with the Devil. It is young Melmoth's wilfulness in choosing to read the manuscript which sets off the supplemental detours of textuality that make up the bulk of the novel, conducting him into a perplexingly labyrinthine archive of texts associated both with illegibility and insurrection, documents which oppose themselves to those texts associated with paternal and legal authority such as the will itself.

In keeping with their dubious provenance, the found narratives that now make their appearance within the novel are extremely difficult to read, as a result partly of the ravages of history, partly of the documents' own inability or reluctance to write the incommunicable secret of the illicit contract with which the Wanderer attempts to seduce a succession of suffering protagonists to take over his own fast-expiring lease with Satan; the dilapidated state of these accounts mimes the forbidden nature of what they have to relate. Attempting to decipher the 'discoloured, obliterated, and mutilated' manuscript (67) dating from the 1670s and 1680s that he finds in his uncle's cabinet, for example, John Melmoth is continually hampered by its hiatuses at all the crucial moments at which a reading of the stranger at the heart of a series of mysteries might be possible (70):[3]

The stranger, slowly turning round, and disclosing a countenance which— (Here the manuscript was illegible for a few lines), said in English—(A long hiatus followed here, and the next passage that was legible, though it proved to be a continuation of the narrative, was but a fragment).

*

These gaps, occurring intermittently throughout the course of the novel, are explicitly identified as revolutionary by the story, related

[3] See also e.g. 80, 99, 103–4, 180, 188, 245, 468.

in this first manuscript, of one Stanton's incarceration in a lunatic asylum in England; a story that, featuring the reading of 'the album of a madhouse', identifies fragmentariness with madness, which is, in its turn, identified with revolution through the crazed politics of its inmates, who scream a miniature Civil War at one another in fragments from the sermons of Hugh Peters on the one side and from the songs and plays of Lovelace, Cowley, and Aphra Behn on the other.[4]

If dispersed and disintegrated documents are thus connected by Maturin with revolution, they are also connected, by a familiar logic, with the power of female sexuality to introduce detours into a patrilineal system of inheritance. The burlesque scene in which the servants of the deceased are gathered round the fire wondering at a great storm and attributing it to the carrying off of the dead man by his supernatural ancestor, for instance, contains at its heart an account of the misappropriation of the law of the father by a woman—in this case, of legal papers belonging to the dead man:

'If it's this you want—and this—and this,' cried a young female . . . , 'take them'; and she eagerly tore the papers out of her hair, and flung them into the fire. Then Melmoth recollected a ridiculous story told him the day before of this girl, who had . . . curl[ed] her hair with some of the old and useless law-papers of the family, and who now imagined that they 'who kept this dreadful pudder o'er her head,' were particularly provoked by her still retaining about her whatever belonged to the deceased . . .   (108–9)

This parodic vignette of the 'feminine', not to say Medusan,[5] defacement and misappropriation of the written fabric of patri-lineal law (a misappropriation doubled by the allusion to *King Lear*, a play in which, after all, an illegitimate son fraudulently disinherits his legitimate brother by means of a forged letter), ushers in the second major set of framed narratives, told by the shipwrecked Spanish nobleman Monçada, all of which centrally revolve around familiar stories of sentimental illegitimacy and

---

[4] For an updated version of a contemporary madman who internalized revolutionary philosophy in a contemporary conservative novel see Mary Brunton, *Discipline* (3 vols., London, 1814); for a fascinating account of a contemporary psychiatric case that anatomizes a madman's internalization of revolutionary and Napoleonic politics and plots in something of the same fashion as do Maturin's lunatics, see Roy Porter, 'Reason, Madness, and the French Revolution', *Studies in Eighteenth-Century Culture*, 20 (1990), 55–79.

[5] Cf. Neil Hertz, 'Male Hysteria Under Political Pressure', *passim*.

epistolarity. However, although these narratives all invoke a series of plot motifs related to revolution, they neither ratify the patrilineal nor the sentimental, but, bafflingly, bundle them up together as equally transgressive.

These narratives begin with the birth of Monçada himself, child of a liaison between a woman of lower rank and an aristocrat, a relationship only later regularized by marriage. This familiar story is chamfered onto the fossil sentimental plot as deployed in the 1790s in the inset narrative of the parricide (whom Monçada employs to help him escape the convent in which he is immured as a penance by his guilty parents), albeit offering as pessimistic a version of that plot as Wordsworth's own sentimental vignette, *Vaudracour and Julia*.[6] The parricide's tale describes the fate of another young couple who secretly marry in defiance of social class and the prohibition of their parents: the husband is incarcerated by his family in the convent in the hope of cutting off this 'degrading' alliance, but he is joined there by the wife, who masquerades as a novice (an episode that reworks a similar, albeit absolutely anti-sentimental cross-dressing episode in Lewis's *The Monk*, 1796). This particular pair, however, do not succeed in evading the law; the parricide describes how he tricked them into a supposed escape, luring them into an underground cell where they were walled up and left to die of starvation. Their Gothic sufferings both inhabit and unravel the sentimental genre within which they have up until then been operating:

'All that night, however, I heard their groans,—those groans of physical suffering, that laugh to scorn all the sentimental sighs that are exhaled from the hearts of the most intoxicated lovers that ever breathed. . . . It was on the fourth night that I heard the shriek of the wretched female,—her lover, in the agony of hunger, had fastened his teeth in her shoulder;—that bosom on which he had so often luxuriated, became a meal to him now.' (290–1)

This tale's parodic expansion of the classic sentimental radical plot into the Gothic register—a particularly unpleasant rewriting of the outcome of Wordsworth's story, in which Vaudracour shares the breast of Julia with the baby, who subsequently dies—is underlined

---

[6] This coded account of Wordsworth's affair in Revolutionary France with Annette Vallon was excerpted from the 1805 draft of *The Prelude* and published separately in the volume of 1820, the same year as Maturin's novel.

by the repetition of this story which the parricide proves to be enacting, betraying the unsuspecting Monçada's escape even as he recounts his earlier betrayal. Monçada's frustrated flight itself, since it is planned and initiated through a forbidden quasi-sentimental correspondence with his brother Juan, is formally as well as thematically congruent with the story that interrupts it. The brothers' epistolary exchange conflates, albeit in homosocial terms, all the letters of Héloïse and Abelard and their descendants which breach the walls of convents with those letters that in Helen Maria Williams's version of the story breach the walls of the Bastille. In this late variant, however, the planned escape, however sympathetically portrayed, is doomed (244–5).

That the double agent common to Monçada's story and its inset mirror image is a parricide, who proves to have been reprieved from execution on condition that he enforce the repressive mandates of the *ancien régime*, suggests something of the mandates' at once transgressive and deeply compromised status. If these stories ambiguously align parricide with the oppressive establishment as well as with the sentimental lovers, 'The Lovers' Tale', appearing later in the novel, displays an equal ambivalence over the clash between the paternal and the sentimental. This story, however, would seem to argue for a possible alignment of the paternal will with the sentimental couple, an alignment ultimately frustrated, however, through a redirection of the letter in a Scott-like context of revolutionary history. Set elaborately in the Civil Wars and the Restoration, this tale tells of the fate of the three Mortimer cousins. Their miniature tragedy results from the kink in narrative transmission produced by a deliberately selective reading of the dead father's letters, instigated by John Sandal's mother in order to compel him to marry the loyalist heiress Margaret Mortimer instead of his beloved, but puritan, Elinor Mortimer— the only way, under the terms of their grandfather Sir Roger Mortimer's will, of retaining the Mortimer fortune and lands within the immediate family. Sandal's mother 'had assured John that he was not her son, but the offspring of the illicit commerce of her husband the preacher with the puritan mother of Elinor . . .' (640–1). This false narrative, itself about falsity and illegitimacy, appears to be a direct reworking of the Countess of Glenallan's fabrications in *The Antiquary*; but whereas for Scott the discrediting of the analogous fabrication eventually leads to a happy

reunion of the father and his legitimate son, Maturin's final
exorcism of the shade of incest produces no happy ending: all three
cousins die childless.

Melmoth the Wanderer thus wires in random series a set of
familiar and interchangeable tropes and plots for revolution—
madness, historical analogues, the sentimental plot, the sentimental
letter, illegitimate birth, parricide, female interception of the
father's will, the Gothic—all governed by the sign of illegibility. But
if, like Scott, Maturin connects illegibility through the usual
channels to the revolutionary sentimental, he, unlike Scott, manifests considerable uncertainty when it comes to relocating legitimate
authority with the father and counter-revolutionary modernity. It is
true that the only inset tale to end happily, 'The Tale of Guzman',
seems to promise the restoration of the law of the father by, finally,
restoring the near-maddened Guzman to responsible fatherhood
and simultaneously revealing a true will; however, in general the
oppression suffered by Maturin's protagonists at the hands of
institutions which conventionally appeared in 'Jacobin' novels as
figures for the *ancien régime* (madhouses, convents, and the
Inquisition amongst them) would seem to justify the overturning of
such an order.

Indeed, this possibility may be said fundamentally to trouble the
apparent project of the novel as a whole, a project figured by the
Jewish patriarch Adonijah's obsessive collection, transcription,
transliteration, and translation of the virtually indecipherable
manuscripts of the many inset narratives in the all but inaccessible
subterranean vault, where he has devoted his life to collecting
evidence of the existence and guilt of the Wanderer. Like Adonijah,
Maturin struggles to bring Melmoth to justice by collating all these
disparate narratives into the same register of reference in order to
regulate them and so to compose a comprehensive indictment. The
proliferations of narrative come to an end only when Melmoth's
wanderings are cut short; only when Melmoth appears in the
outermost frame of the novel, in modern time, conflating the long
series of representations with his body, can the circulation and
proliferation of textuality be suspended. Only when the supernatural revolutionary is finally eradicated, only when the Wanderer—
the prime figure throughout of errant, Jacobinical, seductive plot—
is finally consigned to the flames of hell *in propria persona* (in the
same way as his portrait had been earlier, in accordance with the

dictate of the will which initiates the narrative), are the novel's many tales finally subjected to one generic sign, a family name. But it is a huddled-up, hasty, precarious, and quasi-parricidal solution none the less, and, by admitting Melmoth into the outermost frame at all, it involves placing modern time at risk from the supernatural. Given that *The Antiquary* finds it logical to identify the anti-Jacobin villain, Dousterswivel, with both revolution and the supernatural, and desirable to prove that, nevertheless, all three are fraudulent, Maturin's retention of the supernatural seems noticeably risky and ambivalent.

II

If *Melmoth the Wanderer* is radically fissured by an ambivalence over the sentimental (succeeding neither in valorizing nor containing it), so too is William Hazlitt's quasi-autobiographical *Liber Amoris* (1823). As a dysfunctional simulacrum of a Rousseauistic epistolary fiction, *Liber Amoris* meditates upon the availability of sentimental discourse in the years after Peterloo, coming, in the last analysis, to memorialize the decay and slippage of the political meanings of the sentimental. Like *Melmoth the Wanderer*, *Liber Amoris* registers its simultaneous nostalgia for and discomfort with that discourse through a display of a series of figures of textuality which remain obstinately enigmatic; the problem of how to authorize an appropriate reading of the letter (for Scott, soluble by the authority of social consensus, expressed in the genre of historical narrative) remains, in this essentially first-person narrative, unresolved and unresolvable.

Hazlitt's story of his ill-fated infatuation with his landlady's daughter, Sarah Walker, meticulously exploits the conventions of epistolary fiction: not only does Hazlitt literalize the standard editorial fiction of the sentimental novel (which very frequently claimed simply to have collected up scattered letters) by reprinting their (slightly edited) real-life correspondence, but he consciously deploys these conventions in the prefatory fiction of the now-dead sentimental writer who had 'transcribed [the whole] very carefully with his own hand'.[7] As a contemporary review in *The Globe*

---

[7] Gerald Lahey (ed.), *Liber Amoris: or, The New Pygmalion* [1823], (New York, 1980), 63.

makes clear, the generic affiliations of *Liber Amoris* were as a result immediately recognizable:

The *Liber Amoris* is unique in the English language; and as, possibly, the first book in its fervour, its vehemency, and its careless exposure of passion and weakness—of sentiments and sensations which the common race of man seek most studiously to mystify or conceal—that exhibits a portion of the most distinguishing characteristics of Rousseau, it ought to be generally praised.[8]

If Hazlitt's exploitation of the conventions of sentimental authorship thus aligned him with the Rousseau of the *Confessions*, the autobiographical status of the reprinted letters also identified him with the position not only of St Preux but also of Rousseau's Julie and her contemporary descendants; Peter Patmore, the correspondent who actually makes an appearance as a character in *Liber Amoris*, later published Hazlitt's original letters to him in *My Friends and Acquaintance*, remarking of the extracts that they were marked by 'real, intrinsic passion' and, further, that:

Many of the letters in the 'Nouvelle Heloise' are among the most beautiful and affecting effusions which exist in those works of fiction that concern themselves with sentiments and passion rather than with incident and action. But I venture to say that there is nothing in the 'Nouvelle Heloise' equal in passion and pathos to the foregoing extracts. And the reason is, that the letters are actual and immediate transcripts from the human heart. . . .

Perhaps the published writings most resembling these letters in the depth and intensity of the passion they embody and convey, are the celebrated letters addressed by Mary Woolstonecraft to Imlay.[9]

Patmore's conflation of Hazlitt with Mary Wollstonecraft tellingly positions Hazlitt as an erring and politically radical sentimental heroine. That habitual conflation of sentimental heroine and radical politics was in fact prefigured by Hazlitt's essay in *Table-talk*, written during the throes of the affair with Sarah Walker, and in parallel with parts of *Liber Amoris*, 'On Dreams'.[10] Finished in March 1822, the essay appears to make a veiled reference to his surprising failure, given his erotic obsession, to dream of her face;

---

[8] The *Globe*, 7 June: cited in Stanley Jones, *Hazlitt: A Life* (Oxford, 1989), 338. According to Jones, the analogy with Rousseau was also made by the *Examiner*.

[9] Richard Henry Stoddard (ed.), *Personal Recollections of Lamb, Hazlitt, and Others* (New York, 1875), 189–90.

[10] See Jones, *Hazlitt: A Life*, 322.

the essay then swiftly concludes with two dreams, both of which end in lamentation and weeping. The first sorrows over an imaginary despoiling of the pictures of the Louvre, apparently a dream about the fall of Napoleon (to which we shall be returning) and thus about the final failure of revolutionary ideals; the second, which follows hard on its heels, recasts this eruption of a radical, not to say treasonous, political unconscious as frustrated epistolary desire:

I also dreamt a little while ago, that I was reading the New Eloise to an old friend, and came to the concluding passage in Julia's farewell letter. . . . The words are, '*Trop heureuse d'acheter au prix de ma vie le droit de te aimer toujours sans crime et de te le dire encore une fois, avant que je meurs!*' I used to sob over this passage twenty years ago; and in this dream about it lately, I seemed to live these twenty years over again in one short moment.[11]

Hazlitt seems here at once to imagine himself reading *La Nouvelle Héloïse* to Sarah as a form of seduction (comparable to that staged in Lady Sydney Morgan's *The Wild Irish Girl*), to read their relationship in the terms of *La Nouvelle Héloïse*, and, most striking of all, to read himself as the dead Julie; in short, the classically sentimental credentials of this affair, from Hazlitt's perspective at least, are never in question.

In keeping with this cast, 'S—' at first appears to be a canonical, if déclassée, heroine of sensibility, fit consort for the threadbare 'sentimental lover' (162) H—: her first attachment, she confides, was, in splendidly conventional fashion, both formed over common reading and satisfactorily unsuitable, eventually truncated by 'pride of birth . . . that would not permit him to think of an union' (80). Her first lover, moreover, proves to have borne an extraordinary likeness to a little bust of Napoleon owned by H—, suggesting very strongly his desirably revolutionary credentials. Building on this promising foundation, H— then does his best to read both himself and Sarah into a series of scenarios which include amongst them Rousseau's passion for Sophie d'Houdetot, as related both in the *Confessions* and, according to Byron and many other biographical readers, *La Nouvelle Héloïse*: 'As Rousseau said of Madame d'Houptot (forgive the allusion) my heart has found a tongue in speaking to her, and I have talked to her the divine language of

---

[11] *The Complete Works of William Hazlitt*, ed. P. P. Howe, xii. 24.

love' (126–7).[12] Much of the piece—composed largely of letters and quasi-letters—is accordingly preoccupied with H—'s attempt to involve Sarah within a properly sentimental correspondence via a series of appropriate objects and texts, including, in true revolutionary spirit, the little bust of Napoleon, as well as a locket containing Sarah's hair. This correspondence, however, falls short of anything like a full transcription of the sentiments of the heart, being instead markedly fragmentary—towards the end, literally so. It culminates when the fall of Napoleon is closely folded up with fallen female sexuality into a bathetically sentimental letter:

I gathered up the fragments of the locket of her hair, and the little bronze statue, which were strewed about the floor, kissed them, folded them up in a sheet of paper, and sent them to her, with these lines written in pencil on the outside—'*Pieces of a broken heart, to be kept in remembrance of the unhappy. Farewell.*' (214)

The final transaction is more literary still, when H— gives Sarah copies of Oliver Goldsmith's eminently moralistic *Vicar of Wakefield*, Mackenzie's *The Man of Feeling*, and Elizabeth Inchbald's Rousseauistic polemic *Nature and Art* (1796) in exchange for a number of volumes of 'his own writings'—a novel way of requesting the return of letters to mark the end of the affair, recognized by Sarah when she returns his volumes with her name cut out of all the title-pages (215–16).

Hazlitt's dream of reading Sarah within the sentimental genre, a dream which had as its poignant end-point a projected honeymoon—he wished to persuade Sarah 'to have crossed the Alps with me, to sail on sunny seas, to bask in Italian skies, to have visited Vevai and the rocks of Meillerie, and to have repeated to her on the spot the story of Julia and St Preux, and to have shewn her all that my heart had stored up for her' (186)—is sabotaged throughout the affair by her absolute inscrutability.[13] The core of her unreadability seems to be her unpoliced and unpoliceable sexuality—it stems, for Hazlitt, from the unresolved question of whether she is a 'Madonna' or a 'Magdalen', a question that is related to her lower-class status. As a result, while *Liber Amoris* sets out to 'decipher' Sarah Walker by reading her through the medium of a number of

[12] Cf. Byron, *Childe Harold*, Canto iii.
[13] Yet more poignant is the fact that Hazlitt did ultimately travel to Meillerie in June 1825 on honeymoon with his second wife, who left him within the year.

sentimental and radical novels, it actually records only the failure of that reading. The text as a whole, in consequence, is notably mutilated and generically incoherent, composed as it is of 'conversations', an annotation to 'Endymion', letters to and from Sarah, and to and from a friend, P—, isolated effusions, 'thoughts', literary quotations, and lengthy raptures over nature. The inadequacy of any of these essentially sentimental discourses to give form to Hazlitt's story is underscored in the closing first-person narrative (couched in a series of continuous letters by H— to another friend, J. S. K—) that endeavours, with little success, to retell the story implied by the conflicting written evidence presented hitherto. The problem that Sarah presents is succinctly stated in one of H—'s letters to P—:

> To what a state am I reduced, and for what? For fancying a little artful vixen to be an angel and a saint, because she affected to look like one, to hide her rank thoughts and deadly purposes. . . . I ask you first in candour whether the ambiguity of her behaviour with respect to me, sitting and fondling a man (circumstanced as I was) . . . was not enough to excite my suspicions, which the different exposures from the conversations below-stairs were not calculated to allay? . . . My unpardonable offence has been that I took her at her word . . . (85–6)

Sarah is indecipherable because her 'word' does not, apparently, correspond to her body, remaining as slippery as the corrupted sentimental letters identified by Edgeworth and Austen as viciously Jacobinical.[14] However, unlike her generic if rather more well-bred cousins Lady Olivia or Lady Susan, it proves impossible to fix her meaning by appeal to outside authority. H—, for instance, attempts to establish the meaning of his correspondence by submitting it to an outside reader, P— (113–14), who remains dismayingly noncommittal: similarly, H— invokes paternal authority equally inconclusively. Approached by H—, both S—'s brother and her father refuse to exert authority one way or the other; as P— reports of his negotiations with the brother, 'the thing must and does entirely rest with herself' (174). H— even appeals to state authority, in the shape of the list of the members of the House of

---

[14] In this context it is worth considering Mary Poovey's analysis of the ideological construct of the 'proper lady'; viewed as a genre of gender, it is clear that transparency, an absolute correspondence between inner and outer, is the only way to guarantee female 'virtue' or sexual innocence. See *The Proper Lady and the Woman Writer*, Ch. 1.

Parliament: 'You are to understand, this comes in a frank, the second I have received from her, with a name I can't make out, and she won't tell me, though I asked her, where she got franks. . . . **** is the name on the frank: see if you can decypher it by a Redbook' (119). These consistent failures return the whole correspondence back upon its hermeneutically unstable self once again.

H—'s manœuvres thus repeat, albeit unsuccessfully, those disciplinary procedures that more conservative novels, as I have been arguing, regularly adopted. His appeal to social consensus culminates in a comprehensive 'indictment' of Sarah's alleged promiscuity, and his revenge is painstakingly appropriate—he resolves to publish her. In rendering her public property, he deliberately subjects her to a form of prostitution; by exposing her, in the shape of the reproduced letter, to 'public airings', to recirculation and rereading *ad infinitum*, he debases her sentimental value in much the same way as Edgeworth, Austen, and Scott devalued the sentimental letter: 'she will soon grow common to my imagination, as well as worthless in herself' (256). Like Scott, Hazlitt presides over the demystification of the sentimental letter; in direct refutation of Scott's tactics, however, Hazlitt displays, deliberately or not, the rotting of the fabric of genre under the hands of the would-be regulatory reader.

If *Liber Amoris* eventually fails to carry off this disciplinary manœuvre, it is in large part because it appeared so generically indecorous that it called up in its turn analogous disciplinary measures on the part of the public press. The indecorum of *Liber Amoris* was perceived to reside in the social solecism of recirculating actual letters and retailing actual indiscretions—the same social indecorum that had led the town to vilify William Godwin's similar exercise in *Memoirs of the Author of a Vindication of the Rights of Woman*. In publishing Sarah's actual letters in his attempt to discipline her meanings, and in framing them within a recognizably sentimental logic, however ironized, Hazlitt also, paradoxically and accidentally, laid himself open to analogous measures, finding himself, like Sarah, circulated in public through the medium of such hostile right-wing periodicals as *John Bull*, which reprinted one of Hazlitt's actual letters in order to condemn him more effectually for reprinting Sarah's.[15] In this way, Hazlitt became the scandal of the

---

[15] 22 June 1823: cited in Jones, *Hazlitt: A Life*, 338.

town like Wollstonecraft before him. Unlike the Jacobin novelists of the 1790s, Hazlitt is unable consistently to valorize the position associated with Julie, whether occupied by Sarah or by himself, but his attempts to condemn and jettison it, unlike those of the conservative novelists of the early 1800s, are embarrassed and ultimately sabotaged by his radical nostalgia.

III

However unsuccessful, *Liber Amoris* demonstrates that the energies of sentimental genre, albeit devalued, were still circulating at this late date. Because it suffers from an intense, if undermined, desire to conserve the revolutionary sentimental, *Liber Amoris* ultimately fails to discipline the letter, despite its autobiographical investment in doing so. As such, it stands both as a last souvenir of the all-but-obsolete sentimental, and as a telling memorandum of the energies Scott's novels succeeded in rescheduling. But if *Liber Amoris* attempts, however anachronistically, to keep S— in her assigned place as sentimental heroine by reconciling her discourse with her body, James Hogg's *The Private Memoirs and Confessions of a Justified Sinner, Written by Himself; With a Detail of Curious Traditionary Fact and Other Evidence by the Editor* wholeheartedly subverts that process of collating body with text, a process which this novel associates explicitly with the forms of narrative authority favoured by Scott.[16] Like Scott, Hogg foregrounds errant textuality; unlike Scott, however, Hogg deliberately preserves the aberrancy of his competing inset stories, displaying the ways in which the supplemental excess of writing resists the authoritative antiquarian collation, documentation, and narration of historical 'evidence', thereby threatening to overload or elude those activities that guarantee official, national history. Like Maturin, Hogg realizes this excess as the supernatural—the mysterious Gil-Martin is

---

[16] In offering a reading of *Confessions of a Justified Sinner* along these lines, I am expanding upon Gary Kelly's characterization and reading of the novel as attempting 'to deconstruct the great institution of the Romantic socio-historical novel'. *English Fiction of the Romantic Period*, 252. For other discussions of 'counter-fictions' that contest the version of historicity espoused by the Waverley novels see Ina Ferris, *The Achievement of Literary Authority*, 161–94; Kelly, *English Fiction of the Romantic Period*, 184–201.

cousin to Melmoth the Wanderer in his ability to introduce eccentricity into history.

Split into two discrepant narratives which deal with substantially the same set of early eighteenth-century events, *Confessions* actively resists the possibility of reconciling the inconsistencies between the two accounts it offers. The 'Editor's' early eighteenth-century official history, which frames the whole text, is fissured by an unaccountable and unmanageable anomaly in the shape of the Sinner's seventeenth-century first-person narrative. The first half of the frame narrative, compiled by the Editor from a number of accounts (varying, like those that appear in *Melmoth the Wanderer*, in their provenance and reliability, from 'the stores of tradition and old registers' to contemporary gossip, transcribed and edited in conformity with 'the shackles of modern decorum'), tells how the Sinner, one Robert Wringhim, illegitimate and a Covenanter, apparently persecutes and murders his legitimate, Jacobite brother, George Colwan, subseqently inheriting the estate, and eventually coming to a miserable end as a suicide.[17] The second part of the Editor's account tells of the exhumation of what might be Wringhim's body, and the discovery of his autobiographical memoir.

The centre of this frame is occupied by Wringhim's own confession, a buried narrative in the most literal sense, since it is found by the Editor on the Sinner's exhumed body. Part printed pamphlet, part manuscript, this book is finally delivered up to the authorities, under the aegis of the modern Editor's would-be authoritative reading, more than a hundred years after its composition and burial. It recounts Wringhim's seduction and persecution by the devilish Gil-Martin (in an uncanny doubling of his own persecution of his brother),[18] and his subsequent career of vice, which includes the murder of a clergyman (a crime for which Wringhim allows another innocent clergyman to be executed) and the killings of his brother, his mother, and a young lady whom he had previously seduced by means of 'private correspondence'—a

[17] *Confessions of a Justified Sinner* [1824], ed. John Carey (Oxford, 1981), i, 48, 15.

[18] For an extended discussion of this 'seduction' as homosocial, involving 'a genuinely erotic language of romantic infatuation', see Eve Kosofsky Sedgwick, *Between Men: English Literature and Male Homosocial Desire* (New York, 1985), 103–6.

career in the best tradition of the Jacobinical villain.[19] However, despite the Editor's best efforts to frame, in every sense, this narrative as part of the other evidence he has collected—an effort, like those of Scott or Maturin's Adonijah, to 'translate' it all into the same definitive register—a lingering 'unaccountability' persistently leaks out from this first-person record. As the Editor remarks:

We cannot enter into a detail of the events that now occurred, without forestalling a part of the narrative of one who knew all the circumstances— was deeply interested in them, and whose relation is of higher value than anything that can be retailed out of the stores of tradition and old registers; but, his narrative being different from these, it was judged expedient to give the account as thus publicly handed down to us. (48)

Although the Editor attempts to exert discipline upon the Sinner's memoir by editing and framing it, in the last analysis the Sinner's narrative baffles his expert antiquarian exegesis:

With regard to the work itself, I dare not venture a judgment, for I do not understand it. I believe no person, man or woman, will ever peruse it with the same attention that I have done, and yet I confess that I do not comprehend the writer's drift. . . . Were the relation at all consistent with reason, it corresponds so minutely with traditionary facts, that it could scarcely be missed to have been received as authentic; but in this day, and with the present generation, it will not go down . . . (253–4)

The disturbing discrepancy introduced by historical change decomposes the premises of the frame designed to handle it, privileging, as Gary Kelly has noted, 'indeterminacy in the face of the attempt to unify and make coherent'.[20] In presenting these two narratives as crucially incompatible and mutually chafing—one social, official, historiographical and above all modern, the other solipsistic, unverifiable, autobiographical and archaic—the novel conspicuously refuses to close down the unsettling potential of first-person narrative, which conjures here a historical otherness figured

---

[19] See Gary Kelly for an argument to this effect: '*The Private Memoirs and Confessions* has overtones in its language and its plot that could well suggest a contemporary political "parable" to readers aware of recent British and European history and interested in the growing political and social crisis of the 1820s, which was seen in many ways as a continuation of the crises of the 1790s and the Napoleonic wars.' Kelly argues (and I agree) that the language and actions of Wringhim and Gil-Martin 'strongly suggest . . . an analogy between Wringhim and Gil-Martin and the revolutionary Jacobins'. *English Fiction of the Romantic Period*, 261–5.   [20] Ibid. 261.

as questionably supernatural. Furthermore, this unsettling narrative is, as usual, associated with sexual transgression and political radicalism: in keeping with the nagging illegitimacy of his memoir, the Sinner is himself illegitimate, apparently the offspring of the initial adulterous act on the part of Rabina (herself dubiously legitimate, 1), the wife of the Tory and Jacobite Laird of Dalcastle, with the Reverend Wringhim, a Covenanter and supporter of 'revolutionary principles' (20). This lapse produces what amounts to an ellipsis in the family line; his titular father, the Laird, refusing to acknowledge him as his own, Robert is therefore christened with his pastor's and supposed blood-father's name, Wringhim. Robert's illegitimacy is, inevitably, related to his status as a Covenanter 'incendiary', one who is prepared to rebel against a monarchy based upon primogeniture.[21]

Wringhim thus embodies the pervasive discrepancies that are played out at the level of the elliptic form of Hogg's novel, split between the memoir proper and the Editor's would-be disciplinary frame. The intermittent amnesia that begins to overtake Wringhim, which figures in little the fissures that characterize the structure of the narrative as a whole, afflicts him during those periods when Gil-Martin apparently appropriates Wringhim's body in order to commit general mayhem in his name and, most incontrovertibly, under his signature. This misappropriation of Wringhim (now known as Colwan since his inheritance of his brother's birthright) amounts to a forgery or facsimile, the production of a textual 'second self' (177); it is thus reminiscent of Waverley's disturbing doubleness after the fraudulent activities of Donald Bean-Lean, which similarly generate a treasonous second written self through a misappropriated signature. It is not surprising, therefore, that when

---

[21] His illegitimacy in this sense, however, is complicated by the legalization of these revolutionary principles by the Glorious Revolution of 1688, just as the legitimacy of his brother George Colwan is both underwritten and undermined by his Jacobite politics, which are themselves at once revolutionary and utterly invested in the notion of blood-legitimacy. This paradox is put into elegant conjunction with the bearer of the Hanoverian name: 'George . . . exulting to see so many gallant young chiefs and gentlemen about him, who all gloried in the same principles of loyalty, (perhaps this word should have been written *disloyalty*) . . . made speeches, gave toasts, and sung songs, all leaning slily to the same side . . .' (50). The problem of political legitimacy is here firmly joined with the problem of ambiguity in writing, familiar from *Waverley*, an ambiguity that Hogg eventually extends into a systemic textual 'unaccountability', a chronic illegibility.

the disguised Sinner obtains employment in Her Majesty's printing-house, hoping to publish a pamphlet telling his story, his doubleness should be registered as actually subversive. Like the Editor's narrative, the printing-house is a model of State official-dom—as the master says, he 'could take no man into Her Majesty's printing office upon a regular engagement, who could not produce the most respectable references with regard to morals' (221)—and the Sinner's attempts to harness it to the task of justifying his Jacobinical activities (with the assistance apparently of Gil-Martin as a literal printer's devil) amount to nothing less than, in the master's words, 'treason and blasphemy'. Disruptive textuality is here magnified from the errant letter to the contagious dissemina-tion of sedition within national print-culture, a matter of some topical interest in the year which saw the eventual repeal of the Combination Acts, originally passed to suppress the Corresponding Societies. Although, in the event, the Sinner is forced to flee, pocketing the 'printed sheets, the only copy of my unfinished work existing' (223), the 'proof' of his pamphlet, with his handwritten journal appended, survives his eventual suicide to unsettle the Editor's narrative.

The status of vagrant textuality as that which damages narrative authority, whether of the Editor or of the State, is amplified by the final movement of the novel, which insists upon a critical slippage between text and originating body, a slippage that crucially disables the Editor's attempts to collate the two by installing further discrepancies between the fictitious Editor, the author James Hogg, Hogg's various (and inconsistent) self-representations, and those representations of Hogg produced by other writers. The conclusion of the Sinner's journal is framed by the re-entry of the Editor, who tells of the initial arousal of his curiosity by a letter supposedly published in *Blackwood's Magazine* in 1824, signed 'James Hogg', and of his subsequent attempts to authenticate Hogg's account, which locates the grave of the suicide, tells his story, and recounts an amateur exhumation of the body. Although this letter, the Editor remarks, 'bears the stamp of authenticity in every line', he is wary because he had often been 'hoaxed by the ingenious fancies displayed in that Magazine' (245); in particular, he is suspicious because 'Hogg has imposed as ingenious lies on the public ere now!' (246). The inclusion of this letter marks the novel's moment of maximum semiotic discomfort. The generic self-mutilation that ensues is not simply precipitated by Hogg's gesture of citing himself while inhabiting the persona of the Editor, however curious and destabilizing, but rather by the historical fact that this letter is actually 'authentic'—it really was written by Hogg, and it really was published in *Blackwood's* the previous year. Moreover, because it is certainly the source or starting point for Hogg's work on the novel, its authenticity threatens to unravel the entire framing fiction of the *Confessions*. If the letter points confusingly to a different Hogg to the one who successively ventriloquizes both Editor and Sinner, the problem is compounded by the fact that the *substance* of this real letter is none the less verifiably false; 'Hogg's' information on the site of the grave, checked by both the 'Editor' and subsequently by latter-day editors, proves to be actually incorrect and consciously misleading. At this point the letter reveals itself as at once impeccably, empirically authentic, and also, at the same time, absolutely subversive of disciplinary reading and of operative generic codes.

Undeterred by his own comparative fictionality, the rightly suspicious Editor sets out to verify the substance of this letter by application to its author, undertaking a journey to visit Hogg at his home in the Borders. He is accompanied in this inquisitorial project by his friend John Gibson Lockhart (real-life editor of *Blackwood's*, and Scott's son-in-law), and assisted by William Laidlaw, Scott's steward, who provides them with what are presumably some of Scott's own horses (in-jokes which serve to underscore the affinity of the Editor and his project with Scott's own novelistic persona and practice). However, instead of being able to ratify Hogg's letter by reference to its originating body—and here this conservative tactic is revealed, extraordinarily, as utterly sentimental in thrust—the Editor finds himself frustrated; for what he finds at the end of the road is only another textual version of 'James Hogg': the 'Ettrick Shepherd'. Hogg here makes his appearance only as the second self circulated by *Blackwood's*, the bucolic shepherd-poet who was in fact largely the creation of Hogg's colleague, John Croker Wilson, a self who speaks a very different language to that of the letter in question. The letter is therefore revealed as at once making claim to be thoroughly sentimental, in that it invokes an apparently verifiable autobiographical voice, and as fundamentally anti-sentimental, in that it proves to be radically severed from any such guarantee. The marker of the failure of the sentimental is here, conspicuously, the intervention of the mechanics of print, in the form of *Blackwood's*, between authorial body and published first-person anecdote.

A similar divorce between body and text, also associated ultimately with the duplicities and duplications of print-culture, informs the culminating episode of the novel, the final exhumation of the Sinner himself (from which the Ettrick Shepherd absents himself, claiming he has better things to do) and the discovery, on his body, of Wringhim's memoir. Initially it appears that both the body of the Sinner and the pamphlet buried with him undergo parallel fates—exhumation followed by dissemination by mail: 'I have . . . retained a small portion [of the corpse's garments] for you, which I send along with this, being a piece of his plaid, and another of his waistcoat breast, which you will see are still as fresh as that day they were laid in the grave' (244). However, if the body is thus conflated with its accompanying papers in some sort of gruesome archive in an evident effort to affix the memoir firmly to its author, the text itself, like Hogg's multiple personae, remains defiantly independent of the body. The symptom of this indiscipline is, paradoxically, the appended sample of the Sinner's handwriting. Appended in order to guarantee the manuscript's authenticity—to pin it down to one hand, one name, one body—what it actually displays is the latest technical innovation in printing. Sentimental textuality is thus elaborately adulterated by the visible interposition of print.

IV

Not quite adultery, but adulteration.

(Byron, *Don Juan* (xii. 63))[22]

Versions and descendants of the sentimental letter, however degraded, thus continued to trouble Regency texts, continuing to find certain modalities—such as the autobiographical and the Gothic—especially hospitable. Nowhere is its residual itinerary more clearly or startlingly traced than in the affair between Lord

---

[22] All references to *Don Juan* are from *Lord Byron: The Complete Poetical Works*, ed. Jerome J. McGann (6 vols., Oxford, 1986), v.

Byron and Lady Caroline Lamb, which generated a cross-generic literary duel that lasted from 1812 until 1824, the year of Byron's death. This Regency *roman à clef* reveals the ways in which actual subjects inhabited the patterns of generic negotiation which I have been charting in this study, occupying as it does in turn all the possible orientations on the sentimental letter available in the post-revolutionary period; however, as a strangely belated treatment, it recapitulates them in a strikingly vitiated register. As it evolves, the correspondence subjects the sentimental letter to a series of generic deformations which spring once again, as in *Liber Amoris* and *Confessions of a Justified Sinner*, from the problematic relation of sentimental text to body, and by extension, from the peculiar relation of sentimental authorship to print culture. Progressing from a whole-hearted espousal of the subject-position of the Rousseauistic heroine by Caroline Lamb in the lovers' initial correspondence, to her appropriation of Byron's own letters in the wake of the affair to constitute the core of an anti-Jacobin novel, *Glenarvon* (1816), which casts Byron as revolutionary villain, the literary traces of their involvement finally peter out with Byron's re-appropriation and dismemberment of the sentimental letter in *Don Juan* (1818–24), in which, under his treatment, the Lamb imbroglio metamorphoses into a burlesqued Gothic novelette.[23]

The affair between Lady Caroline Lamb and Lord Byron lasted, in a local sense, for about three months. They first met in early 1812 and conducted a wildly flagrant liaison, complete with all the appropriate and inappropriate manœuvres: indiscreet visits by Lamb, cross-dressed as a page-boy, to Byron's apartments; threatened elopement; passionate and consciously sentimental letters and equally sentimental gifts of and requests for jewellery and, interestingly, pubic hair. The aftermath of this clandestine correspondence was considerably longer and even more socially outrageous, culminating in Lamb's mock suicide attempt (worthy of Lady Olivia) at a major ball, which led directly to her exile from London society and to the Lamb family's first attempt to produce a separation from her husband, Sir William Lamb, on the grounds of insanity.

---

[23] For a more extended treatment both of the Lamb/Byron affair and of *Don Juan*, see Nicola J. Watson, 'Trans-figurations of Byronic Identity', in Mary A. Favret and Nicola J. Watson (eds.), *At the Limits of Romanticism: Essays in Cultural, Feminist, and Materialist Criticism* (Bloomington, Ind., 1994).

The body of letters which survives from this *amour*, despite its status as a historically verifiable, authentic correspondence, displays, like *Liber Amoris*, all the generic features of the sentimental/epistolary novel of passion. On her part, Lamb seems at one point to have fashioned their *billets-doux* into some sort of epistolary novel which, from her description, '—250 letters from a young Venetian nobleman—addrest to a very absurd English Lady—', sounds as though it would have borne a remarkable similarity in point of subject-matter to de Staël's *Corinne*.[24] Byron himself, during the prolonged aftermath of the affair, also explicitly read Lamb as casting their adulterous relationship within an extravagantly sentimental plot and discourse, identifying her letters as belonging to the genre of de Staël's *Delphine* and the 'German' sentimental novel in general.[25] As his remarks to his confidante Lady Melbourne (Lamb's mother-in-law), on 13 September 1812 suggest, he was to some large extent complicit in the production of this discourse:

In the mean time I must and do write the greatest absurdities to keep C[aroline] 'gay' & the more so because ye. last epistle informed me that '8 guineas a mail and a packet *could* soon bring her to London' a threat which immediately called forth a letter worthy of the Grand Cyrus or the Duke of York, or any other hero of Madame Scudery or Mrs. Clarke. (*BLJ* ii. 194).

However, in characterizing his own letters as 'worthy of the Grand Cyrus or the Duke of York,' Byron here insists on the conventionality of sentimental discourse and the subject-position it constructs, pointing out that it is available to literary impersonation. In so doing, he institutes a duplicitous gap between body and letter, a gap designed, appropriately enough, to maintain the distance between himself and Lamb. Furthermore, his remarks rewrite the sentimental in terms of Regency politics, conflating the hitherto revolutionary sentimental letter with shady Tory politics, and reserving the stance of literary pastiche to his broadly Whig position; the fantastic fustiness of French romance is collapsed

---

[24] Murray MSS; cited in Leslie Marchand, *Byron: A Biography* (2 vols., New York, 1957), 616.

[25] See Byron's letter to Lady Melbourne, November 10, 1812: '[Caroline's] letter to Ly. O[xford] was a long *German* tirade . . .', *Byron's Letters and Journals*, ed. Leslie A. Marchand (12 vols., London, 1973–82), ii. 244. (*BLJ* hereafter).

into the sordid politico-sentimental scandal of the sale of army commissions by the Duke of York's mistress, Mrs Clarke, on the proceeds of which she maintained her establishment: a scandal which, breaking in 1809, involved the extensive publication of their correspondence, and severely damaged the credibility of the Tory party.

This mobility of the politics of sentimental genre engineered via the mechanics of pastiche is homologous with another pervasive feature of the Lamb–Byron correspondence, a conspicuous deformation of the constitutive premise of the sentimental letter via the mechanisms of forgery. Supposedly functioning as an unironized substitute for the sincere body of the writer, the forged sentimental letter, like the Sinner's facsimile signature, puts into question the relation between originating body and signature.[26]

The first skirmish in what soon became a combat of mutual forgery was one of Lamb's earliest escapades after Byron broke off the affair, when she expertly faked a letter from Byron, supposedly to herself, in order to purloin his favourite portrait of himself—the so-called Newstead miniature—from John Murray, his publisher.[27] In producing this simulation of Byron, Lamb effectively masqueraded as him, in order to obtain a simulacrum of him.[28] So threatening seemed the importation of such 'Carolinish' *errata* into the Byronic text (which figured in a notable incident later when she even quoted his seal against him, strategically misquoting his family motto, 'Crede Byron', on her livery buttons as 'Ne "Crede

[26] Moreover, forgery, in producing a masquerade of authority, not only betrays its ambition of superseding the law of the father, but actually denies it, in the act denying also the law of genre. Cf. Derrida, op. cit.; also Susan Stewart, *Crimes of Writing: Problems in the Containment of Representation* (New York and Oxford, 1991), 146.

[27] For another reading of this episode, concerned with the ways in which Lamb's forgeries of and masquerades as Byron contested Byron's understanding of his own poetic authority, see James Soderholm, 'Lady Caroline Lamb: Byron's Miniature Writ Large', *Keats–Shelley Journal*, 40 (1991), 24–46.

[28] Although it appears that Lamb in the event did not make use of the letter, but simply stole the picture from Murray's empty rooms (*BLJ* ii. 11 n), Byron himself presumed that the forgery had been good enough, both of his handwriting ('the hand she imitates to perfection') and of his signature, to induce Murray to give up the miniature. On 8 Jan. 1813 he wrote to Murray: 'You have been imposed upon by a letter forged in my name to obtain the picture left in your possession . . . if you have the letter *retain* it . . . You will also be more cautious in the future & not allow anything of mine to pass from your hand without my *seal* as well as signature' (*BLJ* iii. 11).

Byron" '—*BLJ* iii. 9), that Byron wrote in March 1813 that he was thankful that at least he would get away without having seen Lamb at all: 'no bad thing for the original whatever may become of the copy' (*BLJ* ii. 26). If Byron registered this forgery as textual impersonation and adulteration—he later remarked to Henry Fox that Lamb 'has the power of imitating [my] hand to an alarming perfection and still possesses many of [my] letters which she may alter very easily'—he also read it in terms of another generic confusion, this time of gender: elsewhere he acknowledges the extraordinarily upsetting gender-inversion to which Caroline's burglary has subjected him by describing the theft as a rape upon himself as sentimental heroine, a parodic abduction of (Miss Harriet?) Byron, in the best traditions of the sentimental novel.[29] Writing again to Lady Melbourne, he requests her to 'recover my *effigy* if you can—it is very unfair after the restoration of her own— to be *ravished* in this way' (*BLJ* iii. 12).

Extricating himself from this perilously sentimental script, Byron evolved a response to this act of forgery on Lamb's part by mimicking its logic precisely, exacting revenge by imitation. Especially anxious to retrieve his likeness from his *quondam* mistress, because it had been requested most particularly by his new paramour, Lady Oxford, Byron eventually offered Lamb a copy of the miniature (*BLJ* iii. 11), and also acceded to Lamb's stipulation of the gift of a lock of Byron's hair—apparently offering a sentimental souvenir in the shape of an authentic and original part of the physical head in exchange for a mere representation of it.[30] In early April 1813, Byron sent to Lamb, along with a copy of the

[29] Ernest J. Lovell (ed.), *His Very Self and Voice: Collected Conversations of Lord Byron* (New York, 1954), 353.

[30] Lamb's fetishization of the original over the copy—while jealously retaining her authority to recirculate multiple facsimiles—is perhaps most poignantly illustrated in the melodramatic bonfire ritual she held at her home, Brocket Hall, some time during the autumn of 1812, in which she burnt both 'effigies' of the miniature of Byron and copies (she was unable to bring herself to part with the originals) of his letters. *The Works of Lord Byron. A New, Revised and Enlarged Edition, with Illustrations, Letters and Journals*, ed. Rowland E. Prothero (6 vols., London, 1898–1901) (*LJ* hereafter), ii. 447; Samuel Rogers, *Table-talk*, ed. G. H. Powell (London, 1903), 235. Lamb was still in the business of making copies of Byron's letters as late as 1824, when she wrote to Medwin: 'I have had one of his letters copied in the stone press for you; one just before we parted' (*LJ* ii. 452: see also *BLJ* ii. 185 n.). *Glenarvon* (as another repository or copy of those letters?) was itself eventually subjected to the same fate when Lamb burnt all her remaining copies of the novel.

miniature, a lock of 'double' hair which, though it resembled his own, was in fact that of Lady Oxford (*BLJ* iii. 36, 40). In effect Byron, under his own seal and signature, sent a clipping of Lady Oxford cross-dressed as 'Byron', sent, in fact, what was indeed a simulacrum. In so dissimulating himself within the structures of a sentimental exchange, he both withheld his own sentimental identity, and ironized the status of the sentimental letter as a metonym for the sentimental body. In short, this episode may be said to take the paradox at the heart of the sentimental epistolary novel—the reproduction and recirculation of the private, intrinsic letter—to its logical conclusion, subjecting it to the replications of the amatory marketplace.

More significantly for its sequel, this episode also recapitulates the systematic and devaluing recirculation of the letter and its analogues that Austen, amongst others, was carrying out in the contemporary novel proper, as Lamb registered by her response. In 1816 she published *Glenarvon*, a novel which retributively recycles Byron's gifts and letters, Lamb supplying its villain Glenarvon with certain passages transcribed directly from Byron's letters to her.[31] The logic of this act of citation precisely repeats that of an earlier letter from Byron; according to Lamb, her practice of quotation of Byron's letter in another context seems both to have been

---

[31] For the letters in question see *BLJ* ii. 242. In recirculating the figure of Byron and his letters, Lamb was simply replicating a practice of extraction, quotation, and recirculation that both she and Byron had indulged almost from the earliest days of the affair, as evidenced, for instance, by Byron's letter to Lady Melbourne of 18 Sept. 1812: 'I am not sorry that C[aroline] sends you extracts from my epistles, I deserve it for the passage I shewed once to you, but remember that was in the *outset* . . . Moreover recollect what absurdities a man must write to his Idol, & that "garbled extracts" prove nothing without the context' (*BLJ* ii. 200–1). The readings and rereadings that this correspondence underwent—what Byron dubbed extra '*winding*[s] to our *Labyrinth*' (*BLJ* ii. 203)—are therefore merely redoubled. The generic appropriateness of Lamb's action, however extreme, seems to be underscored by the curious fact that Byron seems to have anticipated this recirculation of his letters as early as Sept. 1812, when he wrote that 'I am certain that I tremble for the trunkfuls of my contradictions, since like a Minister or a woman she may one day exhibit them in some magazine or some quartos of villainous memoirs written in her 7000th love fit' (*BLJ* ii. 200–1); by December, during the complicated negotiations over the return of gifts and letters, he was writing 'She will not deliver up my letters—very well—I *will* deliver up hers nevertheless—& mine she may make the most of, they are very like the Duke of York's & the Editor of any magazine will treat with her for them on moderate terms. . . . I leave the story entirely to her own telling' (*BLJ* ii. 255–6). Byron himself, it may be remembered, had a reputation as an inveterate circulator of other's letters.

precipitated by and designed to repeat that letter's original frame of production—Byron's signature beneath another's seal: 'There was a coronet on the seal. The initials under the coronet were Lady Oxford's. It was that cruel letter I have published in *Glenarvon* ...'[32] This citation of Byron not only reproduces him under the 'seal' of Caroline Lamb, repeating the structure of the episode of the stolen miniature, but also allows Lamb to position the figure of Byron within a genre, the strategies of which, as I have already suggested, he had himself already begun to deploy—the anti-Jacobin novel.[33] This generic choice is carefully signalled in Lamb's preface to the second edition of *Glenarvon*, which insists that the novel was designed to inculcate an impeccably conservative moral: 'to enforce the danger of too entire liberty either of conduct, or of opinion; and to show that no endowments, no advantages, can insure happiness and security upon earth, unless we adhere to the forms as well as to the principles of religion and morality'.[34] Lamb thus secures the literary authority to produce her own hostile facsimile of Byron, who is figured at the heart of the text in the degenerate genre of the duplicitous (because both replicated and insincere) but nevertheless 'authentic' sentimental letter.

In Lamb's novel the author of Byron's letter is the glamorous but

[32] Lady Sydney Morgan, *Memoirs* (2 vols., London, 1868), ii. 201.

[33] For a differently inflected reading of *Glenarvon* (and parenthetically of Lamb's relationship with Byron) as structured by the conventions of sentimental fiction, see Gary Kelly, 'Amelia Opie, Lady Caroline Lamb, and Maria Edgeworth: Official and Unofficial Ideology', *Ariel* 12(4) (Oct. 1981), 3–24. Kelly rather oddly relates Lamb's novel to those of Amelia Opie, in particular her ambiguously feminist work *Adeline Mowbray* (1804), that meditates upon Mary Wollstonecraft's life and career.

[34] *Glenarvon* (2nd end., 2 vols., Philadelphia, 1816), i. p. vi. The preface to the second edition of *Glenarvon* was necessitated, in fact, by outraged responses to the excesses of the novel; responses that indeed included a self-consciously and indignantly anti-Jacobin novel by Elizabeth Thomas entitled *Purity of Heart* (1816) which conflates Lamb's own scandalous exploits with those of her heroines Calantha and Elinor in the adventures of Lady Calantha Limb, a recirculation of the sentimental heroine reminiscent of that practised upon Hazlitt. As self-exculpation, Lamb's preface is therefore to some extent suspect. None the less, however entangled the novel is between its incompatible impulses on the one hand to ratify or be seduced by the glamour of revolutionary passion and on the other hand simultaneously to condemn it as socially transgressive, the plot-line is recognizably 'anti-Jacobin' despite the disruptive energies that constantly overflow. For a view of this novel as a 'novel of passion' (which would rank it as ambiguously revolutionary in its sympathies), see Kelly, *English Fiction of the Romantic Period*, 185–7.

reprehensible Lord Glenarvon—a stereotypical philosophic free-thinker who seduces on revolutionary principles.[35] Represented both as the leader of the 1798 Irish rebellion and as a seasoned libertine (no fewer than six mistresses appear in the text), Glenarvon seduces the sentimental Calantha (a conflation of Caroline Lamb herself and Julie). Like Scott's Colonel Mannering, her husband, Lord Avondale, succeeds temporarily in suppressing political unrest in the public sphere, only to have it break out more uncontrollably in the domestic register.[36] Surprisingly, Glenarvon is eventually exculpated, undergoing a conversion back to the right cause of Britain—a manœuvre that recalls Morgan's similar attempts to enlist the sentimental in the service of nationalism. None the less, truer at the last moment to anti-Jacobin convention, Lamb provides a thoroughly familiar *grande débâcle* in which Glenarvon is driven to suicide and thence snatched to hell by a ghostly Black Friar, a fate not insignificantly reminiscent of that of another of Glenarvon's avatars, Don Giovanni. Byron is thus identified by Lamb as Don Juan two years before he begins work on his own poem.

Voluminous and vitriolic as Byron's letters are on this subject, his best-known comment upon the whole Lamb affair may be found in Canto II of *Don Juan*, where it appears in the context of a meditation upon the effects on women of frustrated libido: 'Some play the devil, and then write a novel' (ii. 152). The carelessness of this throwaway line (belied by its privileged position as the punch-rhyme) obscures the ways in which *Don Juan* is pervasively engaged with *Glenarvon*—determined, in particular, to wrench to its own uses the figures of the sentimental letter and of the

---

[35] For another attempt to consider the political valences of *Glenarvon* see Malcolm Kelsall, 'The Byronic Hero and Revolution in Ireland: The Politics of *Glenarvon*', in Edwin A. Stürzl and James Hogg (eds.), *Byron: Poetry and Politics* (Salzburg, Austria, 1981), 137–51. Kelsall argues that Lamb's novel 'reveals the inherent contradictions of the Whig ideology in which she was reared and the utility of the Byronic myth in providing a scapegoat for the failure of her society to find a solution to the Irish problem' (138). Kelsall, while registering the presence of Revolution and revolutionary philosophy in the text, fails to recognize the genres upon which it draws.

[36] The mutual imbrication of the narratives of revolution and seduction is further underlined when Glenarvon gives Calantha a ring: 'It was an emerald with a harp engraved upon it—the armorial bearing of Ireland: "let us be firm and united," was written under. "I mean it merely politically," he said, smiling. "Even were you a Clarissa, you need not be alarmed: I am no Lovelace, I promise you" ' (i. 233–4).

supernatural monk.[37] *Don Juan* describes a formally anti-Jacobinical trajectory from the burlesqued sentimental to the travestied Gothic, in the process systematically dismantling both versions of revolutionary genre by deploying in amplified form the strategies evident in the Lamb/Byron correspondence. Just as in his dealings with Lamb, Byron worked his way through available conventions of authentic feeling with increasing levels of duplicity, so in *Don Juan* even the most apparently immutable textual figures—epistolary heroines, sentimental letters, avenging gothic ghosts—are destabilized by their re-circulation (amounting to serial mutation) through incompatible genres and irreconcilable bodies. Quotation of letters out of context and under another 'seal' modulates into cannibalism; forgery expands into cross-dressing. The result is a fundamental undoing of exhausted radical genres, the elegant dance of a 'metrical novel' on the grave of the epistolary heroine. Such an undoing of the sentimental privileges instead adulteration, impersonation, pastiche, and inauthenticity.

As the above account of *Glenarvon* implicitly suggests, Byron's choice of Don Juan as a hero is hardly as carelessly pragmatic and irresponsibly expedient as his breezy opening remarks would imply; despite his impeccable mother (likened to the heroines of Maria Edgeworth and Hannah More, amongst others), the character and adventures of Don Juan neatly approximate, however ironically, to those of the standard Jacobinical villain. According to Byron's advertised plan, his poem was to conclude by consigning Juan to 'The very place where wicked people go' (i. 207); however sketchily and flippantly (especially given that Juan was apparently to die, in this projected ending, of sexual exhaustion), Juan would have repeated the awful fate of Glenarvon—especially since, according to the 'Memoranda' on the Murray manuscript of the last canto of the poem as it stands, 'The D[eath] of J[uan]' was to be specifically associated with 'The Shade of the/Friar'. Byron at one stage explicitly politicized Juan's prospective fate by proposing that his hero should end his days during the Terror at the hands of the French Revolutionaries (again, a fate suffered by a number of similar villains, notably Isaac

---

[37] For an attempt to consider these two texts together as rival versions of the Don Juan myth, see Peter W. Graham, 'A Don, Two Lords, and a Lady', *Don Juan and Regency England* (Charlottesville, Va., 1990), 89–124.

D'Israeli's Vaurien, 1797) courtesy of Madame La Guillotine (which ending Byron, of course, never executed).[38]

Like *Glenarvon*, too, *Don Juan* takes its departure from a sentimental letter—one markedly deflated, however, by its frame. Don Juan's initial escapade, recounted in Cantos I and II (composed in 1818), is firmly based upon *La Nouvelle Héloïse*, and may usefully be glossed by Byron's remark to Murray that *Don Juan* was not liked by women because 'the wish of all women [is] to exalt the *sentiment* of the passions—& to keep up the illusion which is their empire.—Now D.J. strips off this illusion—& laughs at that & most other things.—I never knew a woman who did not protect *Rousseau*' (6 July 1821: *BLJ* viii. 148). Like much of the first two cantos, as I shall show, this comment suggests that Byron at this stage viewed *Don Juan* as antithetical to the sentimental Rousseau. In Byron's Hispanic variant on Rousseau's plot, Donna Julia, the heroine of Juan's first imbroglio, is 'married, charming, chaste, and twenty-three' (i. 59), married, in fact, to a much older man, in parallel to Julie after her marriage to her father's choice, Wolmar. Julia's struggles with her growing passion for Juan, despite her attempts to relegate it to a purely Platonic connection, end at last in adultery, in pregnancy, and at length in discovery, Juan's disgrace and exile, and Julia's banishment to a convent. Byron in fact goes so far as to underline slyly Julia's near relationship to her French sister:

> And if in the mean time her husband died . . .
>   Never could she survive that common loss;
> But just suppose that moment should betide,
>   I only say suppose it—*inter nos*—
> (This should be *entre nous*, for Julia thought
> In French, but then the rhyme would go for nought.)
>
> (i. 84)[39]

---

[38] 'I meant to . . . make him finish as *Anarcharsis Cloots* [Prussian aristocrat imprisoned in the Terror under Robespierre and executed March 1794] in the French revolution' *BLJ* 8, 78 (Feb. 16, 1821). See also Thomas Medwin, *Medwin's Conversations of Lord Byron*, ed. Ernest J. Lovell Jr. (Princeton, NJ, 1966), 165 (*c*.Dec. 1821 and Mar. 1822). For a discussion of the historical frames of *Don Juan*, see Jerome McGann, *The Beauty of Inflections: Literary Investigations in Historical Method and Theory* (Oxford, 1985), 264 ff.

[39] For a reading of Cantos I and II that similarly connects the figure of Donna Julia with Rousseau's Julie see Lawrence Lipking, *Abandoned Women and Poetic*

However, unlike Julie's letters to her lover, St Preux, which always signal a lapse away from the authority of the law of the father, the sentimental letter written by this latest Eloisa from the convent is notably powerless, largely because it appears so intransigently self-reflexive, so narcissistically caught up in its own generic laws.[40] The sardonic detail of the stanza immediately following the close of the letter shows the epistolary heroine to be engaged, not in entirely spontaneous and quasi-bodily effusion, but in the crafting of a conventional and material discourse, a discourse not of revolution but of self-fetishization:

> This note was written upon gilt-edged paper
>   With a neat crow-quill, rather hard but new.
> Her small white hand could hardly reach the taper,
>   But trembled as magnetic needles do,
> And yet she did not let one tear escape her.
>   The seal a sunflower; *Elle vous suit partout*,
> The motto cut upon a white cornelian;
> The wax was superfine, its hue vermilion.   (i. 198)

Tradition (Chicago, 1988), 32–56. Lipking also connects Julia with de Staël (36–7). Lipking's reading registers the aggression encoded within this episode towards the figure of the abandoned woman as primarily autobiographical; as will become clear, while I do connect the autobiographical with the poem, I am not interested in positing a strictly causal relationship, preferring instead to present the generic homologies between Byron's negotiations with Lamb and his negotiations with Rousseau as crucially informed by a politics of genre.

[40] The relationship, mediated through Pope, was noted by one contemporary review, which considered Julia's letter to be 'equal, in its way, to the celebrated epistle of Eloisa'. Quoted in Bernard Blackstone, *Byron: A Survey* (London, 1975), 299. In view of my remarks on Austen's revision of the scene of epistolary desire at the end of *Persuasion* it is of great interest that Austen's scene is apparently itself revised by Byron in this scene. Julia's lament, expressed in this letter, that 'Man's love is of man's life a thing apart, | 'Tis woman's whole existence; man may range | The court, camp, church, the vessel and the mart, | Sword, gown, glory, offer in exchange | Pride, fame, ambition, to fill up his heart . . . | Man has all these resources, we but one, | To love again, and be again undone' (i. 194) bears a remarkable similarity to Anne's remarks to Captain Harville on women's long constancy, against which Wentworth's letter is written antiphonally ('We certainly do not forget you, so soon as you forget us. . . . We live at home, quiet, confined, and our feelings prey upon us. You are forced to exertion. You have always a profession, pursuits, business of some sort or other, to take you back into the world immediately . . .' Austen, *Works*, v. 232). So close is the verbal echo (although it should be noted that Byron emphatically does *not* celebrate women's constancy here), that Jerome McGann has suggested that Byron may actually have seen the manuscript of Austen's novel before publication through the medium of their common publisher, Murray (*Complete Poetical Works*, v. 680).

As Julia Epstein has remarked, 'the "true art of letter-writing" in the eighteenth-century . . . relied upon the letter's concealing its nature as a *written* artifact'.[41] Here, however, the invocation of the material and the calculated, strongly reminiscent of the materialization of the letter carried out by Edgeworth and Austen, intrudes to seal up and alienate the letter's emotional power.

The discrepancy thus inserted between the content and the materiality of the letter is expanded to its fullest extent in the story of the disintegration of this very letter (what Shelley percipiently called its 'appropriation'), which marks the moment of the decisive evacuation of the sentimental epistolary novel.[42] Byron subjects Donna Julia's effusion to the violent demands of a series of emphatically anti-sentimental (although bathetically physical) masculine bodies: Juan's first rereading of it on board ship is interrupted by seasickness, and the second 'rereading' also eventually induces vomiting, when the starving shipwrecked mariners agree to draw lots to decide 'who should die to be his fellow's food' (ii. 73):

> At length the lots were torn up and prepared,
>   But of materials that much shock the Muse.
> Having no paper, for the want of better,
>   They took by force from Juan Julia's letter. (ii. 74)

The dismemberment of the sentimental letter (and, by metonymic inference, of Julia's body, a dismemberment which thus prefigures Maturin's tale of sentimental cannibalism) followed by its promiscuous dissemination, results in the dismemberment, dissemination, and consumption of Juan's surrogate father, his Rousseauistic tutor, Pedrillo; the consequences of this recycling of revolutionary philosophy are, just as always in the anti-Jacobin novel, madness, blasphemy, despair, and death—in this instance with the familiar trope of ideological 'poisoning' rendered grotesquely literal. But if the effects of devouring Rousseau in this fashion are fatal, there is one figure so contaminated that the starving mariners will not even consider taking the risk, a figure similarly related to the genre of *La Nouvelle Héloïse*:

[41] 'Fanny Burney's Epistolary Voices', *The Eighteenth Century*, 27 (1986), 177.
[42] Letter to Byron, 26 May 1820. *Letters of Percy Bysshe Shelley*, ed. Frederick L. Jones (2 vols., Oxford, 1964), ii. 198.

And next they thought upon the master's mate
As fattest, but he saved himself, because,
Besides being much averse from such a fate,
There were some other reasons: the first was
He had been rather indisposed of late,
And that which chiefly proved his saving clause
Was a small present made to him at Cadiz,
By general subscription of the ladies.   (ii. 81)

The venereal infection that saves the master's mate here acts as a model of the novel, published by subscription, and distastefully subject to general circulation among women; indeed, it is only the mate's kinship with the circulating library (regularly castigated for poisoning the young women who consumed its contents) that saves him from a less metaphoric consumption. Rousseau and the novelistic are here connected, as they generally were by contemporaries, as at once poisonous and (sexually) contagious.

Although this sequence would appear to mock, violate, and ultimately suppress altogether the revolutionary power of the sentimental, the voiding of the letter, surprisingly, does not lead to the re-establishment of paternal law as might be expected, but instead actually to the eating of the man who stands, however dubiously, in the place of Juan's father. This unexorcised unlawfulness resurfaces at the end of the poem as it stands, in Canto XVI, in the burlesque Gothic novelette which centres on the problematic ghost of the Black Friar, a figure which, like the letter, persistently puts into question the validity of paternal authority. Affiliated with a series of dubiously legitimate paternal figures, this figure (like the letter, a demystified revenant) finally breaks apart generic expectations; in indulging in this elaborate game of generic deformation, Byron would seem to recast something of the radical vagaries of the letter.

Fetching up in England, guest in Lord and Lady Amundeville's house-party, held at a venue at once Gothic and autobiographical (the house looks altogether very like Byron's family home, Newstead Abbey), Juan encounters what appears to be the resident ghost, the Black Friar. In addition to functioning as a citation or repetition of the Friar who drags Lord Glenarvon off to Hell, this figure also inescapably encodes that of 'Viviani', the initial alias of Lord Glenarvon in Lamb's novel. More mischievously, the Friar also serves as an allusion to the real-life 'masquerade-attitude' adopted by Byron at the most brilliant gathering of the London season of 1814, which itself probably furnished Lamb with trappings for her character, alluding as it did on the one hand to a whole series of Mephistophelean literary monks (most notoriously Ambrosio, the Faustian sensualist of Matthew Lewis's *The Monk* (1796) and Gothic successors such as Mrs Radcliffe's Schedoni in *The Italian* (1797)), and on the other to Byron's own youthful propensities for dressing up as a monk, hiding in coffins, quaffing blood from a specially mounted skull, and supposedly leading satanic orgies at Newstead Abbey. The problematically double nature of this figure—at once a figure of paternal and divine law and a figure for revolutionary transgression—calls up, on its first appearance, a constellation of other literary allusions and generic signals, all of which figure an oddly perverted or detoured paternal interdiction against sexuality. Indeed, Byron mischievously and appropriately puts this faintly absurd, not to say petulant, prohibition under the imprimatur of his friend and rival, Sir Walter Scott; according to the expert pastiche of Scott's ballads that the Lady Adeline Amundeville composes and performs, the monk haunts the family of the Amundevilles, particularly at moments when patrilineal succession is at issue: 'By the marriage-bed of their lords, 't is said | He flits on the bridal eve; | And 't is held as faith, to their bed of Death | He comes—but not to grieve. | When an heir is born, he's heard to mourn . . .' (xvi. 3–4). Most pertinently, however, this supposedly 'supernatural agent' claims a genealogy from old Hamlet, announced as it is on its first materialization by what Juan thinks might be 'a mouse, | Whose little nibbling rustle will embarrass | Most people as it plays along the arras' (xvi. 20–1). This rodent behind the arras, however, will turn out to be neither Claudius nor Polonius, but the figure of a ghostly father perhaps equally dubious, who will show far less interest than we might expect in the revenge that both old Hamlet and his analogue the Commendatore (released according to the traditional account from the precincts of a monastery) conventionally exact.[43]

The equivocal political, etymological, and generic status of this figure of the father—avenging Old Hamlet? burlesque Viviani?

---

[43] In this context it is of interest that Byron finds fault with the logic of the ghost in *Hamlet* in a (possibly apocryphal) conversation with Shelley recorded in the *New Monthly Magazine*, NS 29 (1830), 327–36.

silenced Commendatore?[44]—is reiterated more signally in the episode of the Black Friar's second portentous appearance, appropriately enough, as from Dante's Hell (xvi. 116), and equally appropriately, given the parallel to *Hamlet*, in Juan's bedroom, which finds Juan 'completely *sans culotte*' (xvi. 111), in comic keeping with Byron's projected anti-Jacobin ending. However, Juan's pursuit ends in a transformation scene from 'stony death' to living flesh, that translates *Don Giovanni* into an indecently travestied version of that patrilineal romance, *The Winter's Tale*, which appears so regularly as a subtext to Scott's novels:

> Back fell the sable frock and dreary cowl,
> And they revealed—alas! that e'er they should!
> In full, voluptuous, but *not o'er*grown bulk,
> The phantom of her frolic Grace—Fitz-Fulke! (xvi. 123)

Like Scott, who in *The Antiquary* unmasks Dousterswivel's wizardry as fraudulent, Byron shows the supernatural to be a matter of trickery associated with the revolutionary; Byron's demystification, however, unlike Scott's, shows the real figure to be more rather than less revolutionary.[45] Old Hamlet's 'gracious figure' proving actually to be 'her gracious, graceful, graceless Grace'—an altogether accessible and thoroughly adulterous Gertrude—the father is replaced by the transgressive woman.[46] If

---

[44] The ghost's perplexing generic ambiguity is amplified by Juan's choice of reading matter to exorcise it: retiring to bed after its first appearance, he calms his mind by reading a political pamphlet which attacks the king, a commercial advertisement for 'Patent Blacking' (suggesting the purely external status of the friar's sableness?), and a paragraph about Horne Tooke, noted radical, friend of William Godwin, and author of an iconoclastic philosophy of grammar, *The Diversions of Purley* (1786–1805), an allusion which therefore raises the question of the Treason Trials simultaneously with the problem of the apparition's grammatical and epistemological status (xvi. 26–7). For a consideration of Byron's poetry in the light of Horne Tooke's philosophy of language which nevertheless unaccountably ignores this passage, see L. E. Marshall, ' "Words are *things*": Byron and the Prophetic Efficacy of Language', *SEL* 25 (1985), 801–22.

[45] This is not to deny that Byron also preserves the supernatural as deliberately paternally threatening—there is nothing to suggest that on its first appearance the ghost is not authentically supernatural. In this he is also paralleling the other appearance of the supernatural in *The Antiquary* in the shape of the possible ghost of Old Aldobrand, a figure who is identified at once with patrilinealism and with Hanoverian loyalty.

[46] This figure is thus related to the unsettling properties of the pun, which, Julia Kristeva has argued, are in some sense both 'revolutionary' and feminine. On this point, see *Revolution in Poetic Language*, trans. Margaret Waller (New York, 1984).

adultery bred generic adulteration in the initial Lamb–Byron correspondence, here, contrariwise, generic (and genderic) adulteration actually allows for and sanctions adultery.

The Duchess of Fitz-Fulke is effectively the last appearance of the sentimental letter, however travestied, in the poem as we have it; not only does this figure bear more than a passing resemblance to the unfortunate novice in *Melmoth the Wanderer* (herself related, as I have argued, to the sentimental letter), but she is related to that other woman in an incongruous habit, functioning, as W. Paul Elledge remarks, as 'a ghostly iteration of a habited Julia deceitfully writing from another monastic house'.[47] Moreover, as a hieroglyph of cross-dressing, Fitz-Fulke presents herself as yet another illegible text.[48] She further combines in a vulgarized register a number of features familiarly associated with the sentimental heroine as imagined by conservatives: she is in the habit of conducting adulterous flirtations that make young men into suicidal Werthers (xiv. 64); her name indicates that, like so many Jacobinical villains, she is not only Irish, but from an illegitimate branch of the family; and she refigures Glenarvon's female counterpart, the cross-dressing Irish revolutionary Elinor, herself a figure (albeit a more Amazonian one than the victimized Calantha) for Caroline Lamb.

This radical displacement of the father by this compromised revolutionary precludes punitive closure except in terms of a rather problematic pun: in that the reader is permitted to infer that this ghostly cross-dresser successfully seduces Juan, it might, for instance, be possible to say that Juan is, if not literally, then metaphorically, 'snatched' to 'Hell' in the embraces of the fair Fitz-Fulke. At stake in this replacement of the properly anti-Jacobin with the actually adulterous and quasi-sentimental seems to be an anxiety about the legitimacy of fathers, and a definite preference for their absence, which (coded through a highly critical reading of *Hamlet* which, as Gary Taylor has argued, was a text vivified in the 1790s by anxieties over the status of the monarchy) may translate into a definite distaste for the general process of Restoration that

---

[47] W. Paul Elledge, 'Immaterialistic Matters: Byron, Bogles and Bluebloods', *Papers on Language and Literature*, 25 (1989), 279.

[48] Marjorie Garber, *Vested Interests: Cross-Dressing and Cultural Anxiety* (New York, 1992), 188. On cross-dressing in *Don Juan* see esp. Susan J. Wolfson, ' "Their She Condition": Cross-dressing and the Politics of Gender in *Don Juan*', *ELH* 54 (1987), 585–617.

governed Europe in the post-Napoleonic era.[49] In other words, the sentimental letter is here being re-scripted as radical in Regency terms. *Don Juan* transposes Jacobinical libertinism into Whig liberalism by transforming the Gothic discrepancy that Hogg chose to preserve back into the sentimental letter, albeit in altered, travestied state.

Postscript

As Byron's quite extraordinarily sardonic and sophisticated handling of the sentimental paradigm might suggest, by 1825, the year that the woman featured on my frontispiece, Miss Harriette Wilson, published her celebrated *Memoirs*, the sentimental letter was threadbare and *déclassée* in the extreme. *La Côtérie Debouché* [*sic*], at once censorious and half-seduced, mockingly celebrates the half-French Harriette Wilson for embodying, as one of her admirers ecstatically sighs, 'the soul of sentiment' (her *Memoirs*, indeed, insistently cast her affair with Lord Ponsonby as a tear-jerking sentimental tragedy) while simultaneously identifying her as a sordid and promiscuous entrepreneur, trading in the cheapened, ridiculous sentiments of her ex-lovers (who include Caroline Lamb's brother and brother-in-law), as she re-cycles their indiscreet letters as her extremely lucrative recollections. This pirate illustration to her *Memoirs* thus not only encodes in its 'elegant figure' the connection between the sentimental letter and illicit female sexuality that I have been detailing throughout this study; it also condenses in miniature the evolution of the sentimental letter from the reflection of the genuine, noble, and essentially private sentiments of the heart (a transcription of the body), into a printed commodity, which, like its author, circulates speculatively around the raffish parts of town. The only thing which can close down that circulation, apparently, is the intervention of national authority—

---

[49] *Reinventing Shakespeare: A Cultural History* (New York, 1989), 102 ff. For a reading which notes that Hamlet consistently appears in the work of Coleridge, Byron, and Shelley as the figure of the impotent intellectual in Napoleonic Europe as opposed to the man of action, Napoleon himself, figured by contrast most frequently as the regicide usurper, Macbeth, see Malcolm Kelsall, 'Hamlet, Byron, and an "Age of Despair" ', in Michael Gassenmeier (ed.), *Beyond the Suburbs of the Mind: Exploring English Romanticism* (Essen, 1987), 40–54.

just as Wilson's threatened sequel was suppressed by an embarrassed Establishment, personified in another topical print, 'Doing *Penance on a Black Lamb*', by the most notable of her former associates, the national hero and future Prime Minister, the Duke of Wellington.[50]

However travestied and disgraced by 1825, as the examples of Byron and Wilson demonstrate so vividly (and indeed simultaneously: Wilson's recollections at one point provide what is probably a spurious account of a conversation with Byron about the real letters in *Glenarvon*),[51] the epistolary would remain a surreptitious but troubling ghost in the fiction of the nineteenth century and beyond, still carrying the residual meanings assigned to it by the struggle over the form of the novel that, as I have tried to show, was so intimately connected with the Revolution which is commonly regarded as having ushered in the era in which we live. Retaining something of its scandalously sexualized nature, something of its secretive ability to disrupt the smooth and public process of patrilineal history, the errant letter continued, and even now continues, to appear in the place of forbidden female sexuality: treasonously adulterous, as in Edgar Allan Poe's 'The Purloined Letter'; unsettlingly prone to metamorphose into ghostly (not to say conventual) figurations, as in Charlotte Brontë's *Villette*; equally liable to induce transfiguration by way of cross-dressing, as in Sir Arthur Conan Doyle's 'A Scandal in Bohemia'; or simply as the sign that must be read aright so as to reinstate patrilineal romance and the fortunes of Britain, as in A. S. Byatt's *Possession*. Characteristically taking as their project the detection and discipline of the errant letter, a process that parallels almost invariably the disciplining of the writing woman, such fictions simply extend Mr Knightley's project of right reading; for their well-founded suspicion is, along with that of one of Conan Doyle's country detectives, that however hard it is to decode the letter, it will generally point to the same subversive figure: 'I make nothing of the note except that there was something on hand, and that a woman, as usual, was at the bottom of it'.[52]

[50] Isaac Cruikshank, 1825. Wilson is shown astride a black ram, the traditional penance for unchastity, while Wellington remarks, 'A pretty mess we have made of it but *She must be taught a great moral lesson*'.

[51] *Memoirs of Herself and Others* [1825], ed. James Laver (New York, 1929), 588–93.

[52] Sir Arthur Conan Doyle, 'The Adventure of Wisteria Lodge', in *His Last Bow* [1917] (London, 1962), 17.

Bibliography

ADAMS, M. RAY, 'Helen Maria Williams and the French Revolution', in Earl Leslie Griggs (ed.), *Wordsworth and Coleridge* [1939] (New York, 1962), 87–117.

—— *Studies in the Literary Background of English Radicalism with Special Reference to the French Revolution* (Lancaster, Pa., 1947).

ALEXANDER, PETER F., ' "Robin Adair" as a Musical Clue in Jane Austen's *Emma*', *RES* NS 39 (1988), 84–6.

ALLEN, B. SPRAGUE, 'The Reaction Against William Godwin', *Modern Philosophy*, 16 (1918), 57–75.

ALLISTON, APRIL, 'The Value of a Literary Legacy: Retracing the Transmission of Value through Female Lines', *Yale Journal of Criticism*, 4 (1990), 109–27.

ALTMAN, JANET GURKIN, *Epistolarity: Approaches to a Form* (Columbus, Oh., 1982).

Ambrose and Eleanor, or the adventures of two children deserted on an uninhabited island. (Translated from the French).—'Providence is their Pilot'—To which is added, Auguste and Madelaine. A Real History. By Miss Helen Maria Williams (Wiscasset, Me., 1797).

Analytical Review (London, 1788–1808).

ANDERSON, BENEDICT, *Imagined Communities: Reflections on the Origin and Spread of Nationalism* (London, 1983).

Anti-Jacobin Review and Magazine, The; or, Monthly Political and Literary Censor (London, 1799–1810).

ARAC, JONATHAN, and RITVO, HARRIET (eds.), *Macropolitics of Nineteenth-Century Literature: Nationalism, Exoticism, Imperialism* (Philadelphia, 1991).

ARMSTRONG, NANCY, *Desire and Domestic Fiction: A Political History of the Novel* (Oxford, 1987).

—— and TENNENHOUSE, LEONARD (eds.), *The Ideology of Conduct: Essays in Literature and the History of Sexuality* (New York, 1987).

AUSTEN, JANE, *Jane Austen's Letters*, ed. R. W. Chapman (2 vols., London, 1932).

—— *The Oxford Illustrated Jane Austen*, ed. R. W. Chapman (6 vols., Oxford, 1967), i.e. *The Novels of Jane Austen*, ed. R. W. Chapman (3rd edn., 5 vols., Oxford, 1933), with vol. vi, *Minor Works*, ed. R. W. Chapman (1954), rev. B. C. Southam (Oxford, 1967).

BARRETT, EATON STANNARD, *The Heroine; or, Adventures of Cherubina* [1813] (3 vols., London, 1815).

BARROW, WILLIAM, *An Essay on Education* (2 vols., London, 1802).

BAYFIELD, E. G., *The Corinna of England; and a Heroine in the Shade. A Modern Romance* (2 vols., London, 1809).

BEASLEY, JERRY C., *English Fiction 1610–1800: A Guide to Information Sources* (Ann Arbor, Mich., 1978).

BISSET, ROBERT, *Douglas; or, The Highlander. A Novel* (4 vols., London, 1800).

—— *Modern Literature: A Novel* (3 vols., London, 1804).

BLACK, FRANK GEES, *The Epistolary Novel in the Late Eighteenth Century: A Descriptive and Bibliographical Study* (Eugene, Ore., 1940).

BLACKSTONE, BERNARD, *Byron: A Survey* (London, 1975).

BLOCK, ANDREW, *The English Novel 1740–1850: A Catalogue* (London, 1961).

BOWLES, J[OHN], *Reflections at the Conclusion of the War* (2nd edn., London, 1801).

—— *A View of the Moral State of Society, at the Close of the Eighteenth Century, Much Enlarged, and Continued to the Commencement of the Year 1804, with a Preface Addressed Particularly to the Higher Orders* (London, 1804).

BOWSTEAD, DIANA, 'Charlotte Smith's *Desmond*: The Epistolary Novel as Ideological Argument', in Mary Anne Schofield and Cecilia Macheski (eds.), *Fetter'd or Free? British Women Novelists, 1670–1815* (Athens, Oh., 1986), 230–64.

BRINTON, CRANE, *The Political Ideas of the English Romanticists* (London, 1926).

BRISSENDEN, R. F., *Virtue in Distress: Studies in the Novel of Sentiment from Richardson to Sade* (London, 1974).

BROWN, DAVID, *Walter Scott and the Historical Imagination* (London, 1979).

BROWN, HOMER OBED, 'The Errant Letter and the Whispering Gallery', *Genre*, 10 (Winter 1977), 574–92.

BROWN, JULIA PREWITT, *Jane Austen's Novels: Social Change and Literary Form* (Cambridge, Mass., 1979).

BROWN, LAURA and NUSSBAUM, FELICITY (eds.), *The New Eighteenth Century: Theory, Politics, English Literature* (New York, 1987).

BRUNTON, MARY, *Discipline* (3 vols., Edinburgh, 1814).

BURGES, MARY ANNE, *The Progress of the Pilgrim of Good-Intent in Jacobinical Times* (London, 1800).

BURKE, EDMUND, *Reflections on the Revolution in France* [1790], ed. Conor Cruise O'Brien (Harmondsworth, 1982).

—— *The Works of the Right Honourable Edmund Burke* (6 vols., London, 1882–4).

BURNEY, FRANCES, *The Wanderer; or, Female Difficulties* (5 vols., London, 1814).

BURROW, J. W., *A Liberal Descent* (Cambridge, 1981).

BUTLER, MARILYN SPEERS, *Jane Austen and the War of Ideas* (Oxford, 1975).

—— *Maria Edgeworth: A Literary Biography* (Oxford, 1972).

—— *Romantics, Rebels and Reactionaries: English Literature and its Background 1760–1830* (Oxford, 1981).

—— 'Telling It Like a Story: The French Revolution as Narrative', *Studies in Romanticism*, 28 (Fall 1989), 345–56.

BYRON, GEORGE GORDON, LORD, *Byron's Letters and Journals*, ed. Leslie Marchand (12 vols., London, 1973–82).

—— *Lord Byron: The Complete Poetical Works*, ed. Jerome J. McGann (6 vols., Oxford, 1986).

—— *The Works of Lord Byron: A New, Revised and Enlarged Edition, with Illustrations, Letters and Journals*, ed. Rowland E. Prothero (6 vols., London, 1898–1901).

CALAHAN, JAMES M., *The Irish Novel* (Boston, 1988).

CASTLE, TERRY, *Clarissa's Ciphers: Meaning and Disruption in Richardson's 'Clarissa'* (Ithaca, NY, 1982).

—— *Masquerade and Civilisation* (Stanford, Calif., 1986).

'CLOVER, ANDREW', *Popular Opinions, or, A Picture of Real Life, Exhibited in a Dialogue between a Scotish Farmer and a Weaver, . . . To Which is added, an Epistle from the Farmer to Elizabeth Hamilton, Author of the Cottagers of Glenburnie, in Scotish Verse* (Glasgow, 1812).

[COMBE, WILLIAM], *Letters of an Italian Nun and an English Gentleman. Translated from the French of Jean Jacques Rousseau* [1781] (2nd edn., 2 vols., London, 1784).

Copies of Original Letters recently written by Persons in Paris to Dr. Priestley in America. Taken on Board a Neutral Vessel (London, 1798).

COX, STEPHEN, 'Sensibility as Argument', in Syndy McMillen Conger (ed.), *Sensibility in Transformation: Creative Resistance to Sentiment from the Augustans to the Romantics* (London, 1990), 63–82.

Critical Review (London, 1756–90).

DALLAS, ROBERT CHARLES, *Percival, or Nature Vindicated* (4 vols., London, 1801).

—— *Sir Francis Darrell; or, the Vortex* (4 vols., London, 1820).

D'ARBLAY, MME, *see* Burney, Frances.

DAY, ROBERT ADAMS, *Told in Letters: Epistolary Fiction before Richardson* (Ann Arbor, Mich., 1966).

Defence of the Character and Conduct of the Late Mary Wollstonecraft Godwin, A. In a series of letters to a Lady (London and Oxford, 1803).

DE MAN, PAUL, *Allegories of Reading* (New Haven, Conn., 1979).

DERRIDA, JACQUES, 'La Loi du Genre | The Law of Genre', *Glyph*, 7 (1980), 202–29.

D'ISRAELI, ISAAC, *Flim Flams!* (3 vols., London, 1805).

—— *Vaurien: or Sketches of the Times* (2 vols., London, 1797).

DOBSON, MICHAEL, ' "Remember | First to Possess his Books": The Appropriation of *The Tempest*, 1700–1800', *Shakespeare Survey*, 43 (1991), 99–108.

DOODY, MARGARET ANNE, 'English Women Novelists and the French Revolution', in *La Femme en Angleterre et dans les colonies américaines aux VIIe et XVIIIe siècles* (Lille, 1975).

—— *Frances Burney: The Life in the Works* (New Brunswick, NJ, 1988).

Dorothea; or, A Ray of the New Light (3 vols., London, 1801).

DOYLE, SIR ARTHUR CONAN, *His Last Bow* [1917] (London, 1962).

—— *The Return of Sherlock Holmes* (London, 1905).

DRYDEN, EDGAR, 'Hawthorne's Castle in the Air: Form and Theme in *The House of the Seven Gables*', *ELH* 38 (1971), 310–24.

EAGLETON, TERRY, *The Rape of Clarissa: Writing, Sexuality and Class Struggle in Samuel Richardson* (Oxford, 1982).

EDGEWORTH, MARIA, *Tales and Novels* (10 vols., 1833; New York, 1967).

Edinburgh Annual Register [1809] (Edinburgh, 1811).

Edinburgh Review (Edinburgh, 1802–30).

ELLEDGE, W. PAUL, 'Immaterialistic Matters: Byron, Bogles and Bluebloods', *Papers on Language and Literature*, 25 (1989), 273–81.

Elliott, Marianne, *Partners in Revolution: The United Irishmen and France* (New Haven, Conn., 1982).

ELLISON, JULIE, 'Redoubled Feeling: Politics, Sentiment and the Sublime in Williams and Wollstonecraft', *Studies in Eighteenth-Century Culture*, 20 (1990), 197–215.

—— 'Rousseau in the Text of Coleridge: The Ghost-Dance of History', *Studies in Romanticism*, 28(3) (Autumn 1989), 417–36.

EPSTEIN, JULIA L., 'Fanny Burney's Epistolary Voices', *The Eighteenth Century*, 27 (1986), 162–79.

—— 'Jane Austen's Juvenilia and the Female Epistolary Tradition', *Papers in Language and Literature*, 21 (Fall 1985), 399–416.

Evils of Adultery and Prostitution, The; with an Enquiry into the Causes of their Present Alarming Increase, and Some Means Recommended for Checking their Progress (London, 1792).

FAVRET, MARY, 'The Idea of Correspondence in British Romantic Literature', Ph.D. thesis (Stanford Univ., 1988).

FENWICK, ELIZA, *Secresy; or, the Ruin on the Rock* [1795], ed. Gina Luria (3 vols., New York, 1974).

FERGUS, JAN, *Jane Austen and the Didactic Novel: Northanger Abbey, Sense and Sensibility and Pride and Prejudice* (Totowa, NJ, 1983).

FERRIS, INA, *The Achievement of Literary Authority: Gender, History, and the Waverley Novels* (Ithaca, NY, 1991).

FIGES, EVA, *Sex and Subterfuge: Women Writers to 1850* (London, 1982).

FINCH, CASEY, and BOWEN, PETER, ' "The Tittle-Tattle of Highbury": Gossip and the Free Indirect Style in *Emma*', *Representations*, 31 (Summer 1990), 1–18.

FLANAGAN, THOMAS, *The Irish Novelists 1800–1850* (New York, 1959).

FLEISHMAN, AVROM, *The English Historical Novel* (Baltimore, 1971).

FOSTER, JAMES R., *History of the Pre-Romantic Novel in England* (New York, 1949).

FRITZ, PAUL, MORTON, RICHARD, and STEVEN, SAMUEL (eds.), *Woman in the Eighteenth Century and Other Essays* (Toronto, 1976).

GARBER, MARJORIE, *Vested Interests: Cross-dressing and Cultural Anxiety* (New York, 1992).

GARSIDE, P. D., '*Waverley*'s Pictures of the Past', *ELH* 44 (1977), 659–82.

GARVER, JOSEPH, 'Gothic Ireland: Lady Caroline Lamb's *Glenarvon*', *Irish Unity Review*, 10(2) (Autumn 1980), 213–28.

Gentleman's Magazine, The (London, 1731–1833).

GEORGE, MARGARET, *One Woman's 'Situation': A Study of Mary Wollstonecraft* (Urbana, Ill., 1970).

GILLIS, CHRISTINA MARSDEN, *The Paradox of Privacy: Epistolary Form in 'Clarissa'* (Gainesville, Fla., 1984).

GIRARD, RENÉ, *Deceit, Desire and the Novel: Self and Other in Literary Structure* (Baltimore, 1966).

GODWIN, WILLIAM, *Caleb Williams* [1794], ed. David McCracken (New York, 1977).

—— *An Enquiry Concerning Political Justice, and its Influence on General Virtue and Hapiness* [1793], ed. F. E. L. Priestley (3 vols., Toronto, 1969).

—— *Fleetwood: or, The New Man of Feeling* (London, 1805).

—— *Italian Letters; or, The History of the Count de St. Julian* [1784], ed. Burton R. Pollin (Lincoln, Nebr., 1965).

—— *Memoirs of Mary Wollstonecraft Godwin, Author of 'A Vindication of the Rights of Woman'* [1798] (Philadelphia, 1799).

GOETHE, JOHANN WOLFGANG VON, *The Sorrows of Young Werther* [1774], trans. Elizabeth Mayer, Louise Bogan, and W. H. Auden (New York, 1973).

GOLDBERG, RITA, *Sex and the Enlightenment* (Cambridge, 1984).

GOLDSMITH, ELIZABETH C. (ed.), *Writing the Female Voice: Essays on Epistolary Literature* (Boston, 1989).

GOODWIN, ALBERT, *The Friends of Liberty: The English Democratic Movement in the Age of the French Revolution* (London, 1979).

GORDON, JAN B., 'A-filiative Families and Subversive Reproduction: Gossip in Jane Austen', *Genre*, 21 (Spring 1988), 5–46.

GRAHAM, PETER, *Don Juan and Regency England* (Charlottesville, Va., 1990).

GREGORY, ALLENE, *The French Revolution and the English Novel* [1915] (New York, 1966).

HAGSTRUM, JEAN, *Sex and Sensibility: Ideal and Erotic Love from Milton to Mozart* (Chicago, 1980).

HAMILTON, ELIZABETH, *Translation of the Letters of a Hindoo Rajah* (2 vols., London, 1796).

—— *Memoirs of Modern Philosophers* (3 vols., Dublin, 1800).

—— *The Cottagers of Glenburnie: A Tale for the Farmer's Inglenook* [1801] (2nd edn., Edinburgh, 1808).

HANLEY, KEITH, and SELDEN, RAMAN (eds.), *Revolution and English Romanticism: Politics and Rhetoric* (Hemel Hempstead, 1990).

HANWAY, MARY ANN, *Ellinor; or, The World As It Is* (4 vols., London, 1798).

HARRAL, THOMAS, *Scenes of Life* (London, 1805).

HART, FRANCIS R., *Scott's Novels: The Plotting of Historic Survival* (Charlottesville, Va., 1966).

HAWKINS, LAETITIA-MATILDA, *Letters on the Female Mind* (2 vols., London, 1793).

HAYDEN, JOHN O. (ed.), *Scott: The Critical Heritage* (London, 1970).

HAYES, RICHARD, *Ireland and Irishmen in the French Revolution* (London, 1932).

HAYS, MARY, *Letters and Essays, Moral and Miscellaneous* (London, 1793).

—— *The Memoirs of Emma Courtney* [1796] (3 vols., New York, 1802).

—— 'Memoirs of Mary Wollstonecraft', in *The Annual Necrology for 1797–8; Including Also, Various Articles on Neglected Biography* (London, 1800), 411–60.

—— *The Victim of Prejudice* (2 vols., London, 1799).

HAZLITT, WILLIAM, *Liber Amoris: or, The New Pygmalion* [1823], ed. Gerald Lahey (New York, 1980).

—— *The Complete Works of William Hazlitt*, ed. P. P. Howe (21 vols., London, 1930–4).

HERTZ, NEIL, *The End of the Line: Essays on Psychoanalysis and the Sublime* (New York, 1985).

HOGG, JAMES, *The Private Memoirs and Confessions of a Justified Sinner* [1824], ed. John Carey (Oxford, 1981).

HOLCROFT, THOMAS, *Anna St. Ives* [1795] (London, 1970).

HOLLY, GRANT I., '*Emmagrammatology*', *Studies in Eighteenth-Century Culture*, 19 (1989), 39–51.

HORNER, JOYCE MARY, *The English Women Novelists and their Connection with the Feminist Movement (1699–1797)* (Northampton, Mass., 1930).

IMLAY, GILBERT, *The Emigrants* [1793] (Gainesville, Fla., 1964).

INCHBALD, ELIZABETH, *A Simple Story* [1791], ed. J. M. S. Tompkins (London, 1967).

—— *Nature and Art* (2 vols., Philadelphia, 1796).

JACK, IAN, 'The Epistolary Element in Jane Austen', in *English Studies Today*, ed. G. A. Bonnard (Berne, 1961), 173–86.

JACKEL, DAVID, '*Leonora and Lady Susan*: A Note on Maria Edgeworth and Jane Austen', *English Studies in Canada*, 3 (1977), 278–88.

JACOBUS, MARY, *Reading Woman: Essays in Feminist Criticism* (New York, 1986).

—— *Romanticism, Writing, and Sexual Difference: Essays on The Prelude* (Oxford, 1989).

—— *Women Writing and Writing about Women* (London, 1979).

JAMESON, FREDERIC, *The Political Unconscious: Narrative as a Socially Symbolic Act* (Ithaca, NY, 1981).

JOHNSON, CLAUDIA L., *Jane Austen: Women, Politics and the Novel* (Chicago, 1988).

JOHNSTON, KENNETH R., and NICHOLES, JOSEPH, 'Transitory Actions, Men Betrayed: The French Revolution in the English Revolution in Romantic Drama', *Wordsworth Circle* 23(2) (Spring 1992), 76–97.

JONES, ANN H., *Ideas and Innovations: Best Sellers of Jane Austen's Age* (New York, 1986).

JONES, STANLEY, *Hazlitt: A Life* (Oxford, 1989).

JONES, VIVIEN, 'Women Writing Revolution: Narratives of History and Sexuality in Wollstonecraft and Williams', in Stephen Copley and John Whale (eds.), *Beyond Romanticism: New Approaches to Texts and Contexts* (London, 1992), 178–99.

Julia Stanley, A Novel (2 vols., Dublin, 1780).

KADISH, DORIS Y., *Politicizing Gender: Narrative Strategies in the Aftermath of the French Revolution* (New Brunswick, NJ, 1991).

KAMUF, PEGGY, *Fictions of Feminine Desire; Disclosures of Héloïse* [1982] (Lincoln, Nebr., 1987).

KAPLAN, CORA, 'Pandora's Box: Subjectivity, Class and Sexuality in Socialist Feminist Criticism', in Gayle Greene and Coppelia Kahn (eds.), *Making a Difference: Feminist Literary Criticism* (London, 1985), 146–76.

—— 'Wild Nights: Pleasure/Sexuality/Feminism', in Nancy Armstrong and Leonard Tennenhouse (eds.), *The Ideology of Conduct: Essays on Literature and the History of Sexuality* (New York, 1987), 160–84.

KAPLAN, DEBORAH, 'Female Friendship and Epistolary Form: *Lady Susan* and the Development of Jane Austen's Fiction', *Criticism*, 29 (Spring 1987), 163–78.

KAUFFMAN, LINDA S., *Discourses of Desire: Gender, Genre and Epistolary Fictions* (Ithaca, NY, 1986).

KELLY, GARY, 'Amelia Opie, Lady Caroline Lamb, and Maria Edgeworth: Official and Unofficial Ideology', *Ariel*, 12(4) (Oct. 1981), 3–24.

—— 'Discharging Debts: The Moral Economy of Amelia Opie's Fiction', *Wordsworth Circle*, 11(4) (Autumn 1980), 198–203.

—— *English Fiction of the Romantic Period 1789–1830* (London, 1989).

—— *The English Jacobin Novel 1780–1805* (Oxford, 1976).

—— 'Godwin, Wollstonecraft and Rousseau', *Women and Literature*, 3(2) (Fall 1975), 21–6.

—— 'Unbecoming a Heroine: Novel Reading, Romanticism, and Barrett's *The Heroine*', *Nineteenth-Century Literature*, 45 (1990), 220–41.

KELSALL, MALCOLM, 'The Byronic Hero and Revolution in Ireland: The Politics of *Glenarvon*', in Edwin A. Stürzl and James Hogg (eds.), *Byron: Poetry and Politics* (Salzburg, 1981), 137–51.

—— 'Hamlet, Byron, and an "Age of Despair" ', in Michael Gassenmeier (ed.), *Beyond the Suburbs of the Mind: Exploring English Romanticism* (Essen, 1987), 40–54.

KERR, JAMES, *Fiction Against History: Scott as Storyteller* (Cambridge, 1989).

KIELY, ROBERT, *The Romantic Novel in England* (Cambridge, Mass., 1972).

KING, SOPHIA, *Waldorf* (2 vols., London, 1798).

KIRKHAM, MARGARET, *Jane Austen, Feminism and Fiction* (Brighton, 1983).

KNOEPFLMACHER, U. C., 'The Importance of Being Frank: Character and Letter-Writing in *Emma*', *SEL* 7 (1967), 639–58.

KOTZEBUE, AUGUST FRIEDRICH FERDINAND VON, *Lovers' Vows: From the German of Kotzebue, by Mrs. Inchbald* (London, 1798).

KRISTEVA, JULIA, [*La Révolution du langage poétique*, 1974] *Revolution in Poetic Language*, trans. Margaret Waller (New York, 1984).

LACLOS, PIERRE AMBROISE FRANÇOIS CHODERLOS DE, *Les Liaisons dangereuses* [1782], trans. anon. as *Dangerous Connections. By M C**** de L**** (4 vols., London, 1784).

LAMB, LADY CAROLINE, *Glenarvon* (2nd edn., 2 vols., Philadelphia, 1816).

LASCELLES, MARY, *Jane Austen and Her Art* (Oxford, 1939).

Laura: or Original Letters, A Sequel to the Eloisa of J. J. Rousseau (2 vols., London, 1790).

LEAVIS, Q. D., 'A Critical Theory of Jane Austen's Writings: *Lady Susan* into *Mansfield Park*', *Scrutiny*, 10 (1941), 114–42, 272–94.

LEVINE, GEORGE, *The Realistic Imagination* (Chicago, 1981).

LEWIS, MATTHEW GREGORY, *The Monk: A Romance* (2nd edn., 3 vols., London, 1796).

LINCOLN, ANTHONY, *Some Political and Social Ideas of English Dissent 1763–1800* (Cambridge, 1938).

LIPKING, LAWRENCE, *Abandoned Women and Poetic Tradition* (Chicago, 1988).

LITVAK, JOSEPH, 'Reading Characters: Self, Society and Text in *Emma*', *PMLA* 100 (1985), 758–65.

LIU, ALAN, *Wordsworth: The Sense of History* (Stanford, Calif., 1989).

LLOYD, CHARLES, *Edmund Oliver* (2 vols., Bristol. 1798).

LOVELL, ERNEST J. (ed.), *His Very Self and Voice: Collected Conversations of Lord Byron* (New York, 1954).

LUCAS, CHARLES, *The Infernal Quixote: A Tale of the Day* (4 vols., London, 1801).

LUKACS, GEORG, *The Historical Novel*, trans. Hannah and Stanley Mitchell (London, 1962).

MACARTHUR, ELIZABETH, *Extravagant Narratives* (Princeton, NJ, 1990).

MACCARTHY, B. G., *The Later Women Novelists 1744–1818* (Oxford, 1947).

MCGANN, JEROME, *The Beauty of Inflections: Literary Investigations in Historical Method and Theory* (Oxford, 1985).

MACKENZIE, HENRY, *Julia de Roubigné* (2 vols., London, 1777).

—— *The Man of Feeling* [1771], ed. Brian Vickers (London, 1967).

MCKEON, MICHAEL, *The Origins of the English Novel 1600–1740* (Baltimore, 1987).

MCMASTER, GRAHAM, *Scott and Society* (Cambridge, 1981).

MAGINN, WILLIAM, *The O'Doherty Papers* (2 vols., New York, 1855).

MARCHAND, LESLIE, *Byron: A Biography* (2 vols., New York, 1957).

MARIE, BEATRICE, '*Emma* and the Democracy of Desire', *Studies in the Novel*, 17 (Spring 1985), 1–13.

MARKLEY, ROBERT, 'Sentimentality as Performance: Shaftesbury, Sterne and the Theatrics of Virtue', in Felicity Nussbaum and Laura Brown (eds.), *The New Eighteenth Century: Theory, Politics, English Literature* (New York, 1987), 224–41.

MARSHALL, L. E., ' "*Words* are *things*": Byron and the Prophetic Efficacy of Language', *SEL* 25 (1985), 801–22.

MARSHALL, PETER H., *William Godwin* (New Haven, Conn., 1984).

Massouf; or, The Philosophy of the Day (London, 1802).

MATHIAS, THOMAS JAMES, *The Pursuits of Literature* (London, 1797).

—— *The Shade of Alexander Pope on the Banks of the Thames* [1798] (2nd edn., Dublin, 1799).

MATURIN, CHARLES ROBERT, *Melmoth the Wanderer* [1820], ed. Alethea Hayter (Harmondsworth, 1977).

—— *The Wild Irish Boy* (3 vols., London, 1808).

MEDWIN, THOMAS, *Medwin's Conversations of Lord Byron*, ed. Ernest J. Lovell Jr. (Princeton, NH, 1966).

Men and Women. A Novel (2nd edn., 3 vols., London, 1807).

MERCIER, LOUIS SEBASTIAN, *Seraphina; a novel. From the French of M.*

Mercier. To which is added, Auguste and Madelaine. A Real History. By Miss Helen Maria Williams (Wiscasset, Me., 1797).

MILLER, D. A., *Narrative and Its Discontents: Problems of Closure in the Traditional Novel* (New Haven, Conn., 1984).

—— et al., 'The Novel and the Police', *Glyph*, 8 (1981), 127–47.

MILLER, NANCY K., *The Heroine's Text: Readings in the French and English Novel, 1722–1782* (New York, 1980).

—— 'Novels of Innocence: Fictions of Loss', *Eighteenth-Century Studies*, 11 (1978), 325–39.

MILLGATE, JANE, *Walter Scott: The Making of the Novelist* (Toronto, 1984).

Monthly Mirror (London, 1795–1810).

Monthly Review (London, 1749–1825).

MORE, HANNAH, *Strictures on the Modern System of Female Education* (2 vols., London, 1799).

—— *The Works of Hannah More* (6 vols., London, 1834).

MORGAN, LADY [SYDNEY], see Owenson, Sydney.

MYERS, MITZI, 'Godwin's *Memoirs* of Wollstonecraft: The Shaping of Self and Subject', *Studies in Romanticism*, 20 (1981), 299–316.

—— 'Mary Wollstonecraft's *Letters Written . . . in Sweden:* Toward Romantic Autobiography', *Studies in Eighteenth-Century Culture*, 8 (1979), 165–85.

NEWMAN, BETH, 'Narratives of Seduction and the Seductions of Narrative: The Frame Structure of *Frankenstein*', *ELH* 53 (Spring 1986), 141–63.

NEWMAN, GERALD, *The Rise of English Nationalism: A Cultural History, 1740–1830* (New York, 1987).

NEWTON, JUDITH LOWDER, *Women, Power, and Subversion* (Athens, Ga., 1981).

NICHOLES, JOSEPH, 'Revolutions Compared: The English Civil War as Political Touchstone in Romantic Literature', in Keith Hanley and Raman Selden (eds.), *Revolution and English Romanticism: Politics and Rhetoric* (Hemel Hempstead, 1990), 261–76.

OKIN, SUSAN MOLLER, *Women in Western Political Thought* (Princeton, NJ, 1979).

'Old England to Her Daughters: Address to the Females of Great Britain' (London, 1803), in *Napoleon's Threatened Invasion of England: Original Broadsides*. Houghton Library Collection.

OPIE, AMELIA, *Adeline Mowbray* [1804] (London, 1986).

—— *The Father and Daughter, A Tale in Prose* (London, 1801).

OUTRAM, DORINDA, *The Body and the French Revolution: Sex, Class and Political Culture* (New Haven, Conn., 1989).

[OWENSON, SYDNEY], LADY MORGAN, *O'Donnel; A National Tale* (London, 1835).

—— *Memoirs* (2 vols., London, 1868).

[OWENSON, SYDNEY], *St. Clair; or, The Heiress of Desmond* (London, 1803).

OWENSON, SYDNEY, *The Wild Irish Girl. A National Tale* [1806] (3rd edn., 3 vols., London, 1808).

Palinode, The; or, The Triumph of Virtue over Love; a Sentimental Novel (London, 1790).

PARKE, CATHERINE N., 'Vision and Revision: A Model for Reading the Eighteenth-Century Novel of Education', *Eighteenth-Century Studies*, 16 (1982–3), 162–74.

—— 'What Kind of Heroine is Mary Wollstonecraft?' in Syndy McMillen Conger (ed.), *Sensibility in Transformation: Creative Resistance to Sentiment from the Augustans to the Romantics* (London, 1990), 99–115.

[PATMORE, PETER GEORGE], *Personal Recollections of Lamb, Hazlitt, and Others*, ed. Richard Henry Stoddard (New York, 1875).

PAULSON, RONALD, *Representations of Revolution 1789–1820* (New Haven, Conn., 1983).

PERRY, RUTH, *Women, Letters and the Novel* (New York, 1980).

POLWHELE, RICHARD, *The Unsex'd Females; a Poem* [1798], ed. Gina Luria (New York, 1974).

POOVEY, MARY *The Proper Lady and the Woman Writer* (Chicago, 1984).

POPE, ALEXANDER, *Poetical Works*, ed. Herbert Davis [1966] (Oxford, 1978).

PORTER, JANE, *Thaddeus of Warsaw* [1803] (Chicago, n.d.).

—— *The Scottish Chiefs. A Romance* (5 vols., London, 1810).

PORTER, ROY, 'Reason, Madness, and the French Revolution', *Studies in Eighteenth-Century Culture*, 20 (1990), 55–79.

PUNTER, DAVID, '1789: The Sex of Revolution', *Criticism*, 24 (1982), 210–17.

—— *et al.*, 'Strategies for Representing Revolution', in Francis Barker *et al.* (eds.), *1789: Reading, Writing, Revolution: Proceedings of the Essex Conference* (London, 1982), 81–100.

Quarterly Review (London, 1809–1967).

RAFROIDI, PATRICK, *Irish Literature in English: The Romantic Period (1789–1850)* (2 vols., Gerrards Cross, 1980).

RAJAN, TILLOTAMA, 'Wollstonecraft and Godwin: Reading the Secrets of the Political Novel', *Studies in Romanticism*, 27 (1988), 221–51.

REDFORD, BRUCE, *The Converse of the Pen: Acts of Intimacy in the Eighteenth-Century Familiar Letter* (Chicago, 1986).

REED, ANDREW, *No Fiction* (2 vols., London, 1819).

REEVE, CLARA, *The Progress of Romance* (2 vols., Colchester, 1785).

REILLY, PAMELA, 'The Influence of *Waverley* on Maria Edgeworth's *Ormond*', in J. H. Alexander and David Hewitt (eds.), *Scott and His*

Influence: Papers of the Aberdeen Scott Conference 1982 (Aberdeen, 1983), 290–7.

RENDALL, JANE, *The Origins of Modern Feminism* (Basingstoke, 1985).

RICHARDSON, SAMUEL, *Clarissa* [1747–8] (8 vols., Stratford-upon-Avon, 1930).

—— *'Clarissa': Prefaces, Hints of Prefaces, and Postscript*, introd. R. F. Brissenden (Los Angeles, 1964).

ROBINSON, HENRY CRABB, *Diaries, Reminiscences, and Correspondence*, ed. Thomas Sadler (Boston, 1869).

—— *On Books and Their Writers* (3 vols., London, 1938).

ROBINSON, MARY, *The False Friend: A Domestic Story* (4 vols., London, 1799).

—— *Walsingham; or, The Pupil of Nature* [1798] (2nd edn., 4 vols., London, 1805).

ROGERS, KATHARINE, *Feminism in Eighteenth-Century England* (Brighton, 1982).

ROGERS, SAMUEL, *Table-talk*, ed. G. H. Powell (London, 1903).

ROSS, ALEXANDER M., *The Imprint of the Picturesque on Nineteenth-Century British Fiction* (Waterloo, Ont., 1986).

ROUSSEAU, JEAN-JACQUES, *The Confessions* [1781], trans. J. M. Cohen (Harmondsworth, 1987).

—— *Émile* [1762], trans. Barbara Foxley, introd. P. D. Jimack (London, 1982).

—— *Julie, ou, La Nouvelle Héloïse* [1761] (Paris, 1960).

—— [*La Nouvelle Héloïse*] *Eloisa: or, a series of original letters collected and published by J. J. Rousseau. Translated from the French* [by William Kenrick] (4 vols., London, 1761).

—— [*La Nouvelle Héloïse*] *Eloisa: or, a series of original letters collected and published by J. J. Rousseau. Translated from the French* [by William Kenrick] [1761] (1803 edn.), ed. Jonathan Wordsworth (2 vols., Oxford, 1989).

RUSSELL, WILLIAM, *Julia, a Poetical Romance, by the Editor of the Essay on the Character, Manners and Genius of Women* (London, 1773).

SCHLEUTER, PAUL, and SCHLEUTER, JUNE (eds.), *An Encyclopaedia of British Women Writers* (New York, 1988).

SCHOFIELD, MARY ANNE and MACHESKI, CECILIA (eds.), *Fetter'd or Free? British Women Novelists, 1670–1815* (Athens, 1986).

SCOTT, SIR WALTER, *The Life of Napoleon Buonaparte, Emperor of the French, with a Preliminary View of the French Revolution. By the Author of 'Waverley,' etc.* (3 vols., Philadelphia, 1827).

—— *The Miscellaneous Prose Works of Sir Walter Scott Bart.* (28 vols., Edinburgh, 1848).

—— *Redgauntlet* [1824], ed. Kathryn Sutherland (Oxford, 1985).

SCOTT, SIR WALTER, *The Waverley Novels* [1814–1832] (1830–3 edn., introd. Andrew Lang, 48 vols., Boston, 1893–4).

SEDGWICK, EVE KOSOFSKY, *Between Men: English Literature and Male Homosocial Desire* (New York, 1985).

SHAW, HARRY, *The Forms of Historical Fiction: Sir Walter Scott and His Successors* (Ithaca, NY, 1983).

SHELLEY, PERCY BYSSHE, *Letters of Percy Bysshe Shelley*, ed. Frederick L. Jones (2 vols., Oxford, 1964).

SINGER, GODFREY FRANK, *The Epistolary Novel: Its Origin, Development, Decline and Residuary Influences* [1933] (New York, 1963).

SMITH, CHARLOTTE, *Desmond* (3 vols., London, 1792).

—— *The Young Philosopher* (4 vols., London, 1978).

SMITH, MACK, 'The Document of Falsimilitude: Frank's Epistles and Misinterpretation in *Emma*', *Massachusetts Studies in English*, 9 (1984), 52–70.

SODERHOLM, JAMES, 'Lady Caroline Lamb: Byron's Miniature Writ Large', *Keats–Shelley Journal*, 40 (1991), 24–46.

SOUTHAM, B. C., *Jane Austen's Literary Manuscripts* (Oxford, 1964).

SOUTHEY, ROBERT, *New Letters of Robert Southey*, ed. Kenneth Curry (New York, 1965).

SPACKS, PATRICIA MEYER, *Desire and Truth: Functions of Plot in Eighteenth-Century Novels* (Chicago, 1980).

—— 'Energies of Mind: Plot's Possibilities in the 1790s', *Eighteenth-Century Fiction*, 1(1) (Oct. 1988), 37–52.

—— *Gossip* (New York, 1985).

—— *Imagining a Self: Autobiography and Novel in Eighteenth-Century England* (Cambridge, Mass., 1976).

SPENCER, JANE, 'Minor Women Novelists and Their Presentation of a Feminine Ideal, 1744–1800', D.Phil. thesis (Univ. of Oxford, 1984).

—— *The Rise of the Woman Novelist: from Aphra Behn to Jane Austen* (Oxford, 1986).

STAËL-HOLSTEIN, ANNE LOUISE GERMAINE DE, *Corinne; ou, l'Italie* [1807] (Paris, 1985).

—— [*Corinne*] *Corinna, or, Italy* (New Brunswick, NJ, 1987).

—— *Delphine* (trans. anon., 6 vols., London, 1803).

STEEVES, EDNA L., 'Pre-Feminism in some Eighteenth-Century Novels', in Cheryl L. Brown and Karen Olson (eds.), *Feminist Criticism* (Metuchen, NJ, 1978), 222–32.

STENDHAL [BEYLE, HENRI], *Le Rouge et le Noir: chronique du XIXe siècle* [1831] (Paris, 1989).

STEWART, SUSAN, *Crimes of Writing: Problems in the Containment of Representation* (New York, 1991).

TANNER, TONY, *Adultery in the Novel: Contract and Transgression* (Baltimore, 1979).

TAYLOR, GARY, *Reinventing Shakespeare: A Cultural History* (New York, 1989).

THEWELEIT, KLAUS, *Male Fantasies*, i: *Women, Floods, Bodies, History*, trans. Stephen Conway (Minneapolis, 1987).

[THOMAS, ELIZABETH]. *Purity of Heart, or The Ancient Costume, A Tale . . . Addressed to the Author of Glenarvon* (London, 1816).

THOMPSON, E. P., 'The Crime of Anonymity', in Douglas Hay, Peter Linebaugh, John G. Rule, E. P. Thompson, and Cal Winslow, *Albion's Fatal Tree: Crime and Society in Eighteenth-Century England* (London, 1975), 255–308.

TODD, JANET M., 'The Biographies of Mary Wollstonecraft', *Signs*, 1 (Spring, 1976).

—— *The Sign of Angellica: Women, Writing and Fiction, 1660–1800* (London, 1989).

—— *Sensibility: An Introduction* (London, 1986).

—— (ed.), *A Dictionary of British and American Women Writers, 1660–1800* (London, 1985).

TOMALIN, CLAIRE, *The Life and Death of Mary Wollstonecraft* (New York, 1974).

TOMPKINS, J. M. S., *The Popular Novel in England, 1770–1800* [1932] (London, Nebr., 1961).

TOPLISS, IAN, 'Mary Wollstonecraft and Maria Edgeworth's Modern Ladies', *Études irlandaises*, NS 6 (1981), 8–19,

—— *The Vagabond* (3rd edn., 2 vols., London, 1799).

WALTERS, MARGARET, 'The Rights and Wrongs of Woman: Mary Wollstonecraft, Harriet Martineau, Simone de Beauvoir', in Juliet Mitchell and Ann Oakley (eds.), *The Rights and Wrongs of Women* (Harmondsworth, 1976), 298–327.

WARDLE, RALPH, *Mary Wollstonecraft: A Critical Biography* (Lawrence, Kan., 1951).

WARNER, JAMES, 'Eighteenth-Century English Reactions to *La Nouvelle Héloïse*', PMLA 52 (Sept. 1937), 803–19.

WATSON, NICOLA JANE, 'Trans-figurations of Byronic Identity', in Mary A. Favret and Nicola J. Watson (eds.), *At the Limits of Romanticism: Essays in Cultural, Feminist, and Materialist Criticism* (Bloomington, Ind., 1994).

—— 'Kemble, Scott and the Mantle of the Bard', in Jean Marsden (ed.), *The Appropriation of Shakespeare: Post-Renaissance Reconstructions of the Works and the Myth* (Hemel Hempstead, 1991), 73–92.

—— 'Novel Eloisas: Revolutionary and Counter-revolutionary Narratives in Helen Maria Williams, Wordsworth and Byron', *Wordsworth Circle*, 23 (1992), 18–23.

—— 'Purloined Letters: Revolution, Reaction and the Form of the Novel, 1790–1825', D.Phil. thesis (Univ. of Oxford, 1990).

WEDD, ANN F., *The Fate of the Fenwicks: Letters to Mary Hays 1798–1828* (London, 1927).

WELSH, ALEXANDER, *The Hero of the Waverley Novels* (New Haven. Conn., 1963).

WEST, JANE, *The Advantages of Education; or, the History of Miss Maria Williams, A Tale for Misses and their Mammas, by Prudentia Homespun* (2 vols., London, 1793).

—— *An Elegy on the Death of the Right Honourable Edmund Burke* (London, 1797).

—— *A Gossip's Story and a Legendary Tale* (2 vols., London, 1796–8).

—— *The Infidel Father* (3 vols., London, 1802).

—— *Letters Addressed to a Young Man* (3 vols., London, 1801).

—— *The Loyalists: An Historical Novel* (2nd edn., 3 vols., London, 1812).

—— *A Tale of the Times* (3 vols., London, 1799).

WHITE, HAYDEN, *Metahistory: The Historical Imagination in Nineteenth-Century Europe* (Baltimore, 1973).

WILLIAMS, HELEN MARIA: see *Ambrose and Eleanor*.

—— *Julia: A Novel, Interspersed with some Poetical Pieces* (2 vols., London, 1790).

—— *Letters From France* [1791–6], ed. Janet M. Todd (Delmar, NY, 1975).

—— *Seraphina; a novel. From the French of M. Mercier. To which is added, Auguste and Madelaine. A Real History. By Miss Helen Maria Williams* (Wiscasset. Me., 1979).

WILLIAMS, IOAN (ed.), *Novel and Romance 1700–1800: A Documentary Record* (London, 1970).

—— (ed.), *Sir Walter Scott on Novelists and Fiction* (London, 1968).

WILSON, HARRIETTE, *Memoirs of Herself and Others* [1825], ed. James Laver (New York, 1929).

WILSON, KATHLEEN, 'Inventing Revolution: 1688 and Eighteenth-Century Popular Politics', *Journal of British Studies*, 28(4) (Oct. 1989), 349–88.

WILT, JUDITH, *Secret Leaves: The Novels of Walter Scott* (Chicago, 1985).

WOLFSON, SUSAN J., 'Their She-Condition: Cross-Dressing and the Politics of Gender in *Don Juan*', *ELH* 54(3) (Fall 1987), 585–617.

WOLLSTONECRAFT, MARY, *An Historical and Moral View of the Progress of the French Revolution; and the effect it has produced in Europe* [1794], ed. Janet M. Todd (New York, 1975).

—— *Letters Written During a Short Residence in Sweden, Norway and Denmark* (London, 1796).

—— *Maria; or, The Wrongs of Woman* [1798], ed. Moira Ferguson (New York, 1975).

—— *Mary, A Fiction, and The Wrongs of Woman* [1788, 1798], ed. Gary Kelly (London, 1976).

—— *Original Stories* [1791], ed. E. V. Lucas (London, 1906).

—— A *Vindication of the Rights of Woman* [1792], ed. Charles Hayden (New York, 1967).

WOOD, SARAH, *Julia, and the Illuminated Baron. A Novel: Founded on Recent Facts Which Have Transpired in the Course of the Revolution of Moral Principles in France* (Portsmouth, NH, 1800).

YAEGER, PATRICIA, *Honey-Mad Women: Emancipatory Strategies in Women's Writing* (New York, 1988).

Index